SEATTLE

The Best *of* Emerald City

An impertinent insiders' guide

By Don and Betty Martin

Pine Cone Press, Inc. • Henderson, Nevada

BOOKS BY DON AND BETTY MARTIN

Adventure Cruising ● 1996
Arizona Discovery Guide ● 1990, 1993, 1994, 1996, 1998
Arizona in Your Future ● 1991, 1993, 1998
The Best of the Gold Country ● 1987, 1990, 1992
The Best of San Francisco ● 1986, 1990, 1994, 1997
The Best of the Wine Country ● 1991, 1994, 1995, 2000
California-Nevada Roads Less Traveled ● 1999
Inside San Francisco ● 1991
Las Vegas: The Best of Glitter City ● 1998, 2000
Nevada Discovery Guide ● 1992, 1997
Nevada In Your Future ● 2000
New Mexico Discovery Guide ● 1998
Northern California Discovery Guide ● 1993
Oregon Discovery Guide ● 1993, 1995, 1996, 1999
San Diego: The Best of Sunshine City ● 1999
San Francisco's Ultimate Dining Guide ● 1988
Seattle: The Best of Emerald City ● 2000
The Toll-free Traveler ● 1997
The Ultimate Wine Book ● 1993, 2000
Utah Discovery Guide ● 1995
Washington Discovery Guide ● 1994, 1997, 2000

ᕲᕲᕲ

Library of Congress Cataloging-in-Publication Data
Martin, Don and Betty —
Seattle: The Best of Emerald City
Includes index.
1. Seattle, Washington—description and travel
2. Seattle, Washington—history
3. Puget Sound area—description and travel

ISBN: 0-942053-32-X
Library of Congress catalog card number: 99-97830

COVER DESIGN ● **Vicky Biernacki**, Columbine Type and Design, Sonora, Calif.

JUST THE BEST: NOT ALL THE REST

This is a different kind of guidebook. Instead of saturating readers with details on everything there is to see and do in Seattle and surrounding areas, the authors have sifted through the region's hundreds of lures and selected only the ten best in various categories. It is more than a mere book of lists, however. Each listing is a detailed description, with specifics on location, hours and price ranges.

And there is plenty from which to choose. *Seattle: The Best of Emerald City* offers Ten Best lists in nearly fifty different categories. It is thus a great resource for visitors with limited time, visitors with lots of time and local residents who'd like to make new discoveries about their community.

A guidebook focusing only on the best must, by its very nature, be rather opinionated. Some would even suggest that it's impertinent. Further, many readers may not agree with the authors' selections, which is part of the fun of reading it. In fact, readers are invited to make their own Ten Best selections. Details are below and in the back of the book.

This is the fourth in a series of "Ten Best" city guides by veteran travel writers Don and Betty Martin. Check your local book store for *Las Vegas: The Best of Glitter City, San Diego: The Best of Sunshine City* and *The Best of San Francisco.*

₧ ₧ ₧

A few words of thanks

The authors could not have written such a detailed and opinionated guide to Seattle and its surrounds without the assistance of many other people. We are particularly grateful to **David Blandford**, manager of the Seattle-King County News Bureau and media relations coordinator **Mandy Mahaney.** They loaded us up with many pounds of remarkably useful information about Emerald City. Other key players in this research project were our good friends **Louie** and **Betty Richmond,** staff members **Lorne Richmond, Carry Porter** and others of Seattle's Richmond Public Relations, Inc. Thanks also to **Barry** and **Hilda Anderson,** noted travel writers and longtime Seattle area residents (recently adjourned to Port Townsend), who through the years have helped us discover why Emerald City is such a jewel.

CONTENTS

1 Seattle!
In search of emeralds — 7
An unauthorized history — 11
Getting there and getting oriented — 15
Our ten favorite Seattle moments — 30

2 Visitor lures
The Ten Best attractions — 36
The next Ten Best attractions — 45
The Ten Best museums — 50
The Ten Best things to do in Seattle — 55
The Ten Best overlooked attractions — 61

3 A Seattle dining guide
The Ten Very Best restaurants — 67
The Ten Best seafood restaurants — 72
The Ten Best Asian restaurants — 76
The Ten Best other ethnic restaurants — 80

4 Savoring something special
The Ten Best specialty restaurants — 86
Sunnyside up: The Ten Best breakfast cafés — 90
Food al fresco: The Ten Best outdoor cafés — 94
Vista vitttles: The Ten Best view restaurants — 98
The Ten Best fish & chips places — 102
The Ten Best coffee stops — 106

5 Proud paupers: A budget guide
Frugal fun: The Ten Best free attractions — 110
The Ten Best cheap eats — 114
The Ten Best cheap sleeps — 118

6 Pillow talk
The Ten Best hotels — 122
The Ten Best bed & breakfast inns — 126

7 Nightside: Culture, clubs and cinemas
The Ten Best performing arts groups — 131
Play it again, Jimi: The Ten Best nightspots — 133
The Ten Best places to catch a flick — 136

8 Pub crawling: The best places to sip suds
The Ten Best watering holes — 141
The Ten Best "personality bars" — 144

9 Romance and other primal urges
The Ten Best places to snuggle with your sweetie — 149
The ten most romantic restaurants — 152
The ten friskiest diversions in Seattle — 156

10 **Points of view: Where to stare and shoot**
The Ten Best viewpoints — 161
Photo tips: Shooting Seattle — 164
Aiming your Canon: The Ten Best picture spots — 165

11 **Credit card corruption**
The Ten Best malls and shopping areas — 169
The Ten Best specialty stores — 173

12 **Getting physical**
The Ten Best hike routes — 177
The Ten Best bike routes — 189

13 **Assorted lists that don't fit into other lists**
Odd ends: A miscellaneous Ten Best — 199
The Ten Best places to sit and do nothing — 203
A city celebrates: The Ten Best festivals — 206
The Ten Best specialty guides to the Seattle area — 208
Easy listening: The Ten Best radio stations — 210
The worst of Emerald City — 211

14 **Leaving Seattle**
The Ten Best reasons for getting out of town — 215

15 **Readers' forum**
Now it's your turn: Select your favorite area attractions — 226

TOO MUCH OF A GOOD THING

Seattle is a city with too much bounty—too many fine seafood restaurants, too many charming little coffee houses, too many interesting attractions and fantastic views. It would be difficult to sample all of its allures in a single vacation trip. And when you extend your visit to the surrounding waterways and mountains—which should be included in any Seattle visit—*c'est impossible!* One simply cannot do it all.

A person could spend a lifetime exploring Seattle, the greater Puget Sound and the Olympic and Cascade areas. Indeed, many people do, for this is one of the fastest growing areas in America.

For those whose time is more limited, and for you Washington residents seeking new discoveries, we present another in our series of Ten Best city guides. We spent months canvassing Emerald City, seeking its most interesting attractions, its best espresso and latte stalls, its most succulent slices of steamed salmon, its cutest cafés and grandest shopping areas, and its best places to hike and ride a bike. Having done this, we galloped off in all directions, seeking the Ten Best side trips to other areas of Puget Sound, the gorgeous Olympic Peninsula to the west and the Cascade Range to the east.

After sorting through the attractions of Seattle and beyond, we saved the very best—just for you.

Don W. Martin
Sipping caffé latte at Pike Place Market

㋡ ㋡ ㋡

CLOSING INTRODUCTORY THOUGHTS
Keeping up with the changes

The largest city in the American Northwest, Seattle is a place of constant change. If you discover something afresh during your visit, or if you catch an error in this book, let us know. Drop us a note if you find that a great seafood restaurant has become a laundromat or the other way around.

We'd also like to invite you to make your own nominations for future editions of *Seattle: The Best of Emerald City*. All who submit at least fifteen nominations will receive a free copy of the next edition. Use the form in the back of this book or—if you're reluctant to dismember it—a photocopy thereof.

Address your comments to:

Pine Cone Press, Inc.
631 Stephanie St., PMB 138
Henderson, NV 89014

Toto, I have a feeling we're not in Kansas anymore.
— Dorothy, in *The Wizard of Oz*

Chapter one

SEATTLE!
IN SEARCH OF EMERALDS

Tourist promoters like to call it The Emerald City, a reference to its green setting and its gem-like downtown core that sparkles in the occasional Seattle sunshine. However, we've dropped the "the," since *Emerald City* fits the tongue better, not to mention the cover of this book.

So, welcome to Emerald City, Dorothy and Toto! This glittering jewel fitted between jade blue waters and emerald green mountains is one of the most appealing, versatile and attractive communities in America.

Seattle is the largest city in the Northwest, with more than half a million residents, and an equal number in surrounding King County. The city and county offer a rich brew of urban and suburban lures for visitors. For culture vultures and sports fans, it's one of the few cities in America with a symphony orchestra, ballet, opera and major league baseball, football and basketball teams. As a commentary on the city's diversity, two of the toughest tickets in town are the Seattle Seahawks (when they're winning) and the Seattle Opera. Even tougher to find

7

are tickets to a University of Washington football game. Huskies game tickets aren't sold; they're inherited, passed down from one generation to the next. The team is so adored that the state motor vehicles department sells Huskies license plates.

Seattle is a great outdoor city, rimmed by Puget Sound and Lake Washington and backdropped by the Olympic and Cascade mountain ranges. It's busy with elaborate parklands and biking and hiking trails, and alpine lures are a short drive away. It has the highest per capita boat ownership in the world, and one can even buy detailed kayaking guides to its surrounding waters.

Like San Francisco, with which it often is compared, Seattle is an international city, rich in ethnic neighborhoods and restaurants. It rivals its California sister in the quality and quantity of restaurants and it's particularly noted for its fresh, local seafood and for its many Asian cafés. More than eight million visitors a year come to play, sleep and eat in Seattle. Tourism is Washington's fourth largest industry and more than half of the visitor money—about $4.75 billion—is spent in Emerald City.

A couple of decades ago, Seattle was famous for its gentility and casual pace; its residents liked to say "please" and "thank you." More congested and faster paced today, it's no longer quite so mellow, although it's still one of the safest and least uptight large cities in America. While motorists elsewhere fret about road rage and avoid eye contact with anyone whose neck is larger than their head, Seattle drivers often yield the right-of-way during traffic jams. Even cabbies are remarkably polite and the only really reckless people are bike messengers, who flit and dart through thick downtown traffic like suicidal humming birds.

Many pedestrians patiently wait for "walk" signs at intersections, even if the street is empty. Of course, this obedience is inspired by the fact that Seattle's polite police will not hesitate to cite jaywalkers.

The city's affable attitude has earned it numerous national plaudits. It was selected in 1998 as America's best place to live by *Money* magazine, and as the best city for women by *American Health for Women* magazine. In1966, *Fortune* magazine called it America's most livable city, and *Parade* magazine tabbed it as America's second safest city. It's also a city that likes to keep in shape. In 1999, *Men's Health* magazine ranked it number three in the nation for having the most physically fit residents. Emerald City definitely is not couch potato country!

Latte da

Famed for its coffee houses and espresso bars, Seattle probably leads the nation in per capita coffee consumption. Perhaps this is why its citizens are a bit more wired these days. The coffee craze started in 1971 when three college friends opened a coffee bar near Pike Place Market on Seattle's waterfront. They named it "Starbucks," after the character in *Moby Dick*. A decade later, marketing whiz Howard Shultz joined the firm and eventually made Starbucks the most popular coffee brand in America. Noting its success, other coffee roasters have cropped up throughout Seattle and the rest of the state. Walk-in, take-out, drive-up and drive-through coffee and espresso stands are scattered from the Olympic Peninsula to the Cascades and beyond to the great wheatfields of eastern Washington. The originator of Seattle's caffeine craze is now the nation's largest coffee roaster, with more than a thousand outlets in North America.

Starbucks' chief competitors in the city are Tully's and Seattle's Best. With these three fast-growing firms and many independents, there are nearly a thousand coffee cafés and espresso stands in the city. (In Chapter Four, we choose our Ten Best coffee stops.)

Is likker quicker?

While Seattlites may love their daily caffeine fix, this town is not known for a lot of great watering holes. Although we pick our favorite pubs in Chapter Eight, we found few to compare with the classic bars of serious drinking cities such as San Francisco, Chicago and New York. Early Seattle certainly was a hard-drinking frontier town, although it and the rest of the state had calmed down considerably by the turn of the last century.

Washington voted for prohibition nearly four years before the infamous Volstead Act dried up the rest of America in 1920. While the state reluctantly went along with Repeal thirteen years later, it still has several laws left over from those prohibitionist days. Only wine and beer can be served in taverns or sold in grocery stores and other retail outlets. For a bottle of the hard stuff, you need to seek out a state liquor store, which arbitrarily sets prices and hours of operation. Don't look for many bargains at the state stores and don't run out of booze late at night or on the Sabbath. Most store hours are Monday-Saturday 10 to 8 and *never* on Sunday. (Despite the state's prissy attitude toward booze, its liquor stores are on the web—*www.wa.gov/liq.*)

Don't get caught drinking in public in Washington; it's illegal unless you're at a sidewalk café. A few decades ago, it was even felonious to carry your drink from one area of a bar to another. You had to summon a cocktail waitress or bartender for liquor transport.

However, the state isn't nearly as dry as we may imply. Any licensed restaurant or cocktail lounge can serve mixed drinks, and you can carry your libation to the corner table where that busty blonde is giving you the eye.

Rain today, probably followed by tomorrow

Everybody talks about the weather, particularly in Seattle. Mostly what they talk about is rain. The Convention and Visitors Bureau, intent on attracting tourists, insists that it doesn't really rain that much. Why, it rains more in New York, Boston and Miami, they insist. Yeah, right guys; it also rains more in the upper Amazon.

Locals who don't want to be overrun by tourists and new residents use "rain humor" to keep them away. What dresses like a duck and waddles like a duck? "A downtown office worker in a rain slicker, trying to get to his car." What comes after two days of heavy rain in Seattle? "Monday."

You want the real truth? Seattle is a wet city, with about thirty-eight inches of rainfall a year. It averages only sixty days of full sunshine, although partly sunny days are common. Get real, folks; this isn't L.A., Las Vegas or even San Francisco—despite that city's infamous cold, damp summers. Thirty-eight inches is a lotta rain, particularly when compared with seven inches in Las Vegas, twelve in Los Angeles and less than twenty-one in San Francisco. Sure it rains more in Miami than in Seattle. It's in the *tropics,* f'chrissake!

But, never mind all that. Most of Seattle's rain falls from October through April; it's quite light in the summer. If you really want to enjoy some of those gorgeous days when you can see halfway to Juneau from the Space Needle, come in July. It has less than an inch of rainfall and the average high temperature is a scalding seventy-five degrees. Since Seattle isn't pummeled by tens of millions of annual tourists like Las Vegas or Orlando, you won't be trampled during a summer visit. The town has no theme parks to draw massive school vacation mobs. Except for those sunny summer weekends when thousands flock to Seattle from nearby areas, visitor attractions and favored waterways aren't excessively crowded.

A year-around city

If summer doesn't work for you, bear in mind that Seattle is a great place to visit any time of the year. Its museums and virtually all of its other attractions are open the year around, and the cultural scene is in full swing in the winter. Further, Seattle's rainfall is rarely torrential. It's usually a friendly drizzle and many Seattlites don't even bother with raincoats or umbrellas. They merely wait for a pause in the drizzle, then they make a quick dash for cover. And finally, snowfall is extremely rare here. If it were common, downtown Seattle wouldn't be terraced into a hillside. One good New York style blizzard, and half the traffic would slide into Elliott Bay.

People don't live in northwestern America's largest city and the surrounding Puget Sound area because of the weather. They live here in spite of it. Bill Gates could have moved Microsoft to sunny Silicon Valley. William Boeing certainly could have picked a sunnier place to flight-test his airplanes. Starbucks Coffee would have done just fine in cool, trend-conscious San Francisco. The fact is, the Puget Sound area appeals to residents and visitors because it's beautiful, upbeat and vibrant. Seattle is Emerald City because rainfall paints the trees and grass green and keeps the streams flowing into Puget Sound. You want a suntan? Go to Phoenix. You want gorgeous scenery, cultural lures and a great cup of coffee? Come to Seattle.

In fact, one of the frustrations of visiting Seattle—no matter what time of year—is that there is too much to see, too much to do, too many cups of caffé latte to sip, too many fine restaurants to try. This of course is the purpose of this book—to sort through all of those choices and offer you the very best.

But first a look at the city and how it came to be. One episode during Seattle's early years sounds like a silly plot for a TV series and unfortunately, it was. However, we must go back further to find the city's roots.

An UNAUTHORIZED HISTORY

To begin, Seattle was started in the wrong place, and it went through a couple of really dumb names before being named in honor of a highly respected native chief. Then in true Western pioneer fashion, the settlers promptly took his land and stuck him on a reservation.

Seattle's history could have started as early as 1790 when British navigator Captain George Vancouver sailed into a large inland sea while searching for the elusive Northwest Passage. However, he didn't hang around. He directed one of his officers, Lieutenant Peter Puget, to launch several longboats to explore this inland waterway. He named the sound for this officer, then continued on his way. Vancouver was more intent on finding the Northwest Passage than pressing exploration of this wonderland of waterways and islands.

The native people, members of a clan called Duwamish, probably were relieved to see the palefaces sail away in their great "houses on water." They weren't disturbed again until 1833, when a group from the Hudson's Bay Company built Fort Nisqually between present-day Olympia and Tacoma. This alarmed the Americans, who wanted the area for themselves, so Lieutenant Charles Wilkes of the U.S. Navy was sent to explore and map this complex maze of land and water.

When the international boundary was established along the 49th parallel, safely to the north of Puget Sound, American settlement began in earnest. In 1851, a handful of pioneers led by brothers Arthur and David Denny erected a crude, roofless cabin on wet and windy Alki Point, several miles south of the present downtown area. *Alki* is Duwamish for "bye and bye." They named their settlement New York-Alki, since some of the settlers had come from the Big Apple.

After a soggy, miserable winter, they decided to relocate their settlement in the more sheltered Elliott Bay, where the heart of the city remains today. Initially, the settlers called their new town Duwamps. (Can you imagine a sports announcer saying: "And now, coming onto the field, the Duwamps Seahawks.") Then, perhaps to ease their guilt about intruding on native land, they renamed the town in honor of Duwamish Chief Sealth. He liked the settlers' metal tools and cloth fabric, for which he traded furs and game, so he urged his people to cooperate with them. To reward their cooperation, the settlers con-

Which King for the county?

In 1986, officials of Seattle's surrounding King County decided to salute Martin Luther King, Jr., by "redesignating" the county's name in his honor. As we went to press, discussions were underway to change the image on the county seal from a stylized crown to a portrait of the civil rights leader. Officials did not rename the county; it has been King County since 1853. Ironically, it was named for Franklin Pierce's vice president, a slave holder named William Rufus DeVane King.

vinced the Duwamish to give them two million acres of land in exchange for $150,000 in supplies.

Although Sealth sought only peace with the whites, other native people rebelled against the intrusion, raiding several Puget Sound settlements. Superior American firepower quelled the uprisings and the Duwamish—including the cooperative Sealth—were moved to a 2,400-acre reservation across Puget Sound. Later, as the intruders demanded more land, the original inhabitants were removed to an even smaller reservation, where Chief Sealth died 1866. Before his death, the bewildered and disillusioned leader pleaded:

How can you buy or sell the sky, the warmth of the land? This idea is strange to us. If we do not own the freshness of the air and the sparkle of the water, how can you buy them?

In a final insult, the intruders couldn't even pronounce the great chief's name correctly. They Anglicized it to "Seattle."

It makes a village

Even as the native people faded from the scene, the new village of Seattle grew on the muddy banks of Elliott Bay. In 1852, one Henry Yesler built a sawmill on a pier and began harvesting the thick forests covering the slopes above. Logs were skidded down a board flume, and bawdy houses and lumbermens' shacks sprouted along this "skid road." In later years, Seattle shifted northward and the original city site became a haven for the down and out. "Skid road," later changed to Skid Row, joined the American lexicon to describe the scruffy area of a city.

Like most frontier towns, early Seattle was populated primarily by men. They sought female companionship either by marrying native women or visiting the whorehouses along Skid Road. Then a young, educated idealist named Asa Mercer arrived from Pennsylvania in 1861. He became famous not for his noblest accomplishment—establishing the University of Washington—but for his efforts to bring proper ladies to the lonely frontiersmen. He caught a ship to Boston and began recruiting women to return with him to Seattle. Only eleven "Mercer maidens" accepted his offer and these weren't exactly maidens. Most were Civil War widows willing to brave an unknown frontier to find new husbands.

Within months of their arrival, all were married and Mercer took off for a second—uh—load. This time, he went on a speaking engagement to churches in Boston, New York and Washington and soon had more than 500 women willing to make the trip west. However, the *New York Herald* got wind of the story, accused him of being a white slaver and ridiculed him with headlines about his "Cargo of heifers." Nearly half the women returned home in fits of embarrassment.

Running short on money and patience, Mercer finally set sail with the remainder of his recruits. Several jumped ship in San Francisco and by most accounts, only fifty-seven women completed this second voyage to Seattle. Most of Mercer's maidens supposedly were proper church-going ladies, although some of the womens' diaries suggested a certain amount of hankie-pankie aboard ship. Mercer himself was never accused of any such improprieties. However, he wooed one lady at sea and was turned down; then he won the heart of a second and married her soon after they reached Seattle.

A hundred years later, Mercer's adventures were loosely chronicled in a silly, mercifully short-lived television series called *Here Come the Brides.*

A hot time in the new town

Rimmed by timber, early Seattle was built almost entirely of wood. Then in 1889, a painter's glue pot boiled over on a hot stove and the city was burned back to the mud. As the town was rebuilt—this time of brick and masonry—mud and tides became its most serious problem. The bottomlands along Elliott Bay became bogs when it rained, and high tides caused the sewer system to go into reverse. (If you take the amusing Bill Speidel Underground Tour listed in Chapter Two, you'll be regaled with stories of exploding Crappers.)

City fathers decided to elevate the streets in the lower section of town, and the sidewalks became trenches behind retaining walls. These later were bridged over, and then covered completely, creating a dark and musty basement city suited more to rats than people. After a plague outbreak in 1907, health officials condemned it. However, an underground of opium dens, brothels and moonshiners thrived there for several more years.

The arrival of the Northern Pacific Railroad in 1883 was a major boon to the new town. A second boost came with an event that occurred more than a thousand miles north. In 1896, three prospectors found rich placer deposits on creeks flowing into the Yukon River near Dawson City. As in the California gold rush, it took more than a year for word to get out. Then, tens of thousands of '98ers flocked to the American Northwest, seeking passage to the Klondike. Thanks to an ambitious chamber of commerce publicity committee, Seattle became the main outfitting center for these gold-seekers. More than eighty percent of the supplies taken to the Klondike were sold by Seattle merchants, creating more wealth here than in the goldfields.

Seattle exported more than flour and picks and shovels. Many of its good time girls followed the goldseekers north. Others passed through the city, willingly swept along in the rush to riches. Several became more wealthy than the men who paid for their favors. One Grace Robinson sang her way from New York to Seattle. She then headed north in the company of one Jim Donaldson, a "well-known sporting man," according to Lael Morgan's *Good Time Girls of the Alaska-Yukon Gold Rush* (© 1998). "At Dear Old Dawson, I made my fortune in a little over two years," she told a newsman.

Lottie Burns used her illicit earnings to buy mining claims from impoverished miners. She sold them at a fat profit, then settled in Seattle. She gave a sanitized version of her story to a *Post-Intelligencer* reporter, who praised her in an article headlined: "Lotta Burns in Seattle: Mother of the Klondike Returns to Civilization."

The most celebrated lady of the north was dancer Klondike Kate Rockwell, who had spent part of her childhood in Spokane. She made a small fortune in the Yukon. She then became the lover of theater magnate Alex Pantages and lived in Seattle early in the last century, performing at the Alcazar Theater. Did she make her Klondike fortune strictly as a dancer? "We were not vestal virgins. Far from it," she said in her biography, *Queen of the Klondike.*

Serving as gateway to the Yukon Gold Rush was Seattle's final wild fling. Its future fortunes would be guided by less colorful—although still enterprising—people. Among the area's major movers were Frederick Weyerhauser, who built the world's largest lumber mill in nearby Everett in 1903; William Boeing, who launched the area's aircraft industry in 1909; Starbucks' Howard Shultz, who joined that firm in the 1980s and eventually made it America's largest coffee roaster; and Bill Gates and Paul Allen, founders of Microsoft in 1975.

Southwestern Washington thrived on international misfortune during World War II, becoming a major aircraft and shipbuilding center. The predictable slump followed the war, then Boeing revived the economy by developing America's first commercial jet. Seattle celebrated its good fortunes in 1962 with Century 21, the only world's fair ever to show a profit.

However, as a three-industry town—aviation, lumbering and the military—Seattle suffered a rollercoaster economic ride. Cutbacks at Boeing, arms reductions and environmental concerns over a scruffy-looking owl sent frequent shock waves through the economy. In 1969, this billboard was erected south of town: "Will the last person to leave Seattle please turn out the lights?"

In fact, 37,000 people did leave between 1970 and 1980, dropping the city's population from 531,000 to 494,000. It didn't regain its previous high until the mid-1990s.

However, Emerald City galloped into the Millennium in high gear, spurred by a more diverse economy. Ongoing or recently completed projects include an expansion of the convention center, new ball yards for the Seahawks and Mariners, a new world trade center, more downtown shopping facilities and new hotels. New or expanded visitor attractions include the strangely innovative Experience Music Project, a major Pacific Science Center expansion, a new Museum of History and Industry, and the gorgeous new home of the Seattle Symphony, Benaroya Hall.

It's not likely that anyone will be turning out Seattle's lights.

GETTING THERE

Seattle is an easy reach, served by north-south Interstate 5, east-west I-90, most major airlines and Amtrak. Its attractions are rather scattered so if you're flying or training to Seattle, plan on renting a car once you arrive.

By highway ● Interstate 5 is the main feeder into Seattle from the north and south. I-90 comes in from the east, crossing Lake Washington and merging with I-5 just south of the downtown area. For the uninitiated, Seattle's freeways are about as organized as a dropped bowl of spaghetti. If you don't remain alert, an off-ramp will blend you back onto I-5 and away you go, bound for Canada. It's easy to miss exits in the downtown area, since they can leave the freeway either from the left or the right lanes. Further, rush-hour express lanes change direction from morning to night. If you merge onto one without intending to—an easy trick—you may be expressed halfway to Everett before you can get off again.

All of this said, if you have a detailed map and approach the city during non-commute hours, you should be able to find your destination without winding up in Issaquah. The Madison or Seneca street exits will get you into the heart of downtown. Once there, you'll find a convenient grid of named streets (running southwest to northeast) and numbered avenues (northwest to southeast). Many of these are one-way so again, you'll need a map. As you'll notice on that map, blocks of streets outside the downtown area are often skewed and truncated to accommodate the city's many lakes and waterways.

By air ● Seattle-Tacoma International Airport—Sea-Tac—located midway between those cities, is served by most major airlines. Call (800) 544-1965 or (206) 431-4444 for information on parking, air and ground traffic, arrivals and departures. Of course, all the major rental car agencies are available.

Passenger service downtown is provided by **Gray Line Airport Express,** serving ten hotels with half-hour departures, (206) 626-6088; **Shuttle Express,** a limo van service, (800) 942-7433 or (206) 622-1424; and by **Metro,** the city's public bus system; call (206) 553-

3000 for route and schedule information. Several other firms offer shuttle service to nearby communities; call the airport number above for details.

By rail • The handsome old King Street Station at Third Avenue and King Street is home to **Amtrak.** The **Coast Starlight** has daily service between Seattle and Los Angeles and the **Empire Builder** head east through Montana to Chicago. Frequent service is provided between Seattle and Portland aboard the **Mount Rainier.** Daily service also is offered to Vancouver, B.C., aboard the **Mount Baker International.** Call (800) USA-RAIL for information and reservations; the local number is (206) 464-1930.

By bus • **Greyhound** operates from a terminal at Ninth Avenue and Stewart Street, serving most of the rest of the country via I-5 and I-90; (800) 231-2222 or (206) 624-3456. **Northwest Trailways** provides service from the Amtrak depot and Greyhound terminal to Everett, Whidbey Island and Vancouver, B.C.; (206) 728-5955.

By ferry • Now, that's the *grand* way to travel to or from Seattle! Washington State Ferries sail between Coleman Dock (Pier 52) and Bremerton on the Kitsap Peninsula and Bainbridge Island. Passenger-only ferries run between Seattle's Pier 50 and Bremerton. Other nearby ferry routes are between Edmonds north of Seattle and Kingston on the Kitsap Peninsula; and between Fauntleroy south of the city and Vashon Island and the Kitsap Peninsula. Call (206) 464-6400 or (888) 808-7977 for a service representative or (800) 84-FERRY for automated schedule information; the toll-free numbers are good in Washington state only. The hearing-impaired number is (800) 833-6388. (WEB SITE: www.wsdot.wa.gov/ferries/)

Visitor services

The **Seattle-King County Convention and Visitors Bureau** operates an information center on Level One of the Washington State Convention and Trade Center, open weekdays 8 to 5; (206) 461-5840. The center is sandwiched against and under the freeway between Pike Street and Ninth Avenue. If you're coming into Seattle on I-5, take the Madison Street exit downtown, go northwest on Fourth or Sixth, turn right onto Pike and follow it back toward the freeway to the center's parking garage. If you're afoot, go up Pike Street, enter the Trade Center through its Galleria Shops (between Seventh and Eighth) and walk eastward to the far corner of the ground floor.

The bureau's main office, which also offers visitor information, is at 520 Pike Street, Suite 1300, open weekdays 8:30 to 5; (206) 461-5840. (WEB SITE: www.seeseattle.org; E-MAIL: visinfo@seeseattle.org)

You might want to request the free *Seattle Visitors Guide* in advance by writing or calling the bureau. This thick publication covers a mix of attractions, restaurants, shopping, transportation and assorted other visitor services. However, listings are sometimes confusing, and seem to be dictated primarily by advertising revenue, with some attractions, museums and performing arts groups omitted. (And why listings for the Chimpanzee and Human Communication Institute in Ellensburg, and the Coueur d'Alene Resort in Idaho?) The center also publishes a free *Seattle Lodging Guide.*

GETTING ORIENTED

You'll need a good street map to find your way about. The *Seattle Visitors Guide* contains downtown and area maps. Good, detailed street maps are produced by the American Automobile Association's **AAA Washington**, although you have to be a member to get one. The Seattle AAA office is at 330 Sixth Ave., near Harrison Street just east of Seattle Center; open weekdays 8:30 to 5:30, (206) 448-5353. Its **AAA Travel Store**, which is open to non-members, is a good place to buy travel guidebooks, maps and travel gear. A for-sale version of the AAA map is available here, and at book and travel stores and hotel newsstands.

Free copies of the brightly colored *Seattle Tourmap* and *Where* magazine's *Seattle Map* are available at most hotel and motel desks, and at visitor centers. Both cover the downtown section only. We prefer the *Where* map because it's less cluttered with advertising logos.

Getting around & getting parked

Seattle isn't *quite* as tight on parking as some cities, although available spots are scarce and you don't get much for a quarter on a meter. If you can find an open meter, it'll be color coded according to its time limit—yellow for fifteen minutes, green for thirty and silver for two to four hours. Meters operate Monday through Saturday, generally from 6 or 7 a.m. to 6 p.m.; they don't have to be fed on the Sabbath or legal holidays.

Pay parking facilities are abundant and they generally don't fill up during business days. Most highrise office buildings and hotels have subterranean parking, which is predictably expensive.

Knowledgeable Seattlites park cheaply or free on the periphery and catch a bus downtown, taking advantage of the free ride zone. You can find longer time limit meters—usually two hours—on the outer fringes of Pioneer Square and the International District, and on Alaskan Way along the waterfront.

Public transit

Most of the downtown area is within Metro's free zone, which operates from 6 a.m. to 7 p.m. Simply hop on a bus, take it to your destination and hop off again, with a clear conscience. The fareless zone is bordered by Sixth Avenue, the freeway, Battery Street, the waterfront and Jackson Street. It includes the city's unusual underground bus tunnel, which runs from the International District to Ninth and Pine near the convention center.

Fares beyond downtown are modest. Naturally, drivers don't make change, but the fare boxes do take dollar bills. Call (800) 542-7876 or (206) 553-3000 for route and fare information.

Incidentally, the downtown bus tube was designed for eventual conversion to a light rail subway, which is on the planning boards. It's part of an ambitious multi-billion dollar regional transit system approved by voters in 1996 and slated to begin service in 2005. It will include a mix of light and heavy rail (over existing train tracks) throughout the Puget Sound region. Meanwhile, regional transit authorities have gotten together to offer **Puget Passes,** which provide combined fares on various lines. Brochures describing this rather complicated system are available aboard most buses.

Two other forms of public transit are popular with visitors, and we've worked them into a downtown walking/transit tour, outlined below. The **Monorail,** built for the Seattle world's fair, runs between the original fair site at Seattle Center and Westlake Center shopping mall at Fifth Avenue and Pine Street. It operates every fifteen minutes, daily 9 to midnight in summer, then Sunday-Thursday 9 to 9 and Friday-Saturday 9 to midnight the rest of the year. Fares are modest.

Waterfront Streetcars are quaint 1920s trolleys imported from Australia. They run from Pier 70, along the Seattle waterfront and then inland through Pioneer Square to the International District at Fifth Avenue and Jackson Street. Departures are every half hour, weekdays from 7 a.m. to 6:15 p.m., and weekends and holidays from 10:30 to 5. The fare is modest and you can get a transfer onto the Metro system. Many downtown merchants offer "Easy Street" tokens, which are good for parking discounts and for free rides on Metro, the Monorail and Waterfront Streetcars.

Getting camped?

Big cities aren't RV country and Seattle is no exception. Because of its complex street patterns, thick traffic and a virtual lack of RV parking, anyone who tries to bring a big rig into the city will not be a happy camper. Smaller units probably can survive the traffic crush and wavy-gravy street patterns, although parking will be a problem, except in residential neighborhoods. However, traffic barriers set up in many neighborhoods to discourage through traffic will drive an RVer bonkers. You can find parking for smaller rigs at outlying attractions such as Woodland Park Zoo, the Museum of Flight, Nordic Heritage Museum and at many city parks.

There are a few RV parks in nearby towns, including these:

Aqua Barn RV Park ● *15227 SE Renton-Maple Valley Rd., Renton, WA 98058; (425) 255-4618. RV and tent sites; full hookups; MC/VISA.* ☐ Showers, coin laundry, mini-mart; small indoor pool. From I-405, take exit 4 and drive three miles east on State Route 169.

Saltwater State Park ● *Two miles south of Des Moines on Puget Sound; (206) 764-4128. RV and tent sites, which can be reserved between May 15 and September 15; call Reservations Northwest at (800) 452-5687; MC/VISA.* □ Sites near the water with flush and pit potties and showers; no hookups. Boat dock, scuba diving, nature trails, mini-mart.

KOA Seattle/Tacoma ● *5801 S. 212th, Kent, WA 98032; (800) 562-1892 or (206) 872-8652. (WEB SITE: www.koakampgrounds.com; E-MAIL: seattlekoa@aol.com) RV and tent sites; full hookups; MC/VISA.* □ Some pull-throughs, many shaded sites; showers, coin laundry, mini-mart, car rentals. Clubhouse, pool, playground, game room. Take I-5 exit 152 to the right onto 188th street, then follow Orillia Road south; it blends into 212th and the campground is on the right, about three miles from the freeway.

Trailer Inns, Inc. ● *15531 SE 37th, Bellevue, WA 98006; (800) 659-4684 or (425) 747-9181. RV sites; full hookups; MC/VISA.* □ Showers, coin laundry, indoor pool, sauna, spa, rec room and playground. Take I-90 exit 11 (westbound) or 11A (eastbound) and follow signs.

Vasa Park ● *3650 W. Lake Sammamish Rd. SE, Bellevue, WA 98008; (425) 746-3260. RV and tent sites; hookups.* □ On Lake Sammamish with showers, swimming, fishing, boat ramp and kids' playground. One mile north of I-90 from exit 13.

If you have a tow-along or a fifth-wheel unit, unhitch and leave your mobile home immobilized at the RV park. If you don't have a second vehicle, consider renting one. That's precisely what we did in researching this book and revising our *Washington Discovery Guide*. We set up shop at KOA Seattle/Tacoma and—by avoiding rush hour traffic—we could whisk our rental car into the heart of the city within twenty minutes.

The heart of the city

Downtown Seattle is generally described as the area between Seattle Center (the world's fair site), Safeco Field, the I-5 freeway complex and the Elliott Bay waterfront. Within this area are several easily-defined sections. The shopping, hotel and business district, shaded by some of the tallest highrises west of Chicago, is concentrated between Eighth Avenue, Stewart Street, Third Avenue and Columbia Street. In fact, the 76-story Bank of America Tower at Fourth Avenue and Cherry Street *is* the tallest highrise west of Chicago, topping out at 943 feet. When you look northwest from downtown toward the 605-foot Space Needle, that famous spire looks a bit squat. (Bank of America Tower has a public observation area; see Chapter Two, page 61.)

Just south of downtown is the **Pioneer Square** area, site of Yesler's sawmill, the underground and other relics of Seattle's beginnings. It's home to shops, restaurants, antique stores and galleries tucked into fine old brick buildings. Just above and to the south of Pioneer Square is Chinatown, formally called the **International District** because of the influx of several other nationalities, primarily Asians. The old King Street railroad station, the Mariners' Safeco Field and the Seahawk's new stadium form its western border.

The **waterfront,** just about everyone's favorite locale in Seattle, stretches for three miles along Elliott Bay, immediately below the downtown highrises. Seattle is one of the West Coast's major shipping centers and you'll see giant orange container-lifting cranes in the port area near Safeco Field. Just north of here, the waterfront offers a savory mix of restaurants, shops, parks, public piers and ferry terminals. Its centerpiece is lovable old **Pike Place Market,** at the foot of Pike Street. North of the waterfront and inland is **Seattle Center.** Here, leftover pieces of the world's fair are represented in the Space Needle, Pacific Science Center, Seattle Opera House and assorted carnival rides and exhibit halls.

Downtown is built on a tilt, so a stroll will give you a good workout. Most streets are one-way, so watch your intersection turns. Down at the waterfront, Alaskan Way will get you to its many attractions. To leave the area quickly, get on the elevated Alaskan Way Viaduct, which unfortunately ruins the view of the city from the waterfront and visa versa.

Shopping

The best shopping is centered in three areas of central Seattle—the downtown core, the waterfront and Pioneer Square.

Most downtown malls, major department stores and specialty shops are concentrated along Fifth and Sixth avenues in the heart the highrise district, between Madison Street and Olive Way. The major shopping complexes are **Rainier Square** between Fourth and Fifth avenues and Union and University Streets; **Westlake Center** at Pine Street between Fourth and Fifth avenues (with the Monorail station); **Pacific Place,** cradled by Pine, Olive, Sixth and Seventh; and **City Centre** between Fifth and Sixth avenues and Pike and Union streets. Downtown's two flagship department stores are **Nordstrom,** covering most of the block rimmed by Pine, Pike, Fifth and Sixth; and **Bon Marché** at Pine and Third.

If you must have a Seattle ashtray or made-in-Taiwan totem, head for the waterfront, where most tourist-oriented shopping is based. The main attraction, on a bluff above the waterfront, is **Pike Place Market.** Hardly a tourist gimmick, it's a wonderful collection of produce stands, food stalls, restaurants and eclectic shops. South of Pike, you'll find serious tourist shopping at **Bay Pavilion** on Pier 57, with more shops on piers 56 and 55, and **Ye Olde Curiosity Shop** at Pier 54.

Pioneer Square offers assorted antique stores, curio shops, galleries and book stores, in addition to several cafés and restaurants. Elliott Bay Book Company at 101 S. Main near First, with hundreds of thousands of books and a folksy café tucked into its old brick basement, is one of the great book stores of western America.

Lodging

When visiting Seattle, we'd recommend staying were the action is—in the downtown area—and commute to the peripheral activities. It's great to be able to walk to Pike Place Market for breakfast or a caffé latte and watch the city stretch and yawn as it prepares for another day.

Most of the city's major hotels are in the downtown area, as are a few smaller hotels and an occasional motel. However, most motels are grouped along Aurora Avenue in north Seattle, since that's the original Highway 99 that served the city in pre-freeway days. More lodgings are strung along southbound Highway 99 and at interchanges of I-5 as these two highways head toward Sea-Tac International Airport. And of course, Sea-Tac has the usual cluster of airport hotels and motels.

The neighbors

Several interesting neighborhoods rim downtown Seattle. Immediately north is the newly gentrifying **Belltown,** an old section becoming trendy with galleries, boutiques and restaurants. **Queen Anne Hill** is to the northeast, site of posh Victorian homes. The name comes from its preponderance of Queen Anne style architecture. Farther north is **Ballard,** settled by Scandinavian fisherfolk and site of the Chittenden Locks that elevate boats from Puget Sound to the higher waters of Lake Union and Lake Washington. North of the locks is the fine Nordic Heritage Museum; to the northeast is Woodland Park Zoo.

The **Eastlake** area encompasses Lake Union, rimmed by a commercial-residential district and tied to Puget Sound by a ship canal (along with Lake Washington). About two miles west, on that canal, is Fishermen's Terminal, home to the West Coast's largest commercial fishing fleet. Northeast of Lake Union is the **University District,** locally known simply as the "U District." Therein lies the large University of Washington campus, surrounded by venerable homes and student-focused retail areas with coffee houses, book stores, earthy bakeries and ethnic cafés.

Immediately west of the "U," coved against the north shore of Lake Union, are the **Wallingford** and **Fremont** districts. They're also busy with coffee houses, international cafés and the odd book store, along with some interesting boutiques. The Fremont, gathered around the northern anchorage of the Fremont drawbridge, is a wonderfully goofy area. After local residents declared it to be the center of the universe several years ago, it has become a center of eccentricity, curious art works and really wacky annual celebrations. Fremonters have adopted as their motto *De libertas quirkas*—"The freedom to be peculiar." It's probably our favorite Seattle neighborhood.

Capitol Hill and **First Hill** immediately northeast of downtown are neighborhoods of fine old homes—mostly restored—and stylish boutiques and cafés. A center strip of Capitol Hill that borders Broadway is home to much of Seattle's gay and lesbian community. East of Capitol Hill is huge **Lake Washington,** surrounded by several water-oriented residential areas. The city of **Bellevue** occupies the far shore and **Renton** is at the bottom.

South of downtown—not a neighborhood but certainly a keystone to Seattle's development—is **Boeing Field,** where the Boeing Airplane Company is headquartered. The airstrip is used primarily for charter airlines and general aviation. The Museum of Flight there is one of the country's finest aviation archives.

DOING SEATTLE

Before we begin sorting through Seattle's lists of Ten Best, let's have a good look at the city. First, we suggest that you take the comprehensive driving route that we outline below. Then do a walking route interspersed with public transit links. These routes will take you past most of what makes the city a major visitor attraction, and they will help you get your bearings.

Much of this material has been lifted from the Seattle chapter of our *Washington Discovery Guide* and it has been updated for both publications.

Note: Bold face listings marked with ❖ are described in more detail elsewhere in this book; check the index for page numbers.

Driving tour

Navigational note: Seattle is a sprawling and complex city. Since it's built on hills rising from waterways, many of its street patterns are quite erratic. Some streets make right-angle turns or peel off suddenly, so it's easy to get lost. Transfer our route description onto a detailed city map with a marker pen and designate one in your party as the navigator. If you're the navigator, give adequate warning when a complicated turn approaches and please don't let wrong turns threaten your relationship. ("You should have turned back there!" "Well, why didn't you *tell* me back there?")

Also, don't attempt our driving route all in one day, for it covers more than seventy miles. Take your time, see the sights along the way and—when the sun begins lowering over Puget Sound—mark the spot where you left off and resume your trek tomorrow. This route is best attempted over a weekend, for you'll avoid getting caught in morning and evening rush hours.

To begin, head south along the waterfront on Alaskan Way—not the viaduct but the surface street.

Navigational note: Most downtown streets stop short of the waterfront. However, these three go all the way—Broad Street (coming down from Seattle Center), Wall Street (from the Belltown area) and Madison Street (from the heart of downtown). Take any of these to Alaskan Way and turn south.

You'll pass many items of interest along the waterfront, such as the Seattle Aquarium on Pier 59, Waterfront Park on Pier 58 and Ye Old Curiosity Shop on Pier 54. Ignore them for the moment, since our walking route below will permit a more comprehensive look. Press on past these lures, past the new home of the Seattle Seahawks (due for completion in 2002) and the Seattle Mariners' ❖ **Safeco Field**, whose retractable roof resembles an unfinished airplane hangar.

Just beyond Safeco, you'll enter the working port district. Here, the piers are called terminals, although the sequential numbers continue. Near **Terminal 30,** a sign directs you to the right to ❖ **Jack Perry Memorial Viewpoint.** It's a postage-stamp park offering views of the East Waterway that brings ships into the cargo docks. As you continue south, your route has changed its name to Marginal Way. Just beyond Terminal 25, as you approach a complex of expressways and freeway ramps, turn right either onto Spokane Street or onto the West Seattle Freeway, following signs to West Seattle. This takes you over the tip of **Harbor Island** and across the bottom of the port area. Your destination is Harbor Avenue, which takes you to the right along West Seattle's east shoreline.

Navigational note: This expressway complex—the West Seattle Freeway—is undergoing major revamping and you must stay alert to keep on course. When we last passed, Spokane Street swung to the right about midway across the lower port area, then you hit a stop signal and turned left to stay on course. (If you do it correctly, you'll pass the Chelan Café.) This may have been modified by the time you arrive; you may be able to use the freeway itself, then fork to the right onto Harbor Avenue.

Once you're safely onto Harbor Avenue, you'll pass through the last of the port industrial area, then the route skims the waterfront and travels alongside a series of parklands that mark the shoreline of **West Seattle.** As you approach ❖ **Salty's on Alki** seafood restaurant, you'll get absolutely awesome vistas of the towering Seattle skyline across Elliott Bay. The community through here is known as Alki, although you've not yet reached Alki Point, where the city was first settled.

As your route bends around ❖ **Duwamish Head,** it changes its name to Alki Avenue SW. A walking/biking path travels for several miles along the shorefront here. It extends from the expressway where you picked up Harbor Avenue, past **Don Armeni Park** in the heart of the Alki community, through the long and skinny ❖ **Alki Beach Park** to finally to ❖ **Alki Point,** where Seattle began. (We picked this as our favorite bike route; Chapter Twelve, page 190) Alki Beach Park has one of the few sandy bathing beaches in the area and it's popular with the suntan crowd on warm summer days.

Stay alert and you'll see—on your right—a small obelisk in Alki Beach Park at 63rd Avenue SW, marking the city's birthplace. A stone from Plymouth Rock, another significant American landing site, is embedded into its base. A few blocks beyond, Alki Avenue crosses the nub of Alki Point and passes the **U.S. Coast Guard Light Station.** It's open to visitors May through September, with tours weekends and most holidays noon to 4; (206) 286-5423.

You're now on Beach Drive SW, which you'll follow for several miles through a mix of homes and shorefront parklands. Although you've lost the downtown vista, you'll see offshore islands of the Puget Sound and—on a clear day—the distant Olympics. Hit a stop sign and take a half left (to avoid a dead end), following Vashon Ferry signs. You'll shortly encounter another stop sign, opposite large **Lincoln Park,** a mix of woods and lawns covering the conical lump of Williams Point. Turn left onto Fauntleroy Avenue SW, the main thoroughfare from the Fauntleroy ferry landing. It curves through a mix of homes and businesses and returns you to the West Seattle Freeway over the tip of Harbor Island.

Navigational note: As we indicated above, this freeway was undergoing reconstruction as this book went to press, so stay alert. Instead of linking with I-5, you'll want to return to southbound Marginal Way by following Highway 99 South signs.

Once you're back down on Marginal Way, continue southward. After a short distance, you'll see a ❖ **Diagonal Avenue South Public Shoreline Access** sign on your right. Follow it through several cargo container terminals to a pleasing little park alongside the **Duwamish Waterway,** which is a popular kayaking channel. This cozy little park has several picnic tables and benches, and a brambly path leads down to water's edge. Return to Marginal Way and continue southward, keeping to the left to avoid being skimmed onto the new Freeway 509, which would take you to Burien.

Navigational note: Highway 99 also veers to the right at this point. You'll want to keep left, staying with East Marginal Way South.

After a couple of miles, you'll arrive alongside the extensive **Seattle Boeing Aircraft** facility and ❖ **Boeing Field,** also known as King County International Airport. Press southward through this complex and you'll see the great glass greenhouse style structure of the excellent ❖ **Museum of Flight** on your left. Drive past the museum and turn left into its parking area.

From the museum, continue south on Marginal for less than a mile, then turn left at a State Highway 900 sign. Cross over I-5 and get into the left lane for Martin Luther King Jr. Way. Drive north through a scruffy industrial area and, after about a mile, turn right at a stop light onto Henderson Street. This takes you to ❖ **Beer Sheva Park** on the shore of ❖ **Lake Washington.** Originally called Atlantic City Park, it was renamed to honor a Seattle sister city in Israel. The park offers picnic and swimming areas and a boat launch.

From here, Seward Park Avenue takes you north through a scruffy and then an elegant old neighborhood and —with a right turn onto Juneau Street—to large ❖ **Seward Park.**

Navigational note: A mile and a half after you turn onto Seward from Henderson, fork to the right to stay with Seward. If you continue straight ahead, you'll wind up on Wilson Avenue.

Occupying a lumpy, wooded peninsula that sticks into Lake Washington like a large green thumb, Seward is one of the city's more versatile parks. It has walking/biking paths, a kiddie play area, a Japanese Garden, picnic grounds, a boat launch and a swimming beach. As you leave the park, turn right onto Lake Washington Boulevard, a pleasant tree-canopied lane that you'll follow for several miles along the lakeshore. Like Alki Avenue, it parallels a long park strip with a hiking/biking path. Offering views of boats at play on Lake Washington and Mercer Island across the way, it's one of the city's more attractive drives.

Two of the world's four floating bridges are along this route. Lake Washington Boulevard crosses under the west anchorage of **Lake Washington Floating Bridge,** which carries I-90 traffic to Mercer Island and far beyond. The original bridge, built on hollow concrete pontoons, was completed in 1939 as the first of its kind. It was replaced by two side-by-side bridges after it sank in a storm in 1991.

After passing under the bridge anchorage, your route changes its name to Lakeside Drive and brushes more lakeside parks. To keep you confused and/or alert, it regains its Lake Washington Boulevard name at some point through here. After a couple of miles, as you pass **Denny Blaine Park,** fork to the left and travel inland through a lushly landscaped neighborhood and then into large **Washington Park,** which is fused into **Broadmoor Golf Course.** Stay with Lake Washington Boulevard, forking to the left and following signs toward State Route 520 East and **Evergreen Point Floating Bridge,** which spans upper Lake Washington. However, you won't go that far. Swing westward to parallel Freeway 520, then take a quick right onto 24th Avenue East, crossing the freeway and following signs to the ❖ **Museum of History and Industry.** (By late 2000 or early 2001, the museum will be in the Washington State Convention and Trade Center, near downtown at Eighth Avenue between Union and Pike.)

Return to Lake Washington Boulevard, go a block west and turn right onto Montlake Boulevard. You'll cross the freeway again and enter the extensive campus of the ❖ **University of Washington.** If you want to explore the grounds, pick up a map at the **Visitor Information Center** at 4014 University Way; (206) 543- 2100. To reach it, fork to the left from Montlake onto NE Pacific Street just after you enter the campus. Follow Pacific to University Way and turn right. The center is two blocks up, on your right at the corner of NE Camino.

The university's northern edge is bordered by NE 45th Street, which separates it from the old and mostly well-tended homes of the

"U District." Many are now fraternity and sorority houses. Most of the typical student bookstores, bistros, coffee houses and other hangouts are along 45th and University Way NE.

To continue the driving tour, if you didn't stop to explore the campus, press northward on Montlake, then fork left at a double left turn lane (opposite a large parking lot) onto 25th Avenue NE. If you did take a campus prowl, go east on 45th and cross a viaduct over 25th Avenue. Make a series of right turns in a kind of clumsy cloverleaf and you'll drop down onto 25th. Either way, you'll soon pass the ❖ **University Village** shopping center on your right.

Continue north from the village for a few blocks, go left onto NE 54th Street, curve around the bottom of ❖ **Ravenna Park,** then pick up Ravenna Boulevard NE and follow it northwest. This is an attractive route with a landscaped median strip, passing through a grand old tree-shrouded residential area. Stay alert as you approach 15th Avenue NE, since you'll have to zig right and then zag left to stay with Ravenna Boulevard. You'll zip under Interstate 5, then within a quarter of a mile, blend onto Green Lake Way. The neighborhood surrounding ❖ **Green Lake Park** is an appealing little village of small cafés and shops.

You may be tempted to pause and play at this popular park which offers—among other things—a 2.8-mile walking/biking path around its shoreline. You can rent a canoe, paddleboat or rowboat at **Green Lake Boat Rentals** (206) 527-0171; or a bike from **Gregg's Green Lake Cycle,** just outside the park at Green Lake Way and NE 70th Street, (206) 523-1822. Unlike chilly Puget Sound, Green Lake's protected waters are warm enough for summer swimming.

From here, continue through Green Lake village then, just beyond the business district, leave the lake rim drive and continue straight ahead on Winona Avenue North. After a couple of blocks, turn south on Aurora Avenue (Highway 99). You're headed for ❖ **Woodland Park Zoo,** which is fused into the southwestern edge of Green Lake Park. However, ignore the first marked turnoff (59th Street), since it takes you to a back entrance gate which is sometimes closed. Continue south on Aurora, turn right on 46th Street and then go right again onto Fremont Street, which will take you to the main zoo entrance.

Having talked with the animals, exit the zoo on Fremont, go right on 50th Street then right again onto Phinney Avenue, essentially wrapping around the edges of Woodland Park. Take Phinney about half a mile to North 65th Street, turn left and follow it west. You'll soon enter the community of **Ballard,** settled by Scandinavians and boasting a fine ethnic archive. To reach the ❖ **Nordic Heritage Museum,** go north on 32nd Avenue NW to NW 68th Street and turn right. The museum occupies a large former high school on your right.

Return to 32nd and continue north. At a stop sign at NW 85th Street, veer to the left toward ❖ **Shilshole Bay Marina** and **Golden Gardens Park.** The route takes you down through the park, in a looping spiral to the waterfront, while conveniently pointing you back toward downtown Seattle. More green than golden, the park is thickly wooded and laced with hiking trails. Its shoreline offers sandy beaches, boat ramps and great views of Puget Sound and the distant Olympic Mountains.

This route puts you on the aptly-named Seaview Avenue NW. Press southward through Shilshole Bay Marina, with its forests of masts and aquatic-view restaurants. You'll shortly curve around to the east onto NW 54th Street and arrive at ❖ **Hiram M. Chittenden Locks and English Gardens.** When you see the Lockspot Café ahead, turn right into a parking area alongside a railroad track and walk through the gardens to the locks.

Continue driving briefly east on 54th, which blends onto NW Market Street; follow it several blocks to 15th Avenue NW and turn right for the **Ballard Bridge.** (You also can do a half right onto Leary Avenue short of 15th, at a "City center/Ballard Bridge" sign.) The bridge takes you across Salmon Bay and the Lake Washington Ship Canal. Down to your right, you'll see a great armada of commercial fishing boats, packed tightly against the piers of ❖ **Fishermen's Terminal.** To reach this interesting area, turn onto West Emerson at the end of the bridge and follow signs.

As you leave the terminal, return to westbound Emerson, then shortly do a half right onto Gilman, following Fort Lawton signs. After about half a mile, swerve around to your left onto Government Way and follow it into ❖ **Discovery Park.** Once inside this wooded hilltop park, follow signs to the ❖ **Daybreak Star Cultural Arts Center;** (206) 285-4425. Primarily a meeting hall and activity center for native people, it has a gallery of traditional and contemporary Indian art. Discovery Park is a mix of woodlands, moors and sea cliffs occupying the site of the former Fort Lawson military base. Stop at the visitor center on the left just inside the park entrance for information concerning conducted nature walks and other activities.

Depart the park on Government Way, turn right (south) onto 34th Avenue, then right again onto Emerson. After about eight blocks, turn left at a stop sign onto Magnolia Boulevard and follow it through one of Seattle's prettiest neighborhoods. This area is called **Magnolia Bluffs**, offering grand views down to Puget Sound, Elliott Bay and the city skyline. Most of these views are hogged by expensive homes, although you'll start seeing them when you come alongside pretty little **Magnolia Park.** As you start downhill from the bluffs, watch on your right for a viewpoint where you can pause and enjoy the panorama.

Navigational note: Just below here, watch for one of those exasperating Seattle street patterns. Without warning, Magnolia Boulevard makes a 90-degree righthand turn at a stop sign. If you continue straight ahead, you'll blunder off course and become haplessly lost in a spaghetti tangle of residential streets. (We did so and wondered how anyone who lives up here ever finds their way home.)

Finally, just when you thought you'd never complete this driving route, you will. Magnolia becomes Gaylor, which drops down a steep viaduct into a waterfront industrial area and blends onto the **Garfield Street-Magnolia Bridge** above ❖ **Elliott Bay Marina.** This route puts you onto Elliott Avenue, taking you past the enjoined ❖ **Elliott Bay-Myrtle Edwards parks** and toward the city center. To reach the waterfront, turn right from Elliott onto Broad Street, drop down to Alaskan Way and turn left. If you're headed for the downtown area, veer to the left from Elliott onto Western Avenue.

Walking/transit tour

This covers about six miles but don't panic. Sections of it can be taken aboard public transit.

You *can* drive the walking tour, although you won't see as much and you may get diverted by one-way streets. Also, it's a bother to find parking places while checking out attractions and shops along the way. Seattle has a wonderful collection of public art, and you'll miss most of it if you drive. Further, it's very difficult to make friends with a waterfront seagull from a moving vehicle.

The tour begins in ❖ **Seattle Center,** the site of the 1962 Century 21 Exposition. This is a good starting point since you'll find ample parking here or at nearby private lots. If you're afoot and downtown, catch the Monorail to Seattle Center from Westlake Center at Fifth and Pine streets.

Several original Century 21 structures still survive, including exhibit facilities, some typical Tinkertoy-style world's fair structures and a permanent fun zone. The ❖ **Pacific Science Center** is a good place to park the kids and possibly yourselves. And *everyone* must ascend the ❖ **Space Needle.** The view from on high will provide a preview of your upcoming exploration. Locator maps and graphics on the indoor and outdoor observation decks point out area landmarks.

After you've finished with the center's attractions, exit onto Broad Street and make a right. This takes you downhill to the waterfront, hitting Alaskan Way just below the car barn and the first stop of the ❖ **Waterfront Streetcars.** Before committing yourself to Alaskan Way, turn right and stroll to ❖ **Myrtle Edwards Park.** It and adjoining ❖ **Elliott Bay Park** extend a mile and a half north along the waterfront, offering great views, a walking-jogging- biking path and a public fishing pier. (Our tour route mileage doesn't include walking the length of the two parks.)

Opposite the streetcar barn is Pier 70, the old **Ainsworth and Dunne Wharf.** It may contain a waterfront shopping complex by the time you arrive; it was being reconstructed—and behind schedule— when we last strolled past. Adjacent **Pier 69** is the launching pad for ❖ **Victoria Clipper** cruises. Just beyond is ❖ **Hotel Edgewater** with its harbor-view restaurant, which you might consider as a lunch stop. From here, you can continue your stroll or hop aboard a Waterfront Streetcar to give your feet a rest. (In doing so, however, you'll be shuttled past the fine ❖ **Odyssey Maritime Discovery Center** at Pier 66.)

If you take the streetcar, get off at Pike Street station. ❖ **Pike Place Market** is just above, reached by climbing 143 steps up the **Pike Place Hillclimb.** It's worth the exertion to visit this wonderfully weathered collection of produce stands, food stalls, shops and restaurants. Several shops are terraced into the hillside climb, offering opportunity to pause in mid-hike. If the total hillclimb is too challenging, hike a block up to Western Avenue and you'll find an elevator near the ❖ **Market Heritage Center.** This is a Pike Place Market history exhibit at 1531 Western.

Return from Pike to the Elliott Bay waterfront for visits to the ❖ **Seattle Aquarium** and the ❖ **Omnidome** theater, which shows those wide-angle travel and adventure films. Both attractions are on Pier 59. ❖ **Waterfront Park** at the site of former Pier 58 offers benches, picnic tables and public fishing spots. Adjacent Pier 57 is home to **Bay Pavilion,** with a collection of souvenir shops and seafood restaurants. ❖ **Argosy** sightseeing and dinner cruises and ❖ **Tillicum Village salmon bake tours** depart from docks between piers 56 and 55. Next door at Pier 54 is ❖ **Ye Olde Curiosity Shop,** the waterfront's senior souvenir store, tracing its roots back to 1899.

Waterfront fish and chips take-outs are Seattle's version of the San Francisco Fisherman's Wharf walk-away shrimp and crab cocktails. They're handy for lunch-on-the-go and you'll find several stalls between Seattle Aquarium and ❖ **Ivar's Acres of Clams,** which is the waterfront's oldest seafood restaurant. Beyond Ivar's, you'll encounter the ❖ **Washington State Ferry Terminal** at Pier 52 (Coleman Dock) and beyond that, a public boat landing at the base of ❖ **Pioneer Square.** It was near here that Henry Yesler built his sawmill in 1852. Follow Yesler Way into Pioneer Square and explore the shops and cafés housed in fine old brick and masonry. At Yesler Way and First Avenue, you'll encounter Bill Speidel's ❖ **Underground Tour** office, in Doc Maynard's Public House.

We won't suggest specific routing through Pioneer Square; simply wander about at will. As you wander, learn about the Yukon Gold Rush at the storefront ❖ **Klondike Gold Rush National Historical Park** at Main and Occidental. Pioneer Square was the main staging area for the rush to riches, and this small, well-done museum represents the Seattle element of the historic park. It also has units in Skagway, Alaska, and Dawson City in the Yukon Territory.

Another worthy Pioneer Square area stop is the ❖ **Seattle Metropolitan Police Museum** at 317 Third Avenue between Main and Jackson. Also, stroll into pretty little ❖ **Waterfall Garden Park** at Main and Second Avenue. A cataract tumbles into a landscaped garden in this appealing park, which marks the site of the founding of United Parcel Service in 1907. And check out ❖ **Smith Tower** at Yesler Way and Second Avenue, Western America's first real skyscraper. An elevator will take you forty-two stories to the top for great views.

From Pioneer Square, follow Jackson Street past the brick clock-towered **King Street Station** and **Union Station.** Just to the south, you'll see a large hole in the ground busy with construction activity, or you'll see the new **Seattle Seahawks' stadium.** Just beyond is the Seattle Mariners' ❖ **Safeco Field** with its distinct retractable roof. Continue up King Street to the ❖ **International District,** busy with Asian restaurants and shops. Note the elaborate dragon gate standing in the middle of **Wing Hay Park** at Jackson and Maynard Avenue. Pause at the ❖ **Wing Luke Asian Memorial Museum** at 417 Seventh Avenue, just south of Jackson.

A rather steep hike up Maynard Avenue or Seventh Avenue will take you to **Kobe Terrace Park** and the **Danny Woo Community Garden,** graded into a steep slope below the I-5 freeway. The parks aren't particularly well-kept, although the concept of tiny family garden patches in a city is interesting.

Stroll back through the International District to the **bus terminal** at Jackson between Fourth and Fifth avenues. You can take the third element of Seattle's transit system to return to your starting point. The "tunnel bus" disappears underground here, with several station stops beneath downtown Seattle. If you stay with it to the end, at Ninth Avenue between Olive Way and Pine Street, you can walk down to Eighth Avenue and then stroll south three blocks to ❖ **Freeway Park.** This is a series of terraces and landscaped patios built adjacent to the tanglework of the freeway system. It's near the impressive **Washington State Convention and Trade Center** and the dramatically concave **Two Union Square** highrise. In the ground floor of the convention facility, you'll find the helpful **Visitors Information Center.**

To complete your loop, go downhill on Pike Street (or Pine Street if you're driving), turn right (north) onto Fifth Avenue (Fourth if you're driving) and follow it to Westlake Center. Here, you can catch the Monorail back to Seattle Center.

OUR FAVORITE SEATTLE MOMENTS

1 STARTING THE DAY AT PIKE PLACE MARKET ● *First Avenue and Pike Street; (206) 682-7453. GETTING THERE: Although the market is at the foot of Pike Street, it's one-way coming up, so take either Pine or Union Street from downtown. Two-way First Avenue, paralleling the waterfront, crosses in front of the market.*

Begun as a direct-to-consumer produce and fish market in 1907, Pike Place Market has become Seattle's most loved tourist attraction, with its cheerful hawkers and dozens of produce and fish stands, curio shops and art stalls. We like to get there around 6:30 in the morning, before the rest of the tourists arrive, and watch the produce and fish mongers set up their glittering and colorful displays. It's a quieter time—there's time to talk with the folks in the food and fish stalls; time to watch first light glisten off Elliott Bay; time to smell the fresh-cut flowers and metallic aroma of fish; time for a leisurely breakfast.

Two market restaurants open early—Lowell's and the Athenian Inn (although it's closed Sundays). Or you can start your Seattle day with goodies from the produce stands—a basket of fresh strawberries, a banana or two, some crisp carrots and—to satisfy your sweet tooth— tasty fruit rolls coated in coconut. Need an early morning caffeine fix? The original Starbucks is just across the way at 1912 Pike Place Market Street. It begins serving its legendary caffé latte and other specialty coffees around 7 a.m. Pike Place Market appears frequently in this book; check the index for other references.

2 WATCHING SUNDOWN FROM THE SPACE NEEDLE •
In Seattle Center, just north of downtown.

Built in 1962 for the Seattle world's fair, this long-legged tripod with a flying saucer atop provides the city's finest views. It's particularly grand at sunset, when *auld sol* slips behind the jagged Olympic Mountains, perhaps tinting wispy clouds pink and orange. We like to stroll around the outside observation deck, watching the waters of Elliott Bay turn to shiny slate; watching the lights of downtown warm to the evening as daylight fades; perhaps catching the last pink glow of light on perpetually snowcapped Mount Rainier. Don't plan a sunset dinner up here, since the slowly rotating restaurant—and not your feet—will dictate where you'll be when the sun slips away. For more on the Needle, see Chapter Two, page 55.

3 HAVING A SUNSET DINNER AT THE PALISADE • *At Elliott Bay Marina at 2601 W. Marina Place; (206) 285-1000. Northwest cuisine; full bar service. Lunch and dinner Monday-Saturday, and Sunday brunch. Major credit cards. GETTING THERE: Take Elliott Avenue about two miles northwest from downtown, cross the Garfield Street-Magnolia Bridge and take the Elliott Bay Marina/Smith Cove Park exit.*

The Space Needle is a great place to watch the sunset, but if you want dinner, you're better served—pun intended—by adjourning to the Palisade restaurant. The kitchen is excellent and the views from the restaurant's floor-to-ceiling windows are simply splendid—through the masts of Elliott Bay Marina to the downtown Seattle skyline. On a good evening, you'll see Mount Rainier's snowcap turning a rosy pink as the sun slips into Puget Sound. For more on the Palisade, see Chapter Three, page 71.

4 *FEEDING SEAGULLS FROM A ROOM BALCONY AT THE HOTEL EDGEWATER* • *2411 Alaskan Way, Seattle, WA 98121; (800) 624-0670 or (206) 728-7000. (WEB SITE: www.noble-househotes.com) Major credit cards. GETTING THERE: It's on Pier 67 at the north waterfront, at the base of Wall Street.*

The Edgewater is Seattle's only waterfront hotel and many of its rooms have balconies right over Elliott Bay. We like to lounge against the railing, admiring the city skyline and tossing bits of food to passing gulls. Many become adept at catching their fare in midair. Don't invite them onto the balcony, however; the management likes to keep things neat and clean. The Edgewater listing is in Chapter Six, page 123.

5 *EATING FISH AND CHIPS AT LITTLE CHINOOK'S* • *Fishermen's Terminal at 1900 W. Nickerson St.; (206) 283-4665. Lunch and dinner weekdays and brunch through dinner weekends. Major credit cards. GETTING THERE: Follow Elliott Avenue northwest from downtown, blend onto 15th Avenue West and take the West Emerson exit just before 15th crosses the Ballard Bridge. Little Chinook's is on the east end of the building that houses Chinook's seafood restaurant.*

Seattle is famous for its fish and chips—perhaps not as famous as Great Britain or Australia—although it certainly is the take-out food of choice here. We feature the city's best fish and chips takeouts in Chapter Four, and the winner is Little Chinook's (page 102). We order halibut and chips, then we take our booty out to one of the benches that offers a view of the terminal's huge commercial fishing fleet. We enjoy the fish, the chips and the view, while ignoring the seagulls who try to convince us that they haven't had a decent meal in days.

6 *ATTENDING A CONCERT AT BENAROYA HALL* • *200 University St.; (206) 215-4747. (WEB SITE: www.seattlesymphony.org) GETTING THERE: Benaroya Hall is downtown between Union and University streets and Second and Third avenues.*

Benaroya Hall is the stunning new home of the Seattle Symphony and its many concerts provide some of the city's best musical moments. The main hall is handsomely coiffed, all seats are excellent and the acoustics are perfectly tuned. The Symphony's concerts are so versatile—ranging from brooding classics to light pops—that you're sure to find a suitable program. See Chapter Seven, page 131.

7 *ADMIRING OUTDOOR GEAR AT REI* • *222 Yale Ave. North; (206) 223-1944. (WEB SITE: www.rei.com) Weekdays 10 to 9, Saturday 9 to 7 and Sunday 11 to 6. GETTING THERE: This outdoor mecca is at the corner of Yale and John Street. Head east from downtown* *on Denny way and—just short of I-5—turn left on Minor Avenue, go a block to John and turn right.*

Opened in 1996 as the new flagship of REI, this handsome multi-story space is easily the most interesting retail outlet in Seattle—at least if you're an outdoor type. Near the entrance, a waterfall splashes into a woodland garden. Inside, you can try out hiking shoes on a mini-trail, climb a 65-foot pinnacle, test a mountain bike on an enclosed course and shop for just about every kind of outdoor item imaginable. And when you're shopped out, take a break at the upper floor World Wrapps, where you can enjoy a great city skyline view while munching some sort of strange international burrito. For more on REI, see Chapter Eleven, page 173.

8 STROLLING OR PEDALING THE WEST SEATTLE SHORELINE • *Around Duwamish Head to Alki Point. GETTING THERE: Cross the tip of Harbor Island on the West Seattle Freeway or Spokane Street and go right onto Harbor Avenue.*

This route around the edge of the West Seattle peninsula offers awesome views across Elliott Bay to the Seattle skyline and then—as you round Duwamish Head—pleasing vistas across Puget Sound. It's popular either as a walking/jogging or cycling route; sections of it have separate paths for pedestrians and cyclists. Alki Beach Park offers one of the few sandy beaches (great for sunning; a bit chilly for swimming) in the Seattle area. If you want to take a picnic break here, you can find lunch fare at Alki Spud Fish and Chips at 2666 Alki Avenue. Or for a caffé latte and bakery snacks, try Alki Bakery at 2738 Alki Avenue. This route is featured as a bike path in Chapter Twelve and the two food places are listed in Chapter Four, pages 103 and 107.

9 WATCHING THE "BIRDS" AT THE MUSEUM OF FLIGHT • *9404 E. Marginal Way (beside Boeing Field); (206) 764-5720. Daily 10 to 5 (Thursdays until 9). GETTING THERE: Head south from downtown on Alaskan Way, which becomes East Marginal Way and takes you to Boeing Field. Or take exit 158 from I-5 and follow directional signs.*

The Museum of Flight is our favorite Seattle archive and one of the best aviation museums in the country. We can spend hours out there, admiring the big "birds" displayed in the imposing six-story greenhouse-style main museum and studying the history of flight. Several other historic aircraft are parked outside, including the original Air Force One that flew several of our presidents about the world. Since we're easily amused, we like to adjourn to the museum's mock-up control tower, where we can watch planes land at adjacent Boeing Field while listing to conversations between pilots and air controllers. For more on the museum, see Chapter Two, page 50.

10 *WATCHING RUSH HOUR TRAFFIC FROM JOSÉ RI-ZAL PARK* ● *In the Beacon Hill district, southeast of downtown. GET-TING THERE: Take Jackson Street east from the Pioneer Square area, cross under the I-5 freeway, go right (south) on 12th Avenue for about five blocks, cross over the I-90 freeway, then turn right onto St. Charles Street in front of the Pacific Medical Center.*

So all right, we have strange ways of amusing ourselves. José Rizal Park, tucked onto a slope adjacent to the large Pacific Medical Center, offers one of the city's finest vistas. The panorama reaches from the port district, Safeco Field and the new Mariners stadium, over the city skyline to the Space Needle and beyond to Elliott Bay and the distant Olympic Mountains. And virtually at your feet is the curving concrete juncture of interstates 5 and 90. It becomes a merry mayhem of traffic during commute hours. The nicest thing about being up here, looking down on all of those frustrated motorists, is knowing that you're not among them.

By sheer force of circumstances, Seattle has come to be well recognized throughout the East as the natural point of supply and departure for the Klondike and all Alaska mining points.
— **Article in the Seattle Post-Intelligencer, July 17, 1897.**

Chapter two

VISITOR LURES
SEEING SEATTLE AS A TOURIST

One of Seattle's particular appeals is that many of its attractions are history-based—things preserved from its rollicking past. Very little is contrived here. The area has not a single theme park; there is no Emerald Disneyland or Six Flags Over Puget Sound.

People are drawn to Seattle to visit its waterfront where thousands departed for history's "last grand adventure"—the Klondike Gold Rush. They poke among old brick buildings of Pioneer Square where the city began. They shop for turnips and trinkets at Pike Place, America's oldest farmers market. The area's favorite amusement rides are the green and white vessels of the world's largest ferry fleet. They're intended for public transit, although they're ranked among Washington's most popular tourist attractions.

Even some of Seattle's contrived attractions are historic. The Space Needle—requisite destination for every resident's visiting aunt—was created as the towering logo of a world's fair. The monorail from that fair still hauls commuters as well as tourists. Ye Olde Curiosity Shop, a wonderfully cluttered curio store and museum at the waterfront, is one of the oldest souvenir stores in America.

Many of Seattle's attractions stem from its corporate success stories. There are no tours of hometown boy Bill Gates' Microsoft campus in nearby Redmond, although you can see his shoreline mansion from an Argosy sightseeing cruise. Starbucks Center, the international headquarters of the firm that sent America on a caffeine binge, isn't open to the public, although you can sip designer coffees at hundreds of Seattle coffee houses. The city's newest attraction, the Experience Music Project, was financed by Microsoft co-founder Paul Allen. The outstanding Museum of Flight was born of the achievements of William Boeing, founder of the world's largest aircraft maker. You also can visit the Boeing Assembly Plant in nearby Everett. And you can tour the world's most expensive ballyard, Safeco Field, the impressive new home of the Seattle Mariners. Now, if this grand space would inspire them to win a pennant...

PRICING: Since prices frequently change, we use dollar sign codes to indicate the approximate cost of adult admission to various attractions and activities: **$** = under $5; **$$** = $5 to $9; **$$$** = $10 to $14 ; **$$$$** = $15 to $19; **$$$$$** = $20 or more. And you already know that prices are almost always less for seniors and kids.

☺ **KID STUFF:** This little grinning guy marks attractions that are of particular interest to pre-teens.

Note: The *Seattle CityPass* provides admission to six major attractions for about half the individual ticket prices. Passes are on sale at any of the participating attractions*the Space Needle, Pacific Science Center, Seattle Aquarium, Museum of Flight, Seattle Art Museum and Woodland Park Zoo. For information, call (707) 256-0490. (WEB SITE: www.citypass.net)*

And so we begin our lists of Seattle's Ten Best. In this and most lists that follow, we start with our favorite, then follow with the next nine in alphabetical order. Thus, as we noted in the introduction, we have no losers in this book—only winners and runners-up.

THE TEN BEST ATTRACTIONS

Writers of insiders' travel guides don't like to start with the obvious, but how can we possibly ignore the most historic, lovable and overdone tourist attraction in Seattle? Obvious or not, it tops our list.

1 **PIKE PLACE MARKET** • *First Avenue at Pike Street; (206) 697-4879. Information booth/ticket agency (206) 682-7453. (WEB SITE: www.pikeplacemarket.org) Info booth open Tuesday-Sunday noon to 6; hours may be longer in summer. **Walking tours** of the market* *are sponsored by the Pike Place Merchants Association Monday and Wednesday at 8:30 and 9:30 a.m., Friday at 2 p.m. and Sunday at 9:30 and 10:30. For reservations, call (206) 587-0351. GETTING THERE: Although the market is at the foot of Pike Street, it's one-way coming up, so take either Pine or Union Street from downtown. Two-way First Avenue, paralleling the waterfront, crosses in front of the market.*

Seattle's most unabashed tourist draw also is its most appealing attraction; some even call it the soul of the city. The best time to see it is early in the morning, before all the other tourists come, when venders are setting up their stalls. Most of them arrive between 6 and 7 and you can watch produce sellers arrange their polished fruits and vegetables in neat geometrical stacks and see the fishmongers carefully align their fresh catch on glistening beds of ice.

Pike Place didn't begin as a tourist gimmick. It was established by city officials in 1907 to provide a direct-to-consumer outlet for regional farmers and fishermen, and to give housewives a break on their grocery bill. By the 1930s, more than 600 sellers manned a string of stalls extending for several blocks along First Avenue. Half of these were Japanese-Americans, and when they were wrongfully interred in relocation camps at the onset of World War II by a paranoid American government, the market went into a near fatal decline. It continued struggling into the 1960s and developers began eying the site for apartment and office buildings. Market supporters rallied the people of Seattle, who voted overwhelmingly in 1974 to place it in a protective historical district. It's now operated by a nonprofit preservation and trust group.

Even during its difficult years, the market developed into a tourist attraction. As the visitors came, so came restaurateurs and sellers of trinkets. Today's Pike Place Market is home to dozens of curio shops, specialty stores and some of the city's oldest restaurants. (Since the market is built into a bluff overlooking Elliott Bay, many of those restaurants offer great views and we feature some of them in Chapter Four.) Mimes, street musicians and puppeteers compete with fish and produce mongers and flower sellers for the attention of passersby. Despite this circus atmosphere, Pike Place has resisted tacky carny attractions that have ruined other markets and waterfront tourist lures. (San Francisco's Fisherman's Wharf comes quickly to mind.) Franchise fast food parlors and national store chains cannot operate here. Instead, ninety farmers, fish and meat vendors and 200 artists and crafts people are licensed to sell their wares. (Crafts people cannot sell mass produced goods although, of course, curio shop operators can.)

Pike Place Market is larger than it looks, covering nine acres and terraced down three levels to Western Avenue, with more than 250 vendors and shops. Plan a good part of a day to explore it, starting early, as we suggested. Virtually all of the vendors and many of the shops close in late afternoon and most of the restaurants stop serving by early evening.

A good place to begin is an information booth near the entrance at First Avenue and Pike Place. It also serves as a discount agency for half-price day-of-show tickets. If the booth isn't manned—and it won't be if you arrive at sunup—pick up a free copy of the *Pike Place Market News*, a monthly newspaper with a detailed map in the middle. To begin your tour, follow the bronze "pig tracks" past Rachel, the market's metal mascot. The tracks—each bearing a donor's name—were purchased at $1,000 each to raise funds for various market charities. (It sponsors a day care center, senior center, low rent housing and a free clinic.) Rachel is a giant piggy bank that accepts donations for market activities; tourists love to be photographed astride her broad, slippery back.

After greeting Rachel, wander at will through the market, admiring the glistening displays of fish and Technicolor arrays of produce, and listening to the sellers hawk their wares and kid with the patrons—a market tradition. Pike Place Fish Company opposite the main entrance probably has the most exuberant hawkers. In addition to the market's fresh fruits and vegetables, you can enjoy a startling array of international foods here. Try the fruit rolls coated with coconut, teriyaki on a stick, savory bakery goods, walk-away crepes and—good grief!—even kosher corn dogs. When you've done the main structure, cross Pike Market Street to three more old brick and masonry market buildings, each busy with vendors stalls, shops and international cafés. Post Alley, which runs between two of the buildings, is lined with take-out food places and tables where you can enjoy your culinary booty.

For a specific walking route through the market complex, see Chapter Twelve, page 178.

2 EXPERIENCE MUSIC PROJECT ● *In Seattle Center at Fifth Avenue near Harrison and Broad; (206) 990-0575. Call for hours and prices. (WEB SITE: www.emplive.com)*

Experience music, indeed! Blend the musical lore of Seattle's late Jimi Hendrix with the money of Microsoft billionaire Paul Allen and the weird creativity of architect Frank Gehry and whaddya get? A high tech salute to American music, housed in Seattle's oddest looking structure. Opened in mid-2000, the facility suggests a lumpy freestanding cave—the monorail runs through it—or a great glop of multicolored Play-Doh left too long in the sun. Or perhaps a giant space ship that toppled from its gantry. This 140,000-square-foot, $100 million museum celebrates American popular music with innovative displays, interactive exhibits, live performances and great blasts of audio.

The museum concept was born when Allen wanted a place to display his extensive collection of Hendrix music memorabilia. Working with his sister Jody Allen Patton, they expanded the concept beyond Hendrix to create—for the City of Seattle—a nonprofit center celebrating the "creativity, innovation and rebellious expression that defines

American popular music." They asked Los Angeles architect Gehry to create a structure that evoked guitars, cars and rock stars. (One of his other noteworthy works is Spain's Guggenheim Museum, which resembles the Sydney Opera House ensnared in giant ribbons.) Contained within the rippled stainless steel and aluminum Experience Music structure are exhibit halls for the Hendrix collection and memorabilia from other pop stars, a virtual reality ride called Artists Journey, the Sound Lab where visitors can create and listen to music, and Northwest Passage, which focuses on the Northwest's contribution to American music. Other facilities include a performance hall and restaurant.

3 HIRAM CHITTENDEN LOCKS & CARL S. ENGLISH JR. BOTANICAL GARDENS • *3015 NW 54th St.; (206) 783-7059. Locks and gardens open 7 a.m. to 9 p.m.; visitor center open 11 to 5; free. GETTING THERE: Head northwest from downtown on Elliott Avenue and then north on 15th Avenue West. Cross the Ballard Bridge and go west, following signs to Chittenden Locks.*

We've always wondered why the Army Corps of Engineers didn't just pull the plug on the Lake Washington Ship Canal and let lakes Union and Washington drain down to sea level. Instead, the corps built this system of locks in 1917 to allow ships and pleasure boats to pass between Puget Sound and these two inland ponds. Among its distinctive features are a fish ladder and a special holding basin to prevent Puget Sound salt water from mixing with fresh water in the lakes. Through the years, it has become a major tourist attraction. After watching the parade of pleasure boats and commercial craft rise and fall through the locks, visitors can adjourn to the adjacent garden, which was planted and nurtured by Corps of Engineer employee Carl English. He spent forty-three years transforming once-barren ground into a botanical showplace, with 500 plant species from around the world. Incidentally, the best time to go lock watching is around sundown on a weekend, when great flotillas of pleasure boats head back home from a day of play on Puget Sound.

4 THE INTERNATIONAL DISTRICT • *Just east of Pioneer Square, bounded by Fifth Avenue, Dearborn Street, Eighth Avenue and Yesler Way.*

"Welcome to Chinatown," says the sign at Fifth Avenue and Jackson Street. However, this neighborhood above Pioneer Square is a blend of many Asian cultures—Chinese, Japanese, Korean, Thai and Vietnamese, as reflected by its multi-ethnic restaurants. This was Seattle's original Chinatown, although it was nearly emptied out during brutal anti-Chinese oppression in the 1880s. The Chinese had been brought here earlier to dig in the mines, work the fields and build the railroads. However, when hard times hit in the 1880s, these hard working folks were subject to harsh discrimination that culminated in their forceful exportation to San Francisco in 1886. The area gradually was resettled with a mix of Chinese, Japanese and other Asian ethnic groups and this blend remains today. It came to be known as the International District, although Asian District certainly would be more appropriate.

This former Chinatown isn't as large as Asian enclaves in other west coast cities such as Vancouver, Portland and San Francisco. Further, it has little of the temple-style architecture and colorful congestion typical of those other cities' Asian communities. However, it offers Seattle's best selection of international cafés, and many of them make our Ten Best Asian restaurants list in Chapter Three and our Ten Best Cheap Eats in Chapter Five. Because of its rich ethnic mix, it has a greater variety of Asian restaurants than Oriental enclaves in other West Coast cities. (In San Francisco's famous Chinatown, you'll find lots of *dim sum* and *kung pao chicken*; very little *phó tái* and *tempura*.)

Other than restaurants and shops, the International District offers only a few specific lures. You'll want to see **Kobe Park** at Main Street and Maynard Avenue, **Hing Hay Park** rimmed by Maynard, King, Sixth and Jackson and the **Wing Luke Asian Memorial Museum** at Seventh near Jackson (listed separately below). And check out the freeway support columns where Jackson crosses under Interstate-5; they're painted red and yellow with images of *koi,* the traditional Japanese carp.

Mostly, the International District is a place for idle strolling, and snacking on savories such as moon cakes, almond cookies, glazed duck and pork buns. Try **King's Barbecue House** for pork buns, glazed duck and—if you're willing—cooked chicken or duck feet. It's at 518 Sixth Avenue; (206) 622-2828. For bakery items, we like **A Piece of Cake** at 514 King St., (206) 623-8284; and—great name—**Yummy House Bakery** at 522 Sixth Ave., (206) 340-8838. With all the recent talk about the health benefits of green tea, you might want to stock up at **TenRen Tea Company** at 506 King St.; (206) 749-9855. In addition to basic green, it offers dozens of tea varieties, from black to orange to oolong to herbal to ginseng. You often can get a sip of what's currently brewing. You'll find an extensive selection of Asian groceries—mostly Japanese, Chinese and Korean—at **Uwajimaya** supermarket at the corner of Sixth Avenue and King Street; (206) 624-6248. It has a small café and takeout where you can get sushi rolls, packaged pre-cooked noodle dishes (microwavable) and other Asian food-on-the-run.

5 *KLONDIKE GOLD RUSH NATIONAL HISTORICAL PARK* ● *117 Main St.; (206) 553-7220. Daily 9 to 5; free. Guided tours of Pioneer Square offered in summer. Gold rush history movies shown periodically. GETTING THERE: The interpretive center is in the Pioneer Square area, near an Occidental Street pedestrian way called Occidental Park.*

In a sense, much of Pioneer Square (below) could be considered a part of this historic park, for this is where the vast majority of the gold-seekers started their rush to riches. Seattle outfitted eighty percent of the Klondike stampeders, and more than half the gold yielded wound up in the city's banks to boost local economy. Many returning miners not only left their gold in Seattle; some chose to stay and keep an eye on it, greatly increasing Emerald City's population. Among the notables who settled here after striking it rich in the Yukon was John W. Nordstrom, founder of the department store chain that bears his name.

Klondike Gold Rush National Historic Park has elements in Pioneer Square and Skagway, Alaska, and there's a Canadian historic park in the Yukon Territory's Dawson City where gold was discovered. Seattle's element is focused primarily in a small and handsomely arrayed storefront museum. Several movies and videos recall the history of the continent's last great gold rush. Particularly interesting is a film narrated by Hal Holbrook, using colorized versions of old black and white photos. Exhibits include original and replica artifacts from the gold rush, and photo murals. Piled near the entrance is and an example of the ton of provisions that Canadian Mounties required for each man headed to the gold fields.

6 *PACIFIC SCIENCE CENTER • 200 Second Avenue in Seattle Center; (206) 443-2001 or (206) 443-2880; IMAX theaters (206) 443-IMAX; laser show schedule (206) 443-2850. (WEB SITE: www.pacsi.org) Daily 10 to 6 in summer, weekdays 10 to 5 and weekends 10 to 6 the rest of the year; $$. Separate fees for laser show and IMAX theaters (although they're included in the CityPass price). GETTING THERE: It's easy to find the Pacific Science Center on the extensive Seattle Center grounds; just look for the IMAX Theater dome that resembles a giant Bermuda onion. Or maybe a Walla Walla sweet.* ☺

This center is directed mostly at kids, although it's easy for adults to get caught up in the fun here. It's many things under several roofs. The main center has 200 hands-on exhibits where folks can interact with science and technology. A planetarium does star shows, two IMAX theaters show regular and 3-D wide screen films and the Laser Theater features a "Laser Fantasy Light" show. In the main center, you can make a giant "sheet bubble," play with lots of computers, take a virtual reality hang-gliding trip over the city, and challenge a robot in a game of tic-tac-toe. You also can learn simple things that you probably never knew—such as how a toilet flushes by siphon effect and how a combination lock works. Half-scale models of several Jurassic Park residents roar and grunt in an exhibit called "Dinosaurs: A Journey Through Time." Not all things here are computerized or robotic. You can peer quizzically at ugly little naked mole-rats, which are rare cold blooded mammals that burrow far beneath the earth. Or check out slithery snakes in terrariums and play with starfish in a tidal tank.

7 **PIONEER SQUARE** ● *Bounded roughly by Alaskan Way, King Street, Fourth Avenue and Yesler Way. GETTING THERE: From downtown, First Avenue will take you south into the middle of the square.*

If downtown is Seattle's heart and Pike Place Market is its soul, then Pioneer Square certainly is its roots. It was here, as we noted in the introduction, that the city was first platted in 1851, after settlers Arthur and David Denny wisely relocated from windy, drizzly Alki Point. They were joined by David "Doc" Maynard who—to encourage industry—donated a chunk of waterfront to Henry Yesler to build a steam-powered lumber mill. The town grew up around Yesler's Mill and the "skid road" down which logs were dragged is now Yesler Way. In the years that followed, downtown Seattle grew northward and this area became an urban slum. "Skid Road" eventually became the definition of a down-and-out area. In the late 1960s, officials decided to level the area to create parking for the growing "new" downtown area. Citizens wailed in protest and in 1970, the city set aside several blocks as one of America's first historical preservation districts.

Through the decades, Skid Road gradually has evolved into Pioneer Square, a district of specialty shops, boutiques and restaurants. The neighborhood covers about twenty city blocks, although most of the brick-clad shopping and dining areas are concentrated along a three block stretch of First Avenue between Yesler Way and Jackson Street. For a thorough exploration of the area and its historic buildings, pick up the free *Discovering Pioneer Square Map & Guide* available just about everywhere in the neighborhood. Or you can follow our walking tour in Chapter Twelve, page 180. For a humorous and irreverent look at the area, take one of Bill Speidel's Underground tours; see below.

The square's major attractions, all listed elsewhere in this chapter, are the Klondike Gold Rush National Historic Park interpretive center at Main and Occidental Mall, Waterfall Garden Park at Jackson and Main, Seattle Fallen Firefighters' Memorial on Occidental Mall near Main, and Smith Tower at Second Avenue and Yesler Way. Pioneer Square is not a major dining district, although it has several small cafés and some historic saloons. And if you like to dine *al fresco,* it has more restaurants with outdoor tables than any other place in the city. Several of these places are listed in Chapter Four and elsewhere in this book; check the index.

A three-block section of the area has been converted into **Occidental Mall** and the larger **Occidental Park**, with strings of white lights in the trees to add a bit of nightly sparkle. Despite the sparkle, the Occidental strip isn't as appealing as it might be. It's a major gathering place for Seattle's homeless, huddled on benches or wrapped in dirty sleeping bags. Sorry, ladies and gentlemen, but you just aren't very decorative.

8 *SEATTLE AQUARIUM • Pier 59; (206) 386-4300 or (206) 386-4320 for a 24-hour recorded message. Daily 10 to 8 in summer and 10 to 6 the rest of the year; $$. Combination tickets available with the adjacent Omnidome; see below. Steamer Seafood Café in front of the aquarium and omnidome offers indoor and outdoor dining. GETTING THERE: The aquarium is at the waterfront off Alaskan Way, behind and below Pike Place Market.* ☺

While this isn't a world class aquarium, it does a fine job of focusing on the watery world of Puget Sound. It exhibits a goodly collection of finned, furred and feathered creatures who make the water or shoreline their home. Most of the exhibit tanks are rather small, although they're effectively presented in a simulated grotto setting, giving one the impression of exploring within a sea cave. The "Sound to Mountain" display recently won an award for excellence in museum exhibits. It takes visitors alongside a cascading cutaway stream from Puget Sound to the creek's headwaters. Mockups, graphics and videos describe the changing flora, fauna and geology as folks follow the creek upstream.

Also impressive is a display of giant octopus that seem indeed capable of snaring Captain Nemo's submarine. Two other distinctive features here are a working salmon hatchery and fish ladder, common elsewhere but unusual in aquariums; and the Fish Dome, where visitors are beneath the sea, looking up at the aquatic critters. It's like a glass bottom boat in reverse. Kids will like the touchy-feely tanks where they can fondle—under supervisions of staff members or docents—starfish and other sea creatures. They'll also enjoy attending the scheduled sea lion and sea otter feedings.

9 *SEATTLE WATERFRONT AND THE FERRIES • Along the Elliott Bay shoreline immediately west of downtown, stretching from Myrtle Edwards Park in the north to Pioneer Square in the south. For Washington State Ferry schedules and information, call (206) 464-6400, (800) 84-FERRY (automated) or (888) 808-7977; toll-free numbers good within Washington only. (WEB: www.wsdot.wa.gov/ferries/) Ferry schedules are available at the Washington State ferry Terminal (Pier 52) and all visitor centers.* ☺

If Pike Place market is the most popular place in Seattle, then the waterfront has to be a close second. In fact, we would surmise that many folks who visit the market continue on down the Pike Hillclimb to Alaskan Way and the waterfront. This is Seattle's front porch to Puget Sound and the world—a pleasing stretch of parklands and piers, walking/biking paths, tour boats and ferry docks. It offers grand vistas west across the water to the Olympic Mountains and eastward to the city skyline. Here one finds many of the city's tourist lures, most of which are listed elsewhere in this book—the Seattle Aquarium, the Omnidome, the Waterfront Streetcars, Ye Olde Curiosity Shop, and Odyssey, the Maritime Discovery Center. Some of the city's most popular seafood restaurants and its tackiest souvenir shops thrive here as well. From the waterfront, one can catch an Argosy sightseeing or dinner cruise along Elliott Bay and through the Chittenden Locks; a high speed Victoria Clipper to Victoria and the San Juan Islands; and a boat to Blake Island State Park for the Tillicum Village Salmon Bake. These are all covered elsewhere; check the index.

And of course, this is home to the largest ferry fleet in America. Afoot or in your car, you can catch a green and white Washington State ferry from Pier 52 to Bainbridge or Bremerton, and link with other ferries that will take you throughout Puget Sound and the San Juan Islands. From Seattle's waterfront, you can walk or bike north through Myrtle Edwards and Elliott Bay parks to Elliott Bay Marina. A brief inland walk will take you to Seattle Center. At the southern end, you can stroll to Pioneer Square and the International District. And you can even walk to a Seattle Seahawks or Mariners game.

10 WOODLAND PARK ZOO ● *Woodland Park, off Phinney Avenue between 50th and 59th streets; (206) 684-4800. (WEB SITE: www.zoo.org) Daily 9:30 to 6 (closes at 4 from mid-October to mid-March). $$ plus parking fee. GETTING THERE: Head north from downtown on Aurora Avenue (Highway 99) to Woodland Park, take the Green Lake/Zoo exit and follow signs. ☺*

One of America's best zoos just keeps getting better. Major improvements include an expanded Asian elephant exhibit, tropical rain forest and tropical Asia. This large, lushly landscaped complex shelters more than a thousand critters. Most are in open-air compounds where they have room to roam. Experts call this one of the most humane zoos in America because of these large enclosures. Virtually all of the original cages have been removed and replaced with simulated natural habitats. Smaller enclosures needing special containment for their critters use Plexiglas instead of wire or bars, to improve viewing. Because of Seattle's damp, temperate climate, the zoo is lushly vegetated; with a little help, rainforest plants do quite well here. This is an interactive zoo, with daily activities ranging from elephant baths to raptor demonstrations, plus conservation-oriented videos and docent tours. Some of the old gimmicks such as a kiddie train and amusement ride area have been removed to create larger animal enclosures. (A tip: Because of these larger habitats, it's a good idea to bring a pair of binoculars for close-ups of animal interactions. Of course, you can get up close and personal with many critters in the smaller enclosures.)

The zoo is divided into several world animal environments, including the African Savanna, Tropical Rain Forest, Tropical Asia and Australasia. The gorilla enclosure in the Tropical Rain Forest is impressive;

visitors can watch a family of these imposing beasts interact. Our favorite area is the Northern Trail, simulating three climate zones of the
far north. At the two-level Taiga Viewing Shelter, you can see trout and
river otters swimming in a cut-away stream, while bears snooze in
their dens and mountain goats clamber in rocky hills above.

THE NEXT TEN BEST ATTRACTIONS

Seattle has so many lures that all of them can't make our "A" list. If
you have time after you've seen the very best, here's a list of the rest.

1 UNIVERSITY OF WASHINGTON & THE "U" DISTRICT

• *The university Visitor Information Center is on the west side of the
campus at 4014 University Way NE, at the corner of NE Camino; (206)
543-9198. It's open weekdays 8 to 5; closed weekends. Modest fee for
visitor parking. GETTING THERE: The campus is in northeast Seattle.
Take I-5 north, go briefly east on Freeway 520, then exit north onto
Montlake Boulevard, which goes through the heart of the campus. To
reach the visitor information center, take a half left onto NE Pacific
Street just after crossing the Lake Washington Ship Canal, then go north
for two blocks on University Way NE.*

Occupying a wooded peninsula shaped by Union Bay and Portage
Bay, Washington's senior university is one of the most attractive in the
West. It's also one of the West's largest, with nearly 40,000 students on
a 700-acre campus. This was the site of the 1909 Alaskan-Yukon-Pa-
cific Exposition and several structures were left for use by the school.
Pick up a map at the information center at University Way and NE
Camino and stroll this tree-shaded campus of brick and grass. Among
its lures are the recently renovated **Burke Museum of Natural
History and Culture** at 17th Avenue NE and NE 45th Street (listed
below); and the **Henry Art Gallery,** 15th Avenue NE and NE 41st
Street. The gallery is open daily except Monday 11 to 5 (until 8 Thursday), exhibiting twentieth century American and European art; (206)
543-2280. It's just around the corner from the visitor information center. From here, follow 15th Avenue NE about a quarter of a mile, turn
right onto NE 45th and you'll cross in front of the Burke Museum.

The University District, locally called the "U District," is immediately north of the campus, with the usual collection of frat houses, coffee galleries, student bookstores and bistros. Most of the commercial
section is along University Way NE and NE 45th Street.

2 THE CENTER FOR WOODEN BOATS • 1010 Valley St.;

*(206) 382-BOAT. (WEB SITE: www.cwb.org; E-MAIL: cwb@cwb.org)
Open 11 to 6 daily from May through Labor Day and 11 to 5 Wednesday-Monday the rest of the year; closed Tuesdays; free. GETTING THERE:*

The facility is adjacent to Northwest Seaport (see below). Both are in front of the old Naval Reserve building at the southern tip of Lake Union. Take West Denny Way from downtown, then go north on Westlake and east on Valley.

A Lake Union peninsula that once housed the Naval Reserve training center is evolving into a maritime heritage complex with three different archives—Northwest Seaport, the Center for Wooden Boats and the Puget Sound Maritime Museum. Our favorite of the trio is the wooden boat center. If you admire those sturdy skiffs, dories and sailing vessels built before the days of Fiberglas, Kevlar and composites, you'll love this place. This is "hands-on history," says the brochure, where you can attend boat-building classes or watch skilled boat builders at work. You can stroll docks where dozens of finely crafted old boats are on display. And if one appeals to you, step into the floating Boathouse and inquire about a rental. The "livery fleet" includes a variety of small sailboats, rowboats, fishing dories and—when we last visited—a beautiful varnished wooded kayak. The Boathouse also has exhibits and photos of classic wooden boats, and the center offers sailing lessons. (To rent a sailboat, you must first demonstrate your sailing skills.)

3 DISCOVERY PARK ● *Northwest of downtown on a bluff overlooking Puget Sound. Visitor center at 3801 W. Government Way; (206) 386-4236. Visitor center hours 8:30 to 5 daily; park hours 6 a.m. to 11 p.m. GETTING THERE: From downtown, follow Westlake, Nickerson and then Emerson past Fishermen's Terminal. Take a half right from Emerson onto Gilman Avenue West, a half left onto Government Way and follow it into the park.*

This is Seattle's largest park and one of its most appealing open spaces. It occupies 513 acres of a key hilltop site that once was a major military reservation guarding the entrance to Salmon Bay. Only a few government housing units and an Army Reserve facility remain from its military days. Most of the park is open to the public, and facilities include a 2.8-mile hiking trail (Chapter Twelve, page 185), spur trails leading to several beaches, nature ponds, birdwatching areas and picnic sites. The visitor center has exhibits on the park's military history and its flora and fauna. You also can learn about nature walks and talks and other special activities, and pick up a modest-priced park brochure and map. Only one park road is open to the public; it enters the east side as Government Way and winds along the northeastern edge to the **Daybreak Star Cultural Arts Center**; listed below. This is mostly a park for walking, running, cycling and getting next to nature while still being next to a major city. If someone in your car is sixty-five or over, five or under, or is handicapped, get a parking pass from the visitor center and follow Utah Avenue past some government housing areas and down to West Point Lighthouse. Passes are limited because there's only ten parking spaces down there. For the rest of us, it's an easy walk—a 2.6-mile round trip. Once there, you can scuff along a driftwood-littered beach, enjoy some nice aquatic views and admire—but not enter—West Point Lighthouse, which dates from 1881. A beachside trail leads north to Daybreak Star.

4 **FISHERMEN'S TERMINAL** • *3919 18th Ave. West on Salmon Bay Waterway, just west of the Ballard Bridge; (206) 728-3395. GETTING THERE: Take Elliott Avenue northwest from downtown, blend onto 15th Avenue West and take the West Emerson exit just before 15th crosses the Ballard Bridge.*

Washington fishing vessels harvest 2.3 billion pounds of seafood a year, more than half the total U.S. catch. A good many of them—more than 700—tie up here at the West's largest commercial fishing dock. The terminal was established in 1913 and it remains one of the most active in America. Fishermen love the place because its fresh water cleans saltwater barnacles from the hulls of their boats. Step onto the dock, where plaques discuss the history of the terminal and help you identify the trollers, crab boats and huge factory ships that range the nearby seas.

The **Seattle Fishermen's Memorial** on the dock honors local fisherfolk lost at sea since 1900. Look for the column with the halibut fisherman on top and a copper *bas relief* of fish around the base. Stroll out on the piers and try figure which boats are trollers and which are trawlers. **Chinook's Restaurant** offers views with its seafood menu, and the small take-out has Seattle's best fish and chips; see chapters three and four. For really fresh fish, crabs, shellfish, lox, smoked salmon and a serious selection of white wine to go with them, step into **Wild Salmon Seafood Market**; (206) 283-3366. It's open Monday-Saturday 10 to 6 and Sunday 11 to 6; major credit cards.

5 **GAMEWORKS** • *Seventh Avenue and Pike Street downtown; (888) 880-4263. Monday-Thursday 10 to 1 a.m., Friday-Saturday 10 to 2 a.m. and Sunday 11 to midnight. Free entry; various charges for games and other activities.* ☺

This multi-level complex with industrial strength décor, kaleidoscopic neon, a heavy rock sound system and high tech effects is the ultimate kid-vid parlor. The good news is that it's chaperoned by cool teens who don't allow its young visitors to smoke, do drugs or drink. The bad news is that most of the games focus on maiming, dismembering and otherwise killing video screen opponents. Facilities include not only video games but old fashioned pinball machines and even good old Skee-Ball. The most elaborate Gameworks game is a thirty-foot Vertical Reality tower, where you're strapped into a seat that elevates you as you blast away at alien rocket ships. If you're skillful, you rise to the top; if you're aim is bad, you crash—gently, of course. A cheerfully decorated grill serves surprisingly good and inexpensive food, including spring rolls, meat loaf, chicken salad and such. The garlic fries, served in huge portions, are particularly tasty.

6 *GREEN LAKE PARK* • *In the Green Lake district of north Seattle. GETTING THERE: Follow I-5 north from downtown, take exit 170 north to Ravenna Boulevard, go left (northwest) under the freeway and the park is within a quarter of a mile.* ☺

Rimming the lake of the same name, this large park is one of Seattle's most popular recreation areas. Facilities include a 2.8 mile walking/running/biking trail, kiddie playground, motorless boat rentals, ball fields and a basketball court. Expect it to be crowded most weekends. Green Lake Park's best appeal is its loop trail, with separate lanes for walkers and cyclists, and even a sand strip for serious runners who disdain asphalt. The water is warm enough for swimming in summer, although it gets pretty rank with algae. You can rent a canoe, paddleboat or rowboat at **Green Lake Boat Rentals**; (206) 527-0171. Rental bikes are available from nearby **Gregg's Green Lake Cycle,** at the juncture of Ravenna Boulevard, Green Lake Way and NE 70th Street; (206) 523-1822.

The adjacent neighborhood is particularly appealing, with small cafés, shops and such. We like to take a break at Zí Paní café and bakery, opposite the park at the corner of Green Lake Way and NE 72nd St. It offers specialty coffees and baked goods, with indoor and outdoor tables.

7 *NORTHWEST SEAPORT* • *On Lake Union at 1002 Valley St.; (206) 447-9800. Tuesday-Sunday noon to 5. GETTING THERE: The facility is in front of the old Naval Reserve building at the southern tip of Lake Union. Head north from downtown on Westlake Avenue, then go east on Valley. The "Seaport" is immediately west of the Center for Wooden Boats.*

Sharing the Maritime Heritage Center with the Center for Wooden Boats (see page 45 above), this small privately endowed facility seeks to preserve the seagoing legacy of the Northwest. Although this outdoor museum looked a bit scruffy—an impolite way of saying underfunded—when we last visited, it has great potential. Volunteers are restoring three historic ships—the 1897 lumber schooner *Wawona;* the 1889 tugboat *Arthur Foss* and the 1904 lightship *Relief.* The *Wawona* is open to the public and the other two may be available for exploration by the time you arrive. Meanwhile, visitors can poke about an outdoor scatter of anchors, pilot houses, rigging and other fragments of maritime lore.

8 **OMNIDOME** • *Pier 59; (206) 622-1868. Show times vary with the season; call for schedules. $$; combination tickets available for two shows and/or Seattle Aquarium admission. MC/VISA. GETTING THERE: The dome is at the waterfront off Alaskan Way, beside the Seattle Aquarium. ☺ Of interest to children, depending on film.*

This is one of those super wide-angle movie theaters with tilt-back seats and surround sound. The Omnidome alternates the showing of two films, generally produced by the IMAX or Omnimax companies. Plan on at least one episode in each film that's intended to make you queasy. Rollercoasters and banking aircraft in narrow canyons seem to be the most effective.

9 **SMITH TOWER** • *Second Avenue at Yesler Way; (206) 622-4004. Observation deck recently reopened after renovation; call for new hours. GETTING THERE: This lofty bit of brick is at the northeast corner of the Pioneer Square area.*

L.C. Smith of typewriter and revolver (Smith and Wesson) fame wanted a monument to his success, so he financed this 500-foot tower, completed in 1914. It stood as the tallest building west of the Mississippi until 1959 when several highrise office buildings rose higher. It was the Seattle's most lofty structure until the Space Needle topped it in 1962, at 605 feet. Step inside to admire its newly-scrubbed marble walls and wrought iron trim, then board an elevator for a swift ride to the top. Once there, you'll emerge into the Chinese Room, with some beautifully carved Asian screens and furniture. Step onto the wrap-around observation deck to enjoy a predictably grand panorama of the city.

10 **YE OLDE CURIOSITY SHOP** • *1001 Alaskan Way; (206) 682-5844. Daily 9 to 9. Free; MC/VISA accepted for purchases. GETTING THERE: This curiosity is at the waterfront on Pier 54, below the foot of Madison Street.*

"Mexican jumping beans just arrived," reads a sign out front and you know you're headed into a tourist trap. However, make no hasty judgments about Ye Olde Curiosity Shop. It's part souvenir shop, part museum and part parlor of kinch. It has been attracting visitors since the turn of the last century. The shop was founded by J.E. "Daddy" Standley on August 8, 1899, and it hasn't missed a day of business since. (The City of Seattle declared August 8, 1999, "Ye Olde Curiosity Shop Day" to honor one of its longest continually operating businesses.)

Among its myriad souvenir ashtrays and T-shirts you'll find such wonders as the mummy of a gut-shot Arizona cowboy that was perfectly preserved in the hot desert sand, stuffed animals, Inuit and

Northwest native art, shrunken heads and enough other odds and ends to fill three ordinary museums. For a "lifetime keepsake" you can spend fifty cents to squish the impression of another mummy—Sylvia—onto a penny. The real Sylvia, a grotesquely gnarled Central American highlands Indian lady, is in a display case beside that poor cowboy.

THE TEN BEST MUSEUMS

Seattle does not have a large selection of museums, although its short list includes some of the finest exhibit centers in western America. In selecting the Ten Best, we've listed nearly every museum in the city. We wouldn't want you to miss anything.

1 MUSEUM OF FLIGHT

1 *MUSEUM OF FLIGHT* ● *9404 E. Marginal Way (beside Boeing Field); (206) 764-5720. Daily 10 to 5 (Thursdays until 9); $$. GETTING THERE: Head south from downtown on Alaskan Way, which becomes East Marginal Way and takes you to Boeing Field. Or take exit 158 from I-5 and follow signs.* ☺

This is Seattle's finest museum. If you're an aviation nut, it's the *Northwest's* finest museum and one of the best aviation archives in the country. Housed in a modernistic six-story greenhouse, this imposing facility covers the full spectrum of flight, from earliest attempts at soaring through the jet age to the first moon landing. Several full-sized aircraft, including an entire DC-3 "Gooney Bird" and the pedal-powered Gossamer Albatross, dangle from the rafters of the main building, like a close-formation squadron. Other aircraft are parked below and outside; they include a rare Boeing 1929 tri-motor, an F4U gull-wing Corsair and a wickedly sleek M-21 Blackbird.

Assorted movies and videos trace the history of aviation, and videos in the large moon landing exhibit show those dramatic moments when man first set foot on the lunar surface. A new feature is a mock-up control tower where you can listen to voices from the real control tower and watch aircraft take off and land at adjacent Boeing Field. Another recent addition—which kids will love—is a Navy flight simulator ride.

Next to the main building is a replica of the "red barn" where William Boeing began building airplanes in 1909. It adds another dimension to this full-dimensional museum, focusing on the design and construction of early aircraft. In a full-scale mockup, mannequins stitch fabric over wooden wing frames. Parked outside the main museum are legendary Boeing aircraft such as the B-17 and B-29 and the first Air Force One built specifically to haul American presidents about. This modified Boeing 707—which you can tour—flew presidents Eisenhower, Kennedy, Johnson and Nixon, until it was retired in favor of the present Boeing 747.

2 BURKE MUSEUM OF NATURAL HISTORY AND CULTURE

● University of Washington campus at 17th Avenue NE and NE 45th Street; (206) 543-5590. (WEB SITE: www.washington.edu/burke-museum) Daily 10 to 5 (until 8 Thursday); $. GETTING THERE: From downtown, take Aurora north across the Washington Memorial Bridge. About a mile beyond, turn right onto NE 45th Street and go east 1.75 miles to the campus. The museum is on your right, between 15th and 17th avenues.

This innovative museum has two important stories to tell and it does so with style. "The Life and Times of Washington State" exhibit begins during the Paleozoic era 545 million years ago when the state was below sea level, and continues to the present, ending with a strong conservation message. At each of five displays covering a different era, "newscasters" in cleverly done videos describe how the land, animals and plants developed. Prehistoric skeletons, relics, graphics and interactive videos help complete the story. It's directed to school children, although adults will appreciate the gentle sophomoric humor of the "newscasts," and there are plenty of exhibits to study.

The second major display is "Pacific Voices," a more mature look at the customs, cultures and religions of Pacific Rim countries. It features fine exhibits of native art, artifacts, costumes and lots of videos. Particularly impressive are brilliantly colored Haida carvings and a fine collection of Javanese shadow puppets and Indonesian masks. The museum also has changing exhibits, plus an excellent gift shop, and a cozy little coffee shop in the lower level.

3 MUSEUM OF HISTORY AND INDUSTRY

● 2700 24th Avenue East; (206) 324-1126. (WEB SITE: www.historymuse-nw.org) Daily 10 to 5 in summer; weekdays 11 to 5 and weekends 10 to 5 the rest of the year; $. GETTING THERE: It's in McCurdy Park, just north of the western anchorage of the Evergreen Point Floating Bridge and south of the University of Washington Campus. The easiest approach is from downtown via 23rd Avenue East, which shifts onto 24th Avenue East and goes into McCurdy Park. **NOTE:** *By late 2000 or early 2001, the museum will be relocated to the Washington State Convention and Trade Center, near downtown at Eighth Avenue between Union and Pike.*

The focal point of this older, nicely done museum is a Seattle boardwalk scene of the 1880s. It features a full-scale replica of Henry Yesler's Wharf, store façades and a batwing door saloon that doesn't bat. A nicely done video recalls that awful day in 1889 when the city burned, leaving the "hideous remains of the feast of fire." In a hands-on history room, visitors can operate model ship cranes and try on old fashioned hats. A "Seattle hits" display features items that originated here, from Almond Roca to Rainier beer to Boeing aircraft. Expect additional exhibits when the museum moves to its new home.

4 **NORDIC HERITAGE MUSEUM** • 3014 NW 67th St. (near 32nd Avenue NW); (206) 789-5707. (WEB SITE: www.nordicmuseum.com; E-MAIL: nordic@intelistep.com) Tuesday-Saturday 10 to 4, Sunday noon to 4, closed Monday; $. GETTING THERE: The museum is in the Ballard district of north Seattle. From downtown, go northwest on Elliott Way, curve north onto 15th Avenue West and cross the Ballard Bridge. Continue north about a mile on 15th, then go west for a mile on NW 65th Street to 32nd Avenue NW and go north; it's two blocks away.

Nearly three million Danes, Swedes, Finns, Norwegians and Icelanders came to America in the last half of the nineteenth century, and many headed for the Northwest. At the turn of the that century, nearly twenty-five percent of Washington's residents were Nordic. This fine museum, housed on three floors of an old brick school, tells their story. The main exhibit, "The Dream of America," focuses on the Scandinavians who found their way to the Northwest. Professionally done displays follow the adventures and perils of immigrants from lurching ships to New York's Ellis Island and across the country. Full-sized mockups depict a farmhand's hovel in a barn (many immigrants were poor farm workers), a slum alley in New York, a sod homesteader's cabin and—as the Vikings' lot improved—prim farms and Scandinavian-American storefronts.

Other exhibits focus on their trades in the Northwest, particularly fishing, boat building and logging. Looms, period costumes, furnished rooms and modern and traditional Nordic art add more dimension to the museum. "Nordic Heritage Northwest" is series of five galleries, each focusing on one of the Viking countries. The museum also has a gift shop, reference library and Scandinavian language school.

5 **ODYSSEY, THE MARITIME DISCOVERY CENTER** • 2205 Alaskan Way at Pier 66; (206) 374-4000. (WEB SITE: ody.org) Sunday-Wednesday 10 to 9 and Thursday-Saturday 10 to 5 in summer; daily 10 to 5 the rest of the year; $$. GETTING THERE: This odyssey is on the north central waterfront, part of the Bell Street Pier complex.

The main focus of this fine exhibit center is Elliott Bay, Puget Sound and the North Pacific, and mankind's impact on their environments. Modern interactive exhibits and videos feature the area's fishing and cargo industries and the attempts to clean up the environment that has been fouled by generations of misuse and overuse. You can climb into a kayak and paddle—with computer video activation—through a Puget Sound waterway. A multi-screen video traces containerized cargo across America by train, to the Seattle container port by truck and then across the Pacific. You can stand on a simulated ship bridge and eavesdrop on radio conversations between the U.S. Coast Guard and ship traffic; or watch—via video—the charting of Puget Sound by sophisticated sonar.

A major exhibit on commercial fishing and "sustainable use quotas" focuses on an interesting political-environmental-economic coup. Several years ago, the U.S. government extended its fishing rights 200 miles off the shore of Alaska. Officials booted out the large Japanese factory ships and replaced them with their own, to harvest millions of pounds of pollack and other fish. And who's the main customer for this huge American catch? Japan.

You may be able to tour one of the American factory ships, or other sorts of vessels. Museum officials work with the fishing industry and the U.S. Navy and Coast Guard, encouraging them to park temporarily inactive ships at the museum's dock and open them to public visits.

6 *PUGET SOUND MARITIME MUSEUM* • *In Chandler's Cove on Lake Union at 901 Fairview Ave. North; or in the old Naval Reserve building on the southern tip of Lake Union; (206) 624-3028. Monday-Saturday 11 to 7 and Sunday noon to 5. (Hours may change when the museum is relocated.) Free or modest admission fee.*

Depending on when you arrive, the Puget Sound Maritime Museum will still be stuffed into a tiny storefront in Chandler's Cove, or rattling around in the huge warehouse-like Naval Reserve Armory. Negotiations to transfer the building from the Navy to the City of Seattle and then to the Puget Sound Maritime Historical Society were completed in 1999. The society has a large collection of ship models and artifacts, photos and documents and you'll see lots of them or only a few, depending on relocation progress. One of its stars is a beautifully detailed model of *HMS Discovery,* the ship aboard which Captain George Vancouver sailed into Puget Sound in 1792. In its new location, the museum will share—or is sharing—the large Maritime Heritage Center complex with the Northwest Seaport outdoor maritime museum and the Center for Wooden Boats; both are listed above. Each is independent of the other and we do wonder why they don't all get together in their common cause to preserve Northwestern America's rich maritime legacy.

7 *SEATTLE ART MUSEUM* • *100 University St. (First Avenue); general information (206) 625-8900; program information (206) 654-3100. (WEB SITE: www.seattleartmuseum.org) Tuesday-Sunday 10 to 5 (until 9 Thursday), closed Monday; $$. GETTING THERE: The museum is downtown, at the foot of University, just above the Harbor Steps.*

Seattle's dramatic art museum is terraced down the slope of University Street, with several galleries of permanent and changing exhibits and a fine little café. Out front is a monumental kinetic sculpture of a metal-working artist. Inside, the Grand Stairway leading to the main exhibit halls is guarded by several huge Ming Dynasty sculptures. Major exhibits feature artifacts from Northwest coastal Indians; African tribal art; and an excellent collection of paintings, carvings, pottery and screens from several Asian countries. Brilliantly colored totems, masks and carved panels in the Northwest native gallery are particularly imposing. Providing international balance are small and select assemblies of European paintings, vases and glassware, and Egyptian tomb artifacts.

Changing exhibits generally are more contemporary—often the blobs, gobs, scrawls and "formulations" of op art and pop art. The changing exhibit area has its own special shop, where you can purchase mementos of whatever's currently on display.

8 *SEATTLE ASIAN ART MUSEUM* • *1400 E. Prospect St.; (206) 654-3100. (WEB SITE: www.seattleartmuseum.org) Daily except Monday 10 to 5 (until 9 Thursday); $$. GETTING THERE: The museum is in Volunteer Park northeast of downtown. Take Olive Way or Madison Street northeast, go left (north) on Fifteenth Avenue East, left again onto East Prospect at the edge of the park, and then right to the museum.*

The home of the Seattle Art Museum from 1933 until 1991, this grand old masonry building was remodeled in 1994 to house the museum's extensive Asian art collection. The venerable building's lofty spaces have been modernized with crisp white walls and track lighting to provide fine exhibit spaces for the treasures of Korea, Japan, China, India and Southeast Asia.

Exhibits change frequently, although you can expect to find some splendid examples of Japanese and Chinese ceramics, paintings and scrolls; Buddhist religious sculptures of India and southern Asia; and temple *bas reliefs* and fragments from throughout the Orient. If you're into ceramics, you'll love the "Wonders of Clay and Fire: Chinese Ceramics through the Ages." It contains ceramic examples from the Bronze Age as far back as 2000 B.C. to gorgeous porcelain items from recent centuries. Particularly striking is an exhibit of stone and bronze Chinese Buddhist works, displayed in a dimmed room with each item bathed in a spotlight. The most stunning piece is a bronze 16th century *guanyin* from the Ming Dynasty, a thousand-arm, eleven headed temple goddess.

9 *SEATTLE CHILDREN'S MUSEUM* • *In Seattle Center, downstairs in the Center House; (206) 441-1768. Weekdays 10 to 5 and weekends 10 to 6; $$. GETTING THERE: Seattle Center is just northwest of downtown, two blocks up from the waterfront off Broad Street.* ☺

One of America's more innovative kid venues, the Children's Museum brims with things to do, things to touch, things to learn. At the entrance, kids crawl through hollow logs, crawl into a backpacker's tent and explore the wonders of nature in a pretend forest. Inside, they learn about other cultures in an international village with mini-houses. Exhibits change frequently and mentors are on hand to teach, direct and motivate. The museum's mission statement says it best: "To make learning a joy by enabling every child and adult to stretch their minds, muscles and imagination in surroundings that stimulate creativity, self-confidence and an understanding of the world."

10 SEATTLE METROPOLITAN POLICE MUSEUM ● 317

Third Ave. South; (206) 748-9991. Tuesday-Saturday 11 to 4; $. GETTING THERE: The museum is between Main and Jackson in the Pioneer Square area, a block north of King Street Station.

This fine museum, missed by many visitors since it's on a back street in the Pioneer Square area, focuses on the Seattle Police and King County Sheriff's departments. One of America's largest police archives, it also tells the story of law enforcement in general, starting with Sir Robert Peel's creation of the first public police agency in London in 1829. You'll learn that the word "sheriff" came from "shire," which means an estate or landholding; and "reeves," the term for a British nobleman's overseer and tax collector. Old photos, newspaper clippings, weapons, handcuffs and badges trace Seattle's law enforcement from 1861, when the frontier town of 400 appointed U.H. "Uncle Joe" Surber as its first marshall. More contemporary exhibits include a dispatch center where you can hear police calls, and a display about the U.S. Customs Service.

THE TEN BEST THINGS TO DO

Darn the rain and full speed ahead! Seattle is an active city where folks like to get out and do things.

1 GET HIGH ON THE NEEDLE ● The Space Needle in Se-

attle Center; (206) 443-2111. (WEB SITE: www.spaceneedle.com) Observation deck open 8 a.m. to midnight in summer; 9 to midnight the rest of the year; $$. Free to restaurant patrons. GETTING THERE: Seattle Center is just northwest of downtown, two blocks up from the waterfront on Broad Street. The Space Needle is easy to find; just look up. ☺

Several other Seattle structures now rise above the Space Needle, including the 76-story Bank of America Tower, which has its own observation deck; see page 61 below. However, this skinny tripod remains the city's most popular landmark. Since its erection for the 1962 world's fair, it has become Seattle's logo, appearing on everything from souvenir ash trays to guidebook covers. The slowly-revolving restaurant at the 500-foot level is a requisite stop for every Seattlite's visiting cousin; see Chapter Four, page 98. For considerably less than the price of a meal, you can ascend to the cocktail lounge or the observation deck for the same grand view. Graphics placed around the indoor observation deck—which essentially is a wrap-around gift shop—tell you what you're seeing. On the outside deck, you'll really sense the tower's height, particularly when you can feel it sway slightly during a stiff wind.

Other Seattle Center lures include the **Fun Forest** amusement park with thrill rides; the **Food Court**; the **Seattle Opera House**; **KeyArena** (formerly the Coliseum), home to the NBA's Seattle Supersonics; **Seattle Children's Museum** and the fine **Pacific Science Center**. The latter two are listed above on pages 54 and 41.

2 CRUISE THE WATERWAYS WITH ARGOSY • *Argosy Cruises, 1101 Alaskan Way, Pier 55; (800) 642-7816 or (206) 623-1445. (WEB SITE: www.argosycruises.com) Various prices. GETTING THERE: Argosy operates from Piers 55 and 56 off Alaskan Way at the Seattle Waterfront and from AGC Marina (look for the highrise AGC office building) at 1200 Westlake Avenue North on the western shore of Lake Union.*

Started as a water taxi service in 1949, Argosy Cruises operates a fleet of fourteen sightseeing vessels and a new dinner cruise ship (see Chapter Four). These voyages of one or more hours provide a fine aquatic view of this community surrounded by water. Among its offerings are the Harbor Cruise along Elliott Bay waterfront; the Locks Cruise from Elliott Bay through the Hiram Chittenden Locks; and the Lake Cruise—Seattle and Lake Cruise—Kirkland, which launch from the AGC Marina on Lake Union. The Kirkland voyage is aboard a refurbished ferryboat.

Our favorite is the Lake Cruise—Seattle that skims the edge of Lake Union, then sails east through the Washington Ship Canal past the University of Washington campus into Lake Washington. It passes clusters of floating homes including—near the cruise's end—Tom Hanks' bachelor pad for the 1992 film *Sleepless in Seattle*. Considerably more elaborate are waterside homes of the wealthy community of Medina on the east shore of Lake Washington, including the woodsy, rambling 48,000-square-foot home of Microsoft zillionaire Bill Gates. (He bought up and leveled five shoreline homes to get enough room for his little place.) Passengers get a running narrative from the captain as the boat cruises slowly past these palaces of the pampered.

3 CRUISE THE CLIPPER TO VICTORIA AND BEYOND • *Victoria Clippers, 2701 Alaskan Way, Pier 69, Seattle, WA 98121; (800) 888-2535 or (206) 488-5000. (WEB SITE: www.victoriaclipper.com) Prices vary, according to length of the cruises. TO LEARN ABOUT VICTORIA: contact Tourism Victoria, 710-1175 Douglas St., Victoria, B.C. V8W 2EI; (604) 382-2127. Once there, stop by the Info Center at 812 Wharf St.*

While you're visiting Seattle, why not pop over to Victoria for a spot of tea at the legendary Empress Hotel? The wonderfully British city on Canada's Vancouver Island is within easy reach—right across Puget Sound. The high speed catamaran *Victoria Clipper* makes the 75-mile trip in two and a half hours, with plenty of scenery en route. Food and beverage service and duty-free shopping are available in the airline-style cabin. Cruises depart Pier 69 on the Seattle waterfront and sail into Victoria's Inner Harbour, within walking distance of the Empress and attractions such as the Royal British Columbia Museum, Maritime Museum of British Columbia, Undersea Gardens and the Royal London Wax Museum. One-day cruises allow several hours ashore, or you can book longer stays with a variety of hotel packages.

To enter Canada, American citizens need proof of citizenship, such as a passport, birth certificate or naturalization papers. Citizens of other countries should carry their passports.

Victoria Clippers also offers one-day or overnight cruises to Friday Harbor in the San Juan Islands, plus combinations such as a three-day Victoria and the San Juans trip, or a five-day San Juan, Victoria and Vancouver cruise. If you'd like to book a slow boat from Seattle to Victoria, board the *Princess Marguerite III*, a refurbished passenger-vehicle ferry. This cruise takes four and a half hours and you can even rent a private day room equipped with a VCR.

4 **SLIDE INTO SAFECO FIELD** • *First Avenue South and South Atlantic Street. Call Ticketmaster at (206) 622-HITS for tour or game tickets or (800) MY-MARINERS or (206) 346-4003 for general Mariners' info. (WEB: www.mariners.org/newpark/safeco_tours.asp) GETTING THERE: Safeco Field is south of Pioneer Square at First Avenue South and South Atlantic Street.*

There are two ways to visit Safeco Field, the new home of the Seattle Mariners and—to date—America's most expensive ballpark. Modest-priced tours of the imposing facility are conducted daily at 10:30, 12:30 and 2:30 April through October and Tuesday-Sunday at 12:30 and 2:30 the rest of the year. Or you can simply catch a game when the Mariners are in town. Of course, home games will alter tour schedules. Opened in 1999, Safeco Field was built at a cost of $517 million, including a parking garage. It's noted mostly for a $60 million retractable roof, which can be closed to ensure there is never a rain-out, and opened to let the sun shine on the fans, the players and the natural turf. The steel girder roof resembles an unfinished airplane hanger, but beyond that Safeco is quite a handsome stadium. Its front is faced with brick and wrought iron for an old fashioned "downtown ballpark" look that fits into its Pioneer Square location. It's quite posh inside with wide aisles on the seating terraces, public art works, and sit-down restaurants and patio areas. Many seats offer imposing views of Elliott Bay and downtown Seattle. The most impressive piece of art is a sculpture of 1,000 translucent baseball bats hanging over the main entrance, resembling a spiraling string of giant Chinese firecrackers.

Tours take visitors to areas that mere ticket-holders can't reach, such as luxury suites and boxes in the Diamond Club and Terrace Club levels, and the press box. Folks on the tour can stroll onto the field, into a dugout and into the visitors clubhouse.

5 SADDLE UP AND PEDAL SEATTLE • Blazing Saddles,
1230 Western Ave.; (206) 341-9994. (WEB SITE: www.blazingsaddles.com) Daily 8 to 8 in summer and 9 to 5 daily except Tuesday the rest of the year. GETTING THERE: You can saddle up at the base of Harbor Steps, just up from the waterfront.

Blazing Saddles has more or less re-invented the bike rental business. In addition to renting bikes, the firm suggests five recommended routes—from moderate to challenging—and it provides a detailed route sheet inserted in a handlebar holder. Different styles of mountain and street bikes are available and each is equipped with a little computerized odometer that tells you how fast you're going and how far you've traveled. The firm also rents tandems, kids bikes and baby seats, and sells cycling gear. Its two most popular routes are an easy pedal along the waterfront, and a moderate run that continues on to Chittenden Locks, with a challenging optional climb to hilly Discovery Park and along Magnolia bluff for fine city views. (It's featured in Chapter Twelve, page 191.) Among other routes are a 22-mile up-and-down run that links several city parks, a "Chilly Hilly" ride through Bainbridge Island and a "Singletrack Bush Whack" on Vashon Island. The firm's rental outlet is a short pedal from the Seattle ferry terminal.

6 EAT OVERCOOKED SALMON ON BLAKE ISLAND •
Tillicum Village Salmon Bake. Boats depart piers 55 and 56; (206) 443- 1244. (WEB SITE: www.tillicumvillage.com; E-MAIL: mail@tillicumvillage.com) Lunch, mid-afternoon and dinner trips; hours vary with the seasons. Call for schedules and reservations; $$$$$. Prices include cruise to Blake Island, salmon feed and show. Island trips without the salmon bake are about half the salmon bake price; MC/VISA.

Generations ago, settlers took Blake Island from the native people and eventually made it into a state park. Several decades ago, descendants of the original inhabitants were invited back to present Indian-style salmon bakes for tourists. The salmon feed has become the darling of the tour bus set and—like the Space Needle—a requisite outing for visiting relatives. (Former president Bill Clinton hosted Asian leaders at an economic summit here with a salmon feed in 1993.) The boat cruises past Seattle's working waterfront and then across Elliott Bay to thickly wooded Blake Island. Views back at the skyline—day or night—are striking. On the island, visitors are ushered into a reconstructed longhouse for a meal featuring salmon baked over open fires. They then witness *Dance on the Wind,* an excessively slick and stagey portrayal of native dances and legends. (We preferred the simpler, earlier versions without the recorded thunder and strobe lightning.) After the show, there's time to stroll island paths or browse through a small crafts display before catching the boat back to Seattle.

7 GO UNDERGROUND IN SEATTLE'S CATACOMBS •

Bill Speidel's Underground Tour. *Ticket sales at 608 First Ave.; tours start at Doc Maynard's Public House, 610 First Ave.; (888) 608-6337 or (206) 682-4646. (WEB SITE: www.undergroundtour.com) Various tour hours; call for reservations; $$.*

Some things are so corny that they're appealing. This is certainly the case with these underground tours, originated by the late Bill Speidel in 1964. Intrigued with the catacombs formed when the streets of Pioneer Square were elevated, he and teams of volunteers cleared away several tons of rubble and began conducting tours. His lighthearted, irreverent style is maintained in today's outings. The guides' narratives are slightly bawdy, often politically incorrect and rich in history, anecdotes and harmless exaggerations. Visitors descend beneath the sidewalks in three different areas, exploring musty corridors, long-abandoned underground businesses and cobweb-draped corners that would make great sets for Alfred Hitchcock movies. The outing ends in a subterranean museum-gift shop.

8 RIDE AN OLD FASHIONED TROLLEY • Waterfront

Streetcar Line; *it operates daily 7 to 6, with longer hours on weekends and in the summer; $. GETTING THERE: Catch a car anywhere along the waterfront or go to either terminus—Alaskan Way and Broad Street or Jackson Street and Fifth Avenue southwest of Pioneer Square and just below the International District.*

This transit isn't rapid, although it certainly is fun. These cheerful little 1920s wooden trolleys, purchased from Australia, run two to three times an hour (depending on the season), with stops at key points along the waterfront. They're are part of the municipal transit system so you can transfer to regular buses on the line. The Pioneer Square-International District stop is within a short walk of the city's central transit terminal and the Amtrak station. The other terminus is at the north end of the Waterfront, adjacent to Myrtle Edwards Park.

9 DINE AND SIP WINE BY RAIL • Spirit of Washington

Dinner Train, *P.O. Box 835 (625 S. Fourth St.; Renton, WA 98057; (800) 876-RAIL or (206) 227-RAIL. Departures weekdays at 6:30, Saturday noon and 6:30, and Sunday at 11 and 5:30 June through September; then Tuesday-Friday at 6:30, Saturday noon and 6:30, and Sunday 11 and 5:30 the rest of the year. Reservations required; MC/VISA; $$$$. GETTING THERE: The dinner train leaves from Renton, about twelve miles southeast of Seattle via I-5 and I-405.*

Unlike the Space Needle's restaurant, this movable feast doesn't go around in circles. It takes diners on a leisurely 45-mile round trip between the Seattle suburb of Renton and the Columbia Winery in Woodenville. A gleaming red and black diesel locomotive pulls a string of handsomely renovated vintage dining cars along the shores of Lake Washington and across a century-old, 102-foot high wooden trestle. En route, passengers are served a full course dinner over white nappery as the on-board host describes the passing scene and tosses in a few one-liners. "Don't worry about that old trestle. We test it twice a day. The second test will be on the way back."

The food, prepared on board in a special kitchen car, is remarkably tasty for an excursion train. Offerings may include roasted salmon with apricot ginger glaze, roasted chicken breast in a Riesling sauce, prime rib or Dungeness crab crepes. At the winery, passengers hop off for forty-five minutes of sipping, touring and gift-shop browsing, then they finish off the evening with dessert on the return leg. Best seats in the house are in the glass-topped dome cars, which can be reserved for a small additional fee. They're great vantage point for watching a pink sunset over Lake Washington.

10 *TOUR AMERICA'S LARGEST AIRCRAFT FACTORY*

• *Boeing assembly plant tour, Paine Field south of Everett, off State Highway 526; (800) 464-1476 or (206) 544-1264. Tours weekdays 8 to 4. Children under forty-two inches tall not permitted and no cameras are allowed. Gift shop with Boeing logo items accepts MC/VISA. GETTING THERE: The easiest way to get there is to book a Gray Line tour out of Seattle by calling (800) 426-7532 or (206) 626-5208. Tours depart from the main level of the Washington State Convention Center at Pike Street and Ninth Avenue. Hotel pickups also available. Plant tour $$, Gray Line tour $$$$. ☺*

Although it's not in Seattle, a tour of the huge Boeing assembly plant in nearby Everett ranks high on most visitors' lists. Even those who hate to fly will be fascinated by this visit to the firm's 747, 757 and 777 assembly plant, where superlatives flow as freely as a jetfoil. It's the world's largest assembly plant and the world's largest building in volume, covering nearly ninety acres—larger than the total square footage of Disneyland or—if you really love trivia—the size of 911 basketball courts.

Boeing's wide-bodied aircraft are assembled here, and the key word is "assembled." Most of the parts are manufactured elsewhere, then brought here to be put together like giant Tinker-Toys. Your guide will tell you that a Boeing 747—the world's largest commercial aircraft— has six million parts. (However, three million of these are rivets.) The price tag for one of these flying goliaths ranges from $168 million up to $191 million if you want it fully equipped. And the superlatives just keep flowing—the 747 contains 175 miles of wire and it's six stories tall from the landing gear to the tip of the vertical stabilizer. Visitors first see a video about Boeing, then they're taken by bus past the flight line, where shiny new aircraft await delivery to airlines around the world. They walk through an underground utility tunnel and are elevated to a catwalk in the cavernous assembly building. Here, they look down upon wings and fuselages being stitched together by giant cranes and an ant swarm of workers.

THE TEN BEST OVERLOOKED ATTRACTIONS

Some of these attractions are overlooked by visitors because they're overlooked by many other guidebooks. Or they may be in out-of-the-way places and easily missed. Most—except for our first choice—may not be worth a special trip, although they're worthy of a look if you happen to be in the area.

1 **VOLUNTEER PARK** • *Northeast of downtown at Fifteenth Avenue East and East Prospect Street; (206) 684-4075. GETTING THERE: Take Olive Way or Madison Street northeast, go left (north) on Fifteenth Avenue East, left again onto East Prospect Street at the edge of the park, and then turn right.*

This is one of Seattle's most gorgeous parks, sitting in the midst of one of its most magnificent neighborhoods. Tree-canopied avenues of the old money Capitol Hill area are lined with some of the city's grandest mansions. Within the park—home to the fine Seattle Asian Art Museum (above)—ancient trees shelter lily ponds, lawns, tennis courts, paths and hideaway benches. The large Volunteer Park Conservatory, done in Kewe Gardens style with glass and wrought iron and refurbished in 1999, will lure botanical buffs. Stroll the park's trails and you'll encounter vista points and breaks in the thick foliage that offer views of the city, Puget Sound and the distant Olympics.

Looking curiously out of place amongst all this greenery is an old concrete reservoir, sitting in front of the Asian Art Museum. A promenade around the pond has been fenced off and a sign warns: *No trespassing: Danger of drowning, injury and contamination of the water supply.*

Presumably in that order.

2 **BANK OF AMERICA TOWER** • *Southwest corner of Columbia Street and Fifth Avenue downtown. Observation deck open weekdays 8:30 to 4:30; $. GETTING THERE: To reach the observation deck, you must take an elevator to the Sky Lobby, then walk around to a second bank of elevators that continue upward.* **NOTE:** *During summer, tickets* *are sold at the observation deck. In the off-season, you must purchase them at an information desk on the left side of the ground floor lobby, at Columbia and Fifth.*

Many locals still call Seattle's highest structure the SeaFirst Columbia Tower. It gained its new name in late 1999 when Bank of America, which has held controlling interest in SeaFirst for several years, merged the two companies. Locals also know something that visitors may not know—that the 76-story tower has a public observation deck on the 73rd floor. It offers a grand panorama of city and surrounds, from the northwest waterfront and Puget Sound, south to Tacoma and Mount Rainier and northeast to Lake Washington and Mount Baker. The view is nearly as imposing as that from the Space Needle, since it's in the heart of downtown Seattle and it's considerably higher at 1,050 feet, compared with 605 feet. The Needle, in fact, looks rather squat from here. On a good day, says a sign in the BofA tower, you can see 125 miles. Signs on window sills point out distant landmarks. This is the highest office building west of Chicago and the second highest manmade structure in the West, after the 1,149-foot Stratosphere tower in Las Vegas.

3 **DAYBREAK STAR CULTURAL ARTS CENTER** ● *In Discovery Park; (206) 285-4425. Gallery and gift shop open Monday-Saturday 10 to 5 and Sunday noon to 5; free. GETTING THERE: See directions to Discovery Park above, then drive west on the main road to the cultural center, following "Daybreak Star" signs.*

Museum-hoppers often miss this native cultural center, which houses the fine Sacred Circle Gallery of American Indian Art. The center, operated by the United Indians of All Tribes Foundation, is an imposing structure—styled after a Northwest native dwelling and held up by massive cedar posts. The gallery, occupying a second floor balcony, has several pieces of monumental native art on its walls, including traditional *bas relief* woodcarvings and some fine traditional Haida art. Smaller rooms off the balcony are used for changing exhibits; call the gallery to see what's currently showing. The lower floor of the center—not generally open to the public—is used for an assortment of activities by native groups and others. While you're in the area, follow a short trail from the parking lot to a nice overlook that provides vistas of Puget Sound, the Olympics and Shilshole Bay Marina.

4 **THE FREMONT TROLL AND HISTORY HOUSE** ● *The Troll is tucked beneath the north end of the Aurora Bridge. The History House is two blocks below, at the corner of North 34th Street and Aurora Avenue North; it's open Wednesday-Sunday noon to 5. GETTING THERE: The Fremont neighborhood is along the Lake Washington Ship Canal just west of Lake Union. To get there from downtown, go north on Westlake Avenue (skirting the western edge of Lake Union), then cross the Fremont* drawbridge, where the route becomes Fremont Avenue North. To go trolling, go right for one block on North 36th and there he sits, under the north abutment of the George Washington Memorial Bridge (known locally as the Aurora Bridge).

The Fremont Troll isn't really an overlooked attraction, for he's the darling of every guidebook writer and tour bus leader. He's just hard to find, since trolls tend to be elusive. If you follow the directions above, you'll see him, emerging from the dirt beneath the bridge abutment and clutching a crushed VW beetle in one gnarled fist. This presumably demonstrates his dislike for all of that traffic rumbling overhead.

What *is* often overlooked in this neighborhood is the History House, a fine little museum with rotating exhibits focusing on various Seattle neighborhoods. A 120-foot photo mural/collage circles the main exhibit room. The museum's courtyard is enclosed by a fence whimsically decorated with wrought iron figures of people, plants, bugs, ships, fish and Seattle landmarks.

The Fremont Troll is one of several curious pieces of public art you'll encounter in this neighborhood. To see the rest, turn to page 188 in Chapter Twelve and follow our Troll Stroll.

5 GAS WORKS PARK • *On a peninsula extending south into Lake Union, off Northlake Way. GETTING THERE: Go north from downtown on Westlake Avenue (skirting the western edge of Lake Union), then cross the Fremont drawbridge. Immediately beyond the bridge, turn right onto North 34th Street and follow it beneath the Aurora Bridge. It becomes North Northlake and skims the edge of the park.*

Is it urban art or rusting junk? The site of the large Seattle Gas Company, which once produced gas from coal, has been fashioned into the city's most unusual park. It's fortunate that it was, for this nipple of land extending into Lake Union offers one of the city's finest views—a 180-degree panorama across the lake, from the I-5 bridge, along the skyline and Space Needle to the Aurora Bridge and beyond. Several huge boilers, fenced off but tattooed with graffiti, form a giant centerpiece for the park, rising in rusty contrast to the gleaming high-rise skyline beyond. In a huge, former industrial shed that's now called the Playbarn, several other pieces of equipment have been cheerily painted. There's a kids' play area on one side and a covered picnic area on the other. On the wall of an adjacent restroom facility, graphics describe how coal was converted to gas to light the cookstoves and heaters of Seattle.

This facility was active from 1909 until 1938 and its product was called "synthetic natural gas," which sounds like a self-canceling phrase. Several low, treeless hills and a waterfront concrete riser provide fine places to sit and admire the city.

6 **MARKET HERITAGE CENTER** • *1531 Western Ave.; daily 10 to 6; free. GETTING THERE: The center is immediately below Pike Place Market, adjacent to an elevator and stair steps that lead to an elevated pedestrian crosswalk.*

Several graphic panels and ongoing videos present the history of Pike Place Market in this outdoor heritage center. Exhibits, some changing and some permanent, trace the market's founding in 1907 and its success and tribulations during nearly a century of operation. When we last past, a video and graphics display called "The Lost Harvest" focused on Japanese-American farmers. They comprised more than half the market's produce and fish vendors until they were unfairly taken to inland detention camps at the start of World War II. Earlier in the last century, according to the exhibit, Japanese comprised only one percent of the state's population, yet they produced seventy-five percent of the berries and produce in the Puget Sound area. Other exhibits and historic photos cover the establishment of the market and its various activities through the decades.

7 **RAINIER SQUARE "TUNNEL"** • *Stretching from Fifth to Sixth avenue, between Union and University streets downtown.*

Rainier Square is a gathering of downtown shops bounded by Union and University streets and Fourth and Fifth avenues. A subterranean corridor stretches a block northeast to Sixth Avenue, emerging at Union Square. Overlooked by virtually all visitors except those who shop at Rainier Square, its walls are lined with old photos and other historic displays. Strolling beneath the downtown stores and streets, you can learn about the Klondike Gold Rush that left half of its wealth in Seattle, about an upstart airplane company called Boeing and other interesting trivia concerning the city's formative years.

8 **SEATTLE FALLEN FIREFIGHTERS' MEMORIAL** • *Occidental Mall near Main Street in Pioneer Square.*

Monuments to police and firemen who died in the line of duty aren't unusual; they're found in many cities. However this memorial, life-sized bronzes of four modern firemen in full gear attacking a fire, is particularly striking. Advancing in a crouch, they appear to be going into combat and indeed they are; dozens of firemen lose their lives in America every year.

Several rough-cut polished granite slabs seem almost carelessly placed about the figures, like pieces of a collapsed building. However, they're a series of engraved tablets. One lists all the Seattle firefighters who have perished through the years. Others discuss the monument's history and describe the thoughts of the artist, a noted Chinese sculptor who completed this impressive work in 1998.

9 **WATERFALL GARDEN PARK** • *Main Street and Second Avenue in the Pioneer Square area. Daily 6 a.m. to 5:45 p.m.; free.*

This little bit of nature tucked into the city is just far enough from the heart of popular Pioneer Square to be missed by many visitors. However, locals know and love this place; expect the benches to be filled with noontime office workers. Step inside this enclosed space and you've stepped from urban Seattle to a lush woodland retreat. A 22-foot waterfall tumbles over a pile of boulders at the rate of 5,000 gallon a minute in this lushly landscaped indoor garden. Benches invite visitors to sit and enjoy the serenity of this place, where the only sound is the soft rumble of falling water. The park was created by the Annie E. Casey Foundation on the site where one Jim Casey started a small messenger service in 1907. It grew to become the United Parcel Service.

10 **WING LUKE ASIAN MEMORIAL MUSEUM** • *407 Seventh Ave. South; (206) 623-5124. (WEB SITE: www.wingluke.org) Tuesday-Friday 11 to 4:30, Saturday-Sunday noon to 4, closed Monday; $; free on Thursdays. GETTING THERE: It's in the International District near the corner of Jackson Street.*

Don't be put off by the rather scruffy exterior of this small museum. Quite nicely done inside, it tells the story of Asian immigrants in America. Its most touching exhibit concerns the World War II relocation of loyal Japanese-American citizens to inland concentration camps. Other displays include examples of calligraphy and Asian arts and crafts. Changing exhibits focus on the city's various Asian ethnic groups. The museum's name honors Seattle's first Chinese-American city councilman, who perished in a plane crash.

Animals feed; man eats. Only the man of intellect and judgment knows how to eat.
— **Anthelme Brillat-Savarin**

Chapter three

SEAFOOD & SUCH

A SEATTLE DINING GUIDE

Seattle is a serious dining venue. It ranks close behind San Francisco among Western American cities for its variety of restaurants.

This diversity comes both in location and menu. Diners can enjoy splendid views at waterside cafés, elegant cuisine in hotel dining rooms, trendy new fare at designer restaurants, great food at neighborhood bistros or simple fish and chips at a bayfront takeout. They can choose from a rich international brew—French, German, Italian, Greek, Middle Eastern, Spanish, Mexican, Irish, East Indian, and even Ethiopian. Chinese, Japanese, Thai and Vietnamese restaurants are particularly abundant, since more than one in ten Seattle residents is of Asian persuasion.

Obviously, in a city nearly surrounded by water, seafood is prevalent, appearing on practically every menu in town. Salmon is as common as steak at a Texas cookout, although seafood selections reach considerably beyond this ubiquitous flipper. Some of the city's most popular restaurants are fish and shellfish havens, from long-established Anthony's, Elliott Bay, and McCormick and Schmick's to new places such as Flying Fish and Etta's. Most of the seafood venues are along the Elliott Bay waterfront, and these tend to draw the most visitors. Some are fine; others are ordinary. Some overdo their seafood since a few out-of-towners think fish should be cooked to the consistency of an artgum eraser.

American *nouveau* is hardly new these days, having been contrived by Alice Waters at Berkeley's Chez Panisse way back in 1971. Her concept—seeking fresh local ingredients and offering them in curious combinations with interesting spices—has evolved into American regional fare. The local version is called Northwest regional or Northwest *nouveau* or Northwest cuisine or Pacific Rim cuisine. Take your pick. We like the latter reference, since Northwest cooking often comes with Asian accents.

Several local cooks focus on this inventive and changing fare. Notable among them is Seattle's signature chef (he doesn't like that title) Tom Douglas. With no formal culinary training, he started cooking at a small place called Café Sport in 1984. Ten years later, he earned the James Beard Association Award as the Northwest's best chef. Douglas now operates three highly regarded Seattle eateries—Dahlia Lounge, Palace Kitchen and Etta's Seafood, which has taken over the old Café Sport site.

Other noteworthy *nouveau* establishments include Cascadia, which we selected as the city's best overall restaurant, Fullers in the Sheraton Seattle, the Hunt Club in Hotel Sorrento, Lampreia, the Painted Table in the Alexis Hotel and Palisade.

For international fare—at least of the Asian variety—head for the International District, which is Seattle's version of Chinatown. It was called Chinatown originally, although so many folks have settled there from Japan, Korea, Vietnam, Cambodia, Thailand, Malaysia and other Asian nations that the new name is more appropriate.

You already know that the city is famous for its specialty coffees and more than a dozen coffee roasting companies are based here, including three majors—Starbucks, Tully's and Seattle's Best. Coffee houses and coffee carts abound and most restaurants feature designer coffees on their menus. Few of them "dare serve a national brand coffee," commented one visiting writer. We list the city's Ten Best coffee stops (not shops) in the next chapter.

PRICING: In our listings, we use strings of dollar signs to indicate the price of a typical dinner with entrée, soup or salad, not including drinks, appetizers or dessert: *$* = less than $10 per entrée; *$$* = $10 to $19; *$$$* = $20 to $29; *$$$$* = "Did you say you were buying?"

THE TEN VERY BEST RESTAURANTS

We've asked ourselves this same question in our other Ten Best city guides: "With hundreds of restaurants to choose from, how can one possibly select the very best?" And we always come up with the same answer: "By being quite arbitrary."

Our choices lean heavily toward Northwest cuisine, since this is a true reflection of regional cooking. Also, our selections tend to be rather expensive. Excellence doesn't come cheap.

1 **CASCADIA RESTAURANT** • *2328 First Ave.; (206) 448-8884. Northwest cuisine; full bar service. Dinner Monday-Saturday. Major credit cards; $$$$. GETTING THERE: Cascadia is midway between Bell and Battery, in Belltown north of the downtown area.*

When we wrote the original edition of our *Washington Discovery Guide* several years ago, we described Northwest cuisine—perhaps unkindly—as "California *nouveau* with salmon." Chef Kerry Sear has taken salmon and a host of other regional ingredients to new culinary heights in his trendy restaurant. He spares no cost—reflected in the menu prices—in finding the best local and organic produce, game, cheeses and meats, often contacting producers directly and committing them as regular suppliers. Even the wine list is primarily from the Northwest, with a few California wines slipped in for balance.

The best way to approach Cascadia is to set aside an entire evening and indulge in one of the four Tasting Menus that feature six or seven different portions, from soup or a vegetable dish through three or four meat and/or fish entrées to dessert. We nibbled happily through the "Decidedly Northwest" menu of baby spinach with marinated bean curd, raw oysters with three different treatments, king salmon, a cute "Kerry's designer soup in a can," rack of Oregon rabbit with salmon, rosemary lamb with grilled apples and garlic fries, cheeses and assorted desserts. We found not a single flaw in this *procession de cuisine*. The restaurant's name comes from a fanciful term that describes the corridor running from Washington to northern California, between the Cascade Range and the Pacific. Located in the newly trendy Belltown area, Cascadia is tucked into a landmark brick building. The look is fashionably understated, accented by a hallmark "rain curtain" that cascades down a large cut glass window between the main dining area and the kitchen.

2 **CAMPAGNE** • *1600 Post Alley at Pine (the Inn at the Market); (206) 728-CAFE. French and American regional; full bar service. Dinner nightly, breakfast Monday-Saturday plus Sunday brunch; light café fare until midnight. Major credit cards; $$$ to $$$$. GETTING THERE: The Inn at the Market is just northeast of Pike Place Market, and the restaurant is on the lower side, opposite the entrance to Post Alley.*

Crisp white linens and tiny flower vases accent the clean, simple lines of this elegant little café. Milk glass light fixtures add a cozy glow. Considering its ambiance and its excellent reputation among local food critics, Campagne isn't particularly expensive. Most of its evening entrées were under $20 when we last checked. Menu offerings do change, so you may or may not find a classic French cassoulet with pork; duck confit; boneless quail stuffed with barley, caramelized onions and bacon; hot smoked pork loin chops; pan-roasted scallops with potato purée and green peppercorn, tarragon and lemon; or rabbit marinated in mustard. The kitchen features daily rotisserie specials, ranging from guinea hens to lamb leg.

3 DAHLIA LOUNGE • *2001 Fourth Ave.; (206) 682-4142. Northwest regional with Asian accents; full bar service. Lunch and dinner daily. Major credit cards; $$$ to $$$$. GETTING THERE: Dahlia is in the heart of downtown, at the corner of Fourth Avenue and Virginia Street.*

Seattle has its own celebrity chef in the ample form of Tom Douglas, although this casually-garbed owner of three local restaurants doesn't like that term. With no formal culinary training, he has earned numerous awards and critical praise for his creative fare. His Dahlia Lounge, recently moved from its original location, is a pleasing space with Asian accents reflected in both the décor and the menu. The latter changes frequently and you might find roast duck with mango pickles and green peppercorn curry, pan roasted venison with mashed sweet potatoes and caramelized endive, or Malaysian coconut curry *laksa* vegetable stew. You *will* find a Douglas staple—excellent crabcakes with a crunchy crust, served over apple herb salad. And do save room—plenty of it—for a huge slice of his signature coconut cream pie, which arrives cascaded with bits of mango, pineapple and coconut shavings.

4 FULLERS • *In the Sheraton Seattle, 1400 Sixth Ave.; (206) 447-5544. Northwest cuisine; full bar service. Lunch weekdays, dinner Monday-Saturday. Major credit cards; $$$ to $$$$. GETTING THERE: Fullers is on the lobby level of the Sheraton Seattle at Sixth and Pike.*

Rivaling Cascadia for its fine Northwest cuisine, Fullers is one of the town's handsomest dining venues. Works of Northwest artists grace the fabric-covered walls of this softly elegant restaurant, and white nappery and fine crystal graces its tables. Heralded by a national dining guide as one of America's top fifty restaurants, it features skillfully prepared and artfully presented cuisine.

The accent is on Northwest regional fare with international touches, such as Chilean sea bass with mushroom ragout, ahi tuna with *kimchee* and grilled watercress, seared King salmon and duck confit with rice noodles and shiitake mushrooms. For a tasty sampler of the kitchen's creativity, try one of the four or seven-course tasting menus. They come with recommendations for wines and awesomely sinful desserts.

5 **GEORGIAN ROOM** • *In the Four Seasons Olympic Hotel at 411 University St.; (206) 621-7889. (WEB SITE: www.fourseasons.com) American regional; full bar service. Jackets requested for gents. Dinner Monday-Saturday. Major credit cards; $$$$. GETTING THERE: The Olympic is downtown between Fourth and Fifth avenues.*

Beaded chandeliers, intimate table lamps, pink nappery, a gorgeous breakfront set with silver service and a tinkling piano set the mood for one of the city's most handsome—and certainly most romantic (Chapter Nine) dining venues. The menu is what you'd expect in an elegant old money hotel dining room with a modern chef. It features Northwest regional fare such as salmon with morel mushrooms, baked sea bass with Russian caviar butter and poached asparagus, lobster with petrale ravioli, and bacon wrapped chicken with basil and feta. The menu changes seasonally, so you may discover new culinary creations.

6 **THE HUNT CLUB** • *In the Sorrento Hotel at 900 Madison St.; (206) 343-6156. (WEB SITE: www.hotelsorrento.com) Northwest regional; full bar service. Lunch weekdays, brunch weekends and dinner nightly. Major credit cards; $$$$. GETTING THERE: The Sorrento is at the corner of Madison Street and Terry Avenue, just above downtown in the First Hill neighborhood. Madison is one-way downhill, so go uphill on Spring Street, cross under the freeway and turn left on Terry.*

Aptly named, the Hunt Club is a study in Old World dark wood elegance, a serene retreat suited to impressing a client or pleasing your mate on an anniversary date. In addition to being one of Seattle's ten finest restaurants, it's is among its most romantic; see Chapter Nine. While the ambiance is Old World, the fare is contemporary, although it's not cutesy nouveau with raspberry puree and sun-dried tomatoes. Chef Brian Scheeshser's rather small menu features savory fare salmon with artichokes and leeks, oven-roasted trout with potato gnocchi pancetta, roasted breast of duckling with glazed endive, herb and olive oil marinated steak, and grilled lamb chops with butternut squash ravioli.

7 **LAMPREIA** • *2400 First Ave.; (206) 443-3301. Northwest nouveau; full bar service. Dinner Tuesday-Saturday. MC/VISA, AMEX; $$$ to $$$$. GETTING THERE: It's in Belltown just north of downtown, at the corner of Battery Street.*

Although *nouveau* is no longer new, creative chefs continue to improve on the original concept of using fresh ingredients interestingly blended and innovatively spiced, and Lampreia is a particularly good example. You may or may not find—since the menu changes frequently—lamb loin with artichoke salad, oven-roasted veal chops with *fonduta* cheese sauce, five-spice duck breast with fried mustard greens and chanterelle mushrooms, or grilled swordfish with *cous-cous* and truffles. Occupying one of Belltown's old brick buildings, Lampreia is a smartly casual, dimly lit place with white nappery, café curtains, modernistic wall sconces and votive candles on the tables.

8 **THE PAINTED TABLE** • *In the Alexis Hotel, 92 Madison St. (206) 624-3646. Northwest nouveau; full bar service. Breakfast and dinner daily, lunch weekdays. Major credit cards; $$$$. GETTING THERE: This elegant table is off the lobby of the Alexis, which sits at First Avenue and Madison Street downtown, near Pike Place Market.*

The Painted Table is pleasing both to the palate and the eye. The fare focuses on "elegantly simple" Northwest cuisine with Asian and French influences. The emphasis is on locally grown herbs and vegetables, fresh seafood and regional specialties. The chef creates some curiously interesting entrées that sound strange but taste great, such as black cod with shiitake mushrooms and soy ginger, stuffed chicken with pistachios and apricots, or steamed salmon with medjool dates. For a delicious sampler of the kitchen's creativity, try one of the multicourse tasting menus. The Painted Table's look is elegant yet cheerful, with tapestry-draped walls, distinctive geometric light fixtures and curving floral patterned booths. Painted plates and other ceramics provide bright splashes of color.

9 **PALISADE** • *At Elliott Bay Marina, 2601 W. Marina Place; (206) 285-1000. Northwest cuisine; full bar service. Lunch and dinner Monday-Saturday, and Sunday brunch. Major credit cards; $$$ to $$$$. GETTING THERE: Take Elliott Avenue about two miles northwest from downtown, cross the Garfield Street-Magnolia Bridge and take the Elliott Bay Marina/Smith Cove Park exit.*

A creative menu, dramatic décor and fine city views blend seamlessly into one of Seattle's best dining experiences. Palisade is a stunning study in interior design, with a free-form circular ceiling, a saltwater "tidepool" trickling between the dining area and bar, and tropical flora. Window walls provide imposing views across the masts of Elliott Bay Marina to the city skyline and—on a clear day—Mount Rainier. The menu dances from the tropical Pacific to the rainy Northwest with fare such as macadamia nut chicken, seared sea bass in a soy curry marinade, rack of lamb marinated in dijon garlic honey, apple-wood grilled salmon and several steaks—from both steers and ostriches. These emerge from several specialty cooking devices, including an applewood broiler, wood-fired rotisserie and a "searing grill."

10 **SAZERAC** • *At Hotel Monaco, 1101 Fourth Ave.; (206) 621-7755. American with southern and Mediterranean accents; full bar service. Breakfast through dinner daily with Sunday brunch. Reservations advised; required from Thursday through Saturday. Major credit* *cards; $$$. GETTING THERE: Sazerac is on the lobby floor of the hotel, downtown at the corner of Fourth and Spring.*

Sazerac supposedly was America's first mixed drink, created in New Orleans in the 1790s as a potent concoction of rye whiskey, bitters and simple syrup. After a few of these, the room will come alive with vivid Cajun colors, strangely geometric chandeliers, distressed copper sculptures and whimsical art; rhythm and blues will pulse in the background. In Hotel Monaco's splashy-trendy restaurant, you can dine festively on New Orleans fare such as jambalaya, gumbo or grilled pork chops with "soft and sexy grits." Other entrées on the changing menu may include veal rib chops with sweet corn risotto, or New York strip steak with cheddar mashers. Meals begin with a dish of spicy olive oil-dipped breads and can end with an awesome vanilla bean crème brulée in raspberry compote.

THE TEN BEST SEAFOOD RESTAURANTS

Flying in the face of local convention, we chose an inland seafood restaurant as Seattle's best, favoring it over all of those waterfront establishments.

1 *FLYING FISH • 2234 First Ave.; (206) 728-8595. Full bar service. Dinner nightly. Major credit cards; $$ to $$$. GETTING THERE: This fish out of water is in Belltown north of downtown, on the corner of Bell Street.*

This starkly modern restaurant flies high in the culinary minds of local food critics and other serious diners. Patrons crowd the spartan interior and spill onto a sidewalk patio that's reached via window walls that rise like glass garage doors. Seattle visitors, generally drawn to Pike Place Market, Fishermen's Terminal and other waterside seafood sites, often miss this restaurant in the heart of Belltown. While decidedly upscale, Flying Fish is affordable; patrons can choose modestly priced small plates in lieu of more expensive main courses. The restaurant's excellence is based not only on the availability of fresh fish but on creative preparations by chef owner Christine Keff. She employs Asian touches to conjure such savories as seafood hot pot in ginger broth with udon noodles, sea scallops with Thai curry, and Dungeness crabs with Szechuan pepper. The large, frequently changing menu reaches beyond the Puget Sound's fishing grounds to feature flippers from all over the world. Presumably, they fly in.

2 *ANTHONY'S PIER 66 • 2201 Alaskan Way; (206) 448-6688. Full bar service. Lunch and dinner daily. Major credit cards; $$ to $$$. GETTING THERE: Anthony's is on the north waterfront, off Alaskan Way at the foot of Bell Street.*

Anthony's has several seafood venues around the city; this is the largest and generally the most highly regarded by local food critics. It's a three-tier place, with a second floor dining room that serves dinner only (where reservations are strongly urged), a less formal lunch-through-dinner Bell Street Diner downstairs and the Fish-Bar, a side-walk takeout. Menus at the elegantly aquatic upstairs restaurant and industrial-nautical downstairs café are similar, although the upstairs fare is more upscale in culinary creativity and price. Both menus have fresh catches of the day, some interesting seafood pastas and a couple of steak and chicken dishes. Both also have fine views of Elliott Bay, although the finest—and cheapest—may be from outdoor tables at the Fish-Bar. This is mostly a fried fish venue with assorted seafoods and chips, a very good fish taco and a sourdough chowder bowl.

3 **CHINOOK'S AT SALMON BAY** • *Fishermen's Terminal at 1900 W. Nickerson St.; (206) 283-4665. Lunch and dinner weekdays and brunch through dinner weekends. Major credit cards; $$ to $$$. GETTING THERE: Take Elliott Avenue northwest from downtown, blend onto 15th Avenue West and take West Emerson exit just before 15th crosses the Ballard Bridge.*

This cavernous café offers great views of Salmon Bay and its huge commercial fishing fleet. The menu is huge as well, offering 125 items at relatively modest prices. There are *nouveau* touches to some of the dishes, although the simply cooked just-off-the-boat fish filets are best. If you must, there's a small selection of steak and chicken dishes. For the kids, convince them that Chinook's salmon burgers are more interesting and healthier than a Big Mac and fries. Speaking of fries, nearby **Little Chinook's** serves the best fish and chips in town; see Chapter Four, page 102, and order the halibut version. It's open daily from 11, and you can eat inside or on the adjacent dock, where seagulls, pigeons and an occasional crow will try to convince you that they're simply starving.

4 **ELLIOTT'S OYSTER HOUSE** • *Pier 56 at the waterfront; (206) 623-4340. Full bar service. Lunch Monday-Saturday and dinner nightly. Major credit cards; $$ to $$$. GETTING THERE: This oyster venue is just off Alaskan Way near the base of Seneca and Spring streets.*

No longer just a tourists' favorite, Elliott's enjoys a deserved reputation among locals as one of the city's best waterfront restaurants. It's quite handsome, dressed in teak, brass, copper and glass after a recent $2 million renovation. A long and slender greenhouse roof dining area lets the sunshine in. Elliott's offers the most extensive oyster bar in the city and a remarkable array of seafood entrées, some with *nouveau* touches. Selections include several versions of Dungeness crab, pepper-crushed tuna, alder planked salmon and assorted seafood pastas.

5 **ETTA'S SEAFOOD** • *2020 Western Ave.; (206) 443-6000. Full bar service. Lunch weekdays, brunch weekends and dinner nightly. Major credit cards; $$$. GETTING THERE: It's just above the waterfront between Lenora and Virginia streets.*

This Tom Douglas creation is decorated mostly with noisy ambiance, although it does has iron fish sculptures and fishbone shaped coat hooks as conversation pieces. This is one of those restaurants that's always upbeat and crowded, busy with young professionals, office workers and the occasional mover and shaker. "Tom Douglas does seafood," says the Zagat Survey, which is an accurate summation of the menu. Seafood arrives in interesting guises—Alaskan cod in a lobster tomato broth, ahi tuna with ginger soy sauce and spicy longbeans, or salmon over cornbread pudding with a shiitake relish. Don't necessary expect these entrées when you arrive, since the menu changes frequently. However, expect things equally innovative. For those of you who cannot face another entrée from the sea, Etta offers a couple of steak, chicken and vegetarian dishes.

6 **IVAR'S ACRES OF CLAMS** • *Pier 54 at 1001 Alaskan Way; (206) 624-6852. Full bar service. Lunch and dinner daily. Major credit cards; $$ to $$$. GETTING THERE: These clammy acres are on the waterfront, between Madison and Spring streets.*

It might be unkind to call this place "Ivar's Acres of Tourists," and then again it might not. Kidded by local food critics yet loved by visitors, it's often praised for its simple, hearty and rather traditional seafood menu. This old fashioned dark wood place is best known for its steamed Manila clams, sautéed oysters and various treatment of prawns. Established in 1938 by Ivar Haglund, "Acres" is one of the city's oldest fish houses. A bronze of Ivar feeding the gulls stands near the entrance.

7 **McCORMICK & SCHMICK'S** • *1103 First Ave.; (206) 623-5500. Full bar service. Lunch weekdays, dinner nightly. Major credit cards; $$$. GETTING THERE: This legendary fish haus is downtown near Pike Place Market, at the corner of First and Spring.*

For generations, this handsome establishment has been downtown Seattle's favorite seafood restaurant. Although newer cafés such as Flying Fish (above) now offer more creative menus, M&S still can be relied upon to provide a good selection of properly prepared fresh fish, with more than two dozen finned entrées. Emerging from the busy menu are Dungeness crab cakes, Hawaiian mahi mahi, clams linguine, Florida rock shrimp popcorn, coho salmon and so on. There are a few steaks and chickens as well. It's a popular business lunch venue and an after-work stop for the white collar crowd. M&S has a clubby old style look with lots of brass and beveled glass, an island bar and an open kitchen. It's one of several McCormick & Schmick outlets in and about Seattle.

8 *RAY'S BOATHOUSE* • *6049 Seaview Ave. NW; (206) 789-3770. (WEB SITE: www.rays.com) Lunch and dinner daily. Major credit cards; $$ to $$$. GETTING THERE: The Boathouse is just south of Shilshole Marina in northwest Seattle. Head northwest from downtown on Elliott Avenue and then north on 15th Avenue West. Cross the Ballard Bridge and go west, following signs to Chittenden Locks. Continue past the locks on NW 54th Street, which swings north and becomes Seaview Avenue.*

Handsomely remodeled with light woods, rattan accents and copper drop lamps, Ray's is one of Seattle's most popular seafood venues. Expect long waits (and make reservations) on weekends when folks flock here for assorted fresh seafoods, salmon linguine, Canadian halibut cheeks, smoked black cod and a couple of meat and poultry dishes. A dessert specialty is apple bread pudding with Bourbon. Less formal and slightly less expensive Ray's Café occupies a second level deck and diners can adjourn to its outdoor deck on cheerful days. The views from both levels are quite fine—north to Shilshole Marina, west to the Olympic Peninsula and the Olympic Mountains, and south across Salmon Bay to the headlands of Discovery Park. It also makes our list of Ten Best view restaurants in Chapter Four, page 101.

9 *SALTY'S ON ALKI* • *1936 Harbor Ave, SW; (206) 937-1600. (WEB SITE: www.saltys.com; E-MAIL: alki@saltys.com) American, mostly seafood; full bar service. Lunch Monday-Saturday, Sunday brunch, dinner nightly. Major credit cards; $$$ to $$$$. GETTING THERE: It's in West Seattle near Duwamish Head. Take Marginal Way south, then go west on Spokane Street or the West Seattle Freeway, then fork to the right on Harbor Avenue SW.*

Is Salty's just an overpriced chowder house loved mostly by tourists? Not anymore, says the *Seattle Times* food critic, who recently rated it as "outstanding." Indeed, the kitchen has become more creative, offering changing "market dinners" in addition to an extensive regular menu. You may encounter curiosities such as pomegranate salmon with *cous-cous* and lemon *beurre blanc*. These "market dinners" come with wine suggestions, and Salty's has a very good wine list, with a dozen or more available by the glass. There's no question that the restaurant offers one of the finest dining views in Seattle—a splendid panorama of the city skyline across Elliott Bay; it's one of our Ten Best view restaurants in Chapter Four, page 101. Entrées on the large menu reach into the $30s, and range from grilled salmon, Maine lobster, cioppino and mixed seafood grill to chicken breast and a few steaks.

10 SEA GARDEN SEAFOOD RESTAURANT • 509 Seventh Ave. South; (206) 623-2100 or (206) 623-8721. Chinese; full bar service. Lunch through late evening daily. MC/VISA; $$ to $$$. GETTING THERE: This garden of seafood is in the International District between King and Weller streets.

Local critics call this one of Seattle's best Chinese restaurants and one of the its finest seafood parlors. As you enter, you'll brush past the kitchen, where you'll see a tank stuffed with squirming crabs and lobsters who are obviously less excited about dinner than you. The décor is neat and prim, with a few prints on pale walls accented by wall lamps. The focus is on seafood and vegetables, Cantonese style—which means perfectly fresh and lightly cooked. We counted nearly thirty seafood entrées on the large menu, ranging from live lobster and braised cod to cashew nut prawns and geoduck clams in black bean sauce. Anti-fish fans can find the full range of chicken, duck, beef, pork and vegetarian dishes as well. A specialty here is *congee*, a rice broth with meat, fish and/or egg.

THE TEN BEST ASIAN RESTAURANTS

Asians are Seattle's second largest racial group after Caucasians, comprising more than eleven percent of the population. Not surprisingly, Seattle has an impressive number of Asian restaurants, both in the International District and elsewhere. Our dining choices run the full Oriental gamut, and the full economic gamut, from inexpensive family-run cafés to trendy high-profile restaurants.

1 SHANGHAI GARDEN • 524 Sixth Ave. S; (206) 625-1688. Chinese; full bar service. Lunch weekdays, dinner nightly. MC/VISA; $$ to $$$. GETTING THERE: This culinary garden is in the International District near Weller Street.

Seattle's best Asian food is served in this simply attired and mostly pink chef-owned restaurant. It has met with such success with its creative Cantonese, Mandarin and Szechuan cookery that clones have opened in Bellevue and Issaquah, run by family members. A specialty is barleygreen hand-shaven noodles, used in a variety of soups and chow meins. How do you shave a noodle? (Resist the temptation to say: "Very carefully.") Shanghai Gardens noodles are shaved from a solid block of dough and they have a fresh taste not found in the packaged or even freshly extruded kind. (Rice and corn noodles are made the same way here, although the barleygreen are the most nutritious.) Among other tasty menu items are crisply scallops with plum sauce, pepper salted spareribs, orange flavored beef, and perfectly cooked whole steamed fish.

2 *BANH THAI* • *409 Roy St.; (206) 283-0444. Thai; full bar service. Lunch weekdays and dinner nightly. MC/VISA, DISC; $$. GETTING THERE: It's just behind Seattle Center between Fourth and Fifth avenues.*

Our favorite local Thai restaurant offers visual appeal, wonderful spicy food and remarkably modest prices. Several combination dinners are available in the middle to low teens. A specialty is the "Seafood Lover" mix of shrimp rolls, cashew nut prawns, seafood steamed rice and *Tom Yum Chow Koh,* which is a hot and sour seafood soup with mushrooms, lemon grass and chili paste. The menu is *huge,* with more than a hundred different entrées. Those who like it hot can select from several curry dishes. Assorted chicken, pork, beef, seafood and vegetarian dishes range from mild to tongue-toasting. Cool things down with sweet, flowery Thai iced tea and in-house coconut ice cream. All of this is served in a curiously pleasing setting. Occupying an early American Carpenter style house, Bahn Thai has been fashioned into a pleasing and romantic space with dim light, soft music and Thai artifacts. It makes our romantic restaurant list in Chapter Nine.

3 *BANGKOK HOUSE* • *606 S. Weller; (206) 382-9888. Thai; wine and beer. Lunch and dinner daily. MC/VISA; $$. GETTING THERE: It's in the International District near Sixth Avenue.*

The menu here is larger than the restaurant and it offers a wide assortment of traditional Thai dishes, ranging from mellow to spicy. Among its many offerings are basil chicken, sweet and sour chicken with cucumber pineapple, garlic prawns, sautéed prawns in chili sauce, and assorted spicy curries. House specialties include "Swimming Angel," stir-fried chicken on a bed of spinach and topped with peanut sauce; and crab stir-fried with curry powder, garlic, egg and cream sauce. Bangkok House is a prim little place, featuring two cozy dining rooms with wainscotting and a few Thai artifacts.

4 *BUSH GARDEN* • *614 Maynard Avenue South; (206) 682-6830. Japanese; full bar service. Lunch weekdays; dinner nightly. Major credit cards; $$$. GETTING THERE: It's in the International District near Lane Street.*

There are several gardens Bush in major West Coast cities. They're favored by those who like traditional if somewhat Americanized Japanese food and generally ignored by those who prefer something more creative. This Seattle landmark, clothed in old brick with a handsome Japanese garden inside, has survived the earlier decay of the International District and is thriving with the area's renewal. Menu items are what you'd expect in a place with *shoji* screens and stone lanterns— yakitoris, tempuras and teriyakis. Try the *tendon* (deep-fried prawns over rice) or *katsudon* (deep-fried pork cutlets over rice). If you love sushi, the downstairs sushi bar is quite handsome, done in blonde woods and rice paper screens.

5 THE CHINA GATE • *516 Seventh Ave. South; (206) 624-1730. Chinese; full bar service. Lunch through late evening daily. Major credit cards; $$ to $$$. GETTING THERE: This big "gate" is in the International District near Weller Street.*

Every American Chinatown must have a cavernous culinary hall, resplendent with red and gold trim. Seattle's International District has two—China Gate and Ocean City (609 S. Weller; 623-2333). Both have huge high-ceiling dining rooms with huge menus to match. We prefer China Gate because—after a recent fire—it has been completely redone inside with a rather tasteful, understated décor. Gone are the lavish murals and red-tassled lanterns, although the exterior—which was spared the blaze—still looks like a gaudy Chinese temple. The Gate's menu leans toward spicy Mandarin, featuring curry beef hot pot, ginger and green onion chicken and *mu shu* pork. A specialty is live seafood; try the recently-expired Szechuan prawns or the whole braised fish. Local critics rave about the dim sum.

6 CILANTRO • *Marion Street near First Avenue; (206) 652-9300. Multi-Asian; wine and beer. Lunch and dinner Monday-Saturday, closed Sunday. Major credit cards; $ to $$. GETTING THERE: It's on a sidewalk "balcony" extension of Marion Street, several blocks south of Pike Place Market.*

Despite its prime location near the waterfront, this prim, simply decorated little place offers remarkably inexpensive fare, with many entrées under $6. The kitchen features several Asian food disciplines and you can afford to take an Oriental culinary tour at these prices. Among its varied offerings are Chinese sweet and sour pork, Thai meat and cashews sautéed and seasoned with basil leaf and chili, Indonesian fried rice, and deep fried fish with chili and garlic flavored sauce.

7 GIAO'S • *2311 Second Ave.; (206) 770-0270. Vietnamese; full bar service. Lunch weekdays, dinner nightly. Major credit cards; $$. GETTING THERE: Giao's is in Belltown, between Battery and Bell streets.*

One of Seattle's most handsome Asian restaurants, Giao's is decorated with thin woven-wood wall plaques and wing-like fixtures that seem to float above the large, airy dining areas. The fare, artfully presented and relatively inexpensive, ranges from traditional Vietnamese such as *Quyen's chao tom* (tofu sheets filled with shrimp paste) to Seattle-inspired creations such as broiled salmon glazed with tamarind-honey-soy sauce. If you prefer spicier fare, try the lemongrass chicken with garlic and chili pepper. Vegans can choose from five different vegetarian dishes. Our favorite is the "monk's dish," braised vegetables with fried tofu and shiitake mushrooms done in a clay pot.

8 *HO HO SEAFOOD RESTAURANT* • *653 S. Weller St.; (206) 382-9671. Chinese; wine and beer. Lunch through late dinner daily. MC/VISA; $$ to $$$. GETTING THERE: It's in the International District near the corner of Maynard.*

Don't laugh. Some local café critics rate this funnily-named place as Seattle's finest Asian seafood restaurant. The dining room is classically austere, with traditional lazy Susan tables for feeding frenzies by large groups. (It's popular for Chinese family banquets.) Austerity does not extend to the menu, which offers an extensive selection of seafood entrées—more than thirty when we last counted. Among our favorites are curry crab with vermicelli, steamed rock cod and pepper salted prawns. The large menu offers the full range of other chicken, pork, beef and vegetarian dishes, in mild Cantonese and spicier Szechuan versions. Korean style hot pot dishes are a specialty.

9 *NIKKO* • *In the Westin Seattle at 1900 Fifth Ave.; (206) 322-4641. (WEB SITE: www.nikkorestaurant.com) Japanese; full bar service. Lunch weekdays and dinner Monday-Saturday. Major credit cards; $$$ to $$$$. GETTING THERE: The hotel is between Fifth and Sixth avenues near Stewart Street, in downtown Seattle's north end; Nikko is on the Sixth Avenue side.*

"Japanese-Northwest *nouveau*" best describes the fare at this stylish restaurant. Among menu selections are halibut topped with shiitake mushroom sauce, seafood grill and teriyaki versions of chicken, salmon and beef. You also can get good old fashioned *sukiyaki* and tasty—if expensive— *kaiseki* multi-course dinners. The look of Nikko is so stylish that it's almost overdone. The most appealing area is the cocktail bar, with stone accents and wall decorations fashioned of large *origami* cranes. The main dining room is more subdued with the usual blonde woods, *shoji* screens and appealing ceiling fixtures that suggest inverted Japanese umbrellas. The centerpiece here is a large sushi bar, known for serving some of the city's best.

10 *WILD GINGER ASIAN RESTAURANT AND SATAY BAR* • *1400 Western Avenue at the waterfront or Third Avenue and Union Street downtown; (206) 623-4450. Southeast Asian; full bar service. Lunch Monday-Saturday and dinner nightly. MC/VISA, AMEX; $$ to $$$. GETTING THERE? It depends on when you come. At press time, the restaurant was scheduled to move from its Western Avenue and Union Street location uphill into the Mann Building at Third and Union. Call before you go.*

We've seen it in San Francisco and now it's enjoying a successful ride in Seattle—the mixed marriage of several Southeast Asian cuisines. Wild Ginger has gained national culinary attention for spicy creations like Thai beef curry with cardamom and coconut milk, Szechuan style duck, Burmese curry crab and squid with herbs, chiles and garlic. A central focus is the *satay* bar, where you can select toothsome delicacies such as chicken marinated in curry and coconut cream, lemon grass marinated chicken and scallops served with black ginger dipping sauce. *Satay*, should you not know, is the Malaysian version of Japan's *yakitori*—skewered meat and vegetable bits, traditionally seared over a charcoal brassier.

THE TEN BEST OTHER ETHNIC RESTAURANTS

Since we just covered Seattle's Asian scene, the list below focuses on other ethnic food groups. Most are European, although we've included some regional specialties—Cajun-Creole, New Mexico's Southwestern fare and that American *nouveau*-Oriental blend that some call Pan-Asian.

1 *CAJUN-CREOLE: The New Orleans • 114 First Avenue; (206) 622-2563. Full bar service. Lunch and dinner daily. MC/VISA; $$. GETTING THERE: It's in the Pioneer Square area between Yesler Way and Washington Street.*

More of a nightclub than a restaurant, New Orleans nevertheless fills a niche as Seattle's best New Orleans style café. You've got your red beans and rice, pork ribs, seafood *étouffée*, jambalaya and filé gumbo—everything Cajun and Creole except crawfish pie. The look is yesterday Seattle or maybe early Bourbon Street—raw brick walls, high ceilings and bentwood chairs. It's a lively jazz and blues place with photos of performers past and present papering the high walls.

2 *FRENCH: Rover's • 2808 E. Madison St.; (206) 325-7442. (WEB SITE: www.rover-seattle.com) Wine and beer. Dinner Tuesday-Saturday; reservations required. Major credit cards; $$$$. GETTING THERE: Rover's is northeast of downtown near Lake Washington Park, in a courtyard off Madison near 28th Avenue. Follow Spring Street under the freeway (to avoid Madison's one-way grid), then shift over to Madison and follow it nearly two miles.*

French-born Chef Thierry Rautureau has created a sensuous culinary retreat in a courtyard cottage in the charmingly upscale Madison Valley area. One of the city's most expensive restaurants, Rover's is a special occasion place, offering *grand ménus de dégustation*. While frankly French, these multiple-course culinary festivals have a few

Northwest accents. A typical—if one could use that word—dinner might include sturgeon caviar with scrambled eggs, Alaskan prawns, sturgeon with caramelized turnips, a Pinot Noir sorbet and venison medallions with chanterelles and black peppercorn sauce, plus a choice of splendid desserts. The full treatment approaches $100; Rautureau offers slightly more modest *prix fixe* dinners for a few dollars less.

3 *GERMAN-BAVARIAN: Szmania's* • *3321 W. McGraw St.; (206) 284-7305. Full bar service. Lunch Tuesday-Saturday and dinner Tuesday-Sunday; no lunch in summer. MC/VISA; $$$. GETTING THERE: Are we there yet? It's a challenge for visitors to find this restaurant in the isolated Magnolia village, although local critics say it's worth the effort. The simplest approach—which isn't simple—is to take Elliott Way from downtown, cross the Garfield Street-Magnolia bridge above Smith Cove, climb a steep viaduct up to Magnolia Bluff and go right on 28th Avenue West, past the area's gorgeous homes. Turn left onto McGraw Street and you'll fall off the bluff and drop down to the isolated Magnolia business district. The restaurant is at the corner of 34th Avenue West.*

The creativity is all in the kitchen of Seattle's best German restaurant. The dining room is rather austere and would pass at a casual glance as a simple coffee shop. You'll find the classic Bavarian fare here, such as *jagerschnitzel* (breaded pork cutlets and cheese, *spaetzle*), *hasenpheffer* (marinated spiced rabbit) and roast duckling with sweet cherries and roast cabbage. Many of the dishes also have strong American accents, such as Alaskan halibut, salmon and peppercorn steak. Begin your meal here with the notable goulash soup. Szmania's special event winetasting dinners are popular, with themes such as the Hunter Dinner, Bordeaux and Cabernet dinners.

4 *GREEK: Yanni's Greek Cuisine* • *7419 Greenwood Ave. N; (206) 783-6945. Wine and beer. Dinner Monday-Saturday. MC/VISA; $$. GETTING THERE: Seattle's best Greek cuisine is a bit out of your way. Head north on Aurora Avenue (Highway 99), and take the North 65th Street/Green Lake exit. Cross under Aurora, continue north briefly on Woodland Avenue, then curve around to the left onto 65th. Go uphill several blocks to Greenwood Avenue on Phinney Ridge, then go north about ten blocks to Greenwood and 75th Street.*

Classic blue and white Greek colors, splashy murals and wine casks mark this cheerful storefront café on Phinney Ridge. Sit down to spicy fare such as beef, pork or chicken skewered with onions, spice-rubbed and spit-roasted chicken, boneless chicken breast with spices and egg plant, or the classic spinach *spanakopita*. Or try one of the huge salads busy with *kalamata* olives and chunks of feta, and a side of *hummus* to be scooped up with wedges of *pita* bread. Greek music and wine will inspire the proper atmosphere for a lively *taverna* evening.

5 **INDIAN: Chutney's** • *519 First Ave. North; (206) 284-6799. Full bar service. Luncheon buffet Monday-Saturday and dinner nightly. Major credit cards; $$$. GETTING THERE: It's just north of downtown between Republican Street and Mercer Avenue. Note that it's on First Avenue North, on the east side of Queen Anne Avenue, not First Avenue West, which is two blocks west. And yes, it is confusing.*

In pleasing contrast to many Indian restaurants with cluttered temple-like décor, Chutney's look is pleasantly spartan, with light wooden booths, simple table settings and *bas relief* icons tucked into little arched alcoves. A specialty here is *tikka masala*, a chutney and tomato-yogurt dish with chicken, lamb or shrimp. Or diners can choose from a long list of curry dishes, while choosing their degree of hotness. Apparently inspired by the Northwest location, the café also features fresh halibut, mussels and other regional seafoods. However, these entrées are dressed India style with curry and coconut. Our favorite dish here is *hariyali*—boneless chicken filet marinated with mint, coriander and other spices and cooked in a traditional clay oven.

There's a larger although more out-of-the-way Chutneys in the Wallingford neighborhood north of Lake Union, at North 45th and Burke Avenue North, in Wallingford Center. It serves lunch and dinner daily. Consider it on a warm day, since it has outdoor tables.

6 **IRISH: Kells Irish Restaurant & Pub** • *1916 Post Alley; (206) 728-1916. (WEB SITE: www.kellsirish.com) Full bar service. Lunch and dinner daily. MC/VISA; $$. GETTING THERE: Post Alley is in the Pike Place Market area, just inland from the main market. Kells is between Stewart and Virginia streets.*

This wee bit of Ireland tucked into Post Alley consists of a small café and a smaller sidewalk patio. It also features a long and slender barroom with a back bar stacked almost to the ceiling with bottles, for some serious Irish drinking. There are of course some good Irish whiskies in that collection. This is not a fancied up Irish tourist place with shamrocks and Leprechaun posters; it's a rather austere pub with worn tile floors and exposed heating vents. What's mostly Irish about this place is the food—steak and kidney pie, roast *armagh* chicken with rosemary and saffron, Irish stew, and "Kells Bookie," which is aged New York steak. (The name comes from the rough times in Ireland when only bookmakers could afford steak.) Ask for some soda bread with your meal, or take a loaf home. As in any proper Irish pub, live Celtic and other kinds of music are featured several nights a week.

7 **ITALIAN: Il Terrazzo Carmine** • *441 First Ave. South; (206) 467-7797. Full bar service. Lunch weekdays, dinner Monday-Saturday. Major credit cards; $$$. GETTING THERE: Il Terrazzo Carmine is lo-*

cated inside the Merrill Place building in the Pioneer Square area between Jackson and King streets.

The Pioneer Square address would suggest some sturdy old brick-walled *risotteria* with raffia-wrapped bottles and red checkered table-cloths. Not hardly. Seattle's best Italian restaurant also is its most stylish—a light, airy space facing a sunny patio and sheltered from the old brick of Pioneer Square. Light woods, glossy tile floors, potted plants, floral drapes and—from somewhere—the quiet strains of a classic guitar—create an atmosphere of calm elegance. Entry is through the foyer of a small office building called Merrill Place. The menu features a savory range of cacciatores, piccatas and creative pastas, plus rather Americanized New York steak, rack of lamb with garlic and rosemary, and veal chops. Il Terrazzo Carmine is noted for its calamari, done in a tomato and garlic sauté. The large wine list features an excellent selection of Italian reds.

8 *PAN-ASIAN: Nishino • 3130 E. Madison St; (206) 322-5800. Full bar service. Dinner Monday-Saturday. Major credit cards; $$ to $$$. GETTING THERE: Nishino is northeast of downtown near Lake Washington Park, at the corner of Lake Washington Boulevard. Follow Spring Street under the freeway (to avoid Madison's one-way grid), then shift over to Madison and drive just over two miles.*

"Pan-Asian" is what happens when a Japanese-born chef comes to America and becomes enamored with the rich seafood trove and cooking styles of the West Coast. Tatsu Nishino's fare is an interesting and sometimes fun mix of these two cultures. Examples are "Dynamite" baked geoduck clams with scallop and mushrooms, broiled Dungeness crab in a spicy cream sauce, chicken *yakitori* and garlic calamari. He also serves some of the freshest and most innovative sushi in town. His restaurant is housed in a Cape Cod style complex on the edge of trendy Madison Park. The interior is contemporary Japanese, with light woods, impressionistic Asian prints, bentwood chairs and a few select pieces of folkware. The term "austere elegance" comes to mind.

9 *MEXICAN: Galerias • 210 Broadway East; (206) 322-5757. Full bar service with a strong focus on tequilas. Lunch and dinner daily. MC/VISA; $$ to $$$. GETTING THERE: Galerias is in the Capitol Hill neighborhood northeast of downtown. Take Denny Way east or Olive Way northeast to Broadway, then go north; the restaurant is near East John Street. The restaurant is on the second floor, above a record and CD store.*

Broadway is Seattle's street of nonconformists, body piercing parlors and leather shops, a strange place for this formally decorated bit of Old Mexico. However, its second story location provides sanctuary from the gay/lesbian and post-hippie scene on the street below. If you wish to witness that passing parade of nonconformity, you can adjorn to a narrow balcony. The cozy, almost cluttered restaurant is over-dressed in old religious art, wrought iron, earthy pottery and dark carved woods. The menu is clad in hammered tin; be careful not to drop it on your foot. Within that armored document you'll discover ex-cellent Mexican cuisine—not burritos and tacos but savory fare such as veal and pork-stuffed chicken molé, pork loin glazed with guava salsa and creatively spiced giant prawns.

10 *SOUTHWESTERN: Santa Fe Café* • *2255 NE 65th St., (206) 524-7736; and 5910 Phinney Ave. N,; (206) 783-9755. Full bar service. Lunch Tuesday-Friday at 65th Street café and weekends only at the Phinney location; dinner nightly at both. Major credit cards; $$. GETTING THERE: Both of these small cafés are in out-of-the-way neigh-borhoods, worth the drive if you seek traditional New Mexico style cook-ing. To reach the first, take I-5 exit 170 east onto NE 62nd Street, shift up to NE 65th and continue east about three-fourths of a mile; the café is near 23rd Avenue. For the second, head north on Aurora Avenue (High-way 99) and take the North 65th Street/Green Lake exit. Cross under Aurora, continue north briefly on Woodland Avenue then curve around to the left onto 65th. Go uphill several blocks to Phinney Ridge, then head south on Phinney; it's near 60th Street.*

To call Southwestern fare "ethnic" may be stretching a point, al-though it's a blend of Spanish, Pueblo Indian and Mexican and that's certainly an ethnic mix. These two cafés Santa Fe don't serve the Southwest *nouveau* fare that was trendy a couple of decades ago. Theirs is authentic New Mexican, the sort of food you'd find in a small mom and pop café in Santa Fe or Taos. Typical of this fare is *posole* (hominy stew with garlic, lime juice and red chile), *carne adovada* (pork with red chile sauce), green chile stew, and pinto beans—*never* refried beans. In New Mexican cuisine, chiles—red and green—aren't merely used as a garnish; they're cooked into the food. For a taste of old Santa Fe, try the green chile burrito with shredded beef, onion and tomato, served with pinto beans and *posole;* and the *carne adovada* burrito. Now, if they'd just offer some of those legendary Santa Fe breakfast burritos...

He who does not mind his belly will hardly mind anything else.
— Samuel Johnson

Chapter four
SAVORING
SOMETHING SPECIAL
RESTAURANTS WITH AN ATTITUDE

Part of the fun of dining in Seattle is to seek out places with special character—be it in the design of the place, the style of the food or the way it's presented. We begin with an eclectic list—the Ten Best restaurants with a particular designer theme or food specialty. We then start your day with the Ten Best breakfast cafés, followed by the Ten Best outdoor cafés and view restaurants. We end with two categories suited particularly to Seattle—the Ten Best fish and chips places and the Ten Best coffee stops.

While the focus is more on specific styles of restaurants, we haven't sacrificed food quality in our selections. All of our nominees serve interesting, well-prepared and sometimes inexpensive fare.

PRICING: As in the previous chapter, we use simple strings of dollar signs to indicate the price of a typical dinner with entrée, soup or salad, not including drinks, appetizers or dessert: **$** = less than $10 per entrée; **$$** = $10 to $19; **$$$** = $20 to $29; **$$$$** = "Did you say you were buying?"

THE TEN BEST SPECIALTY RESTAURANTS

Since these selections don't relate to one another, they're listed in no particular order.

1 THE BEST FOOD AFLOAT: Argosy Dinner Cruise ● *Argosy Cruises, 1101 Alaskan Way, Pier 55; (800) 642-7816 or (206) 623-1445. (WEB SITE: www.argosycruises.com) American; full bar service. Dinner and lunch cruises; hours vary with the seasons. Major credit cards; $$$$. GETTING THERE: Argosy operates its dinner cruises from Piers 55 and 56 off Alaskan Way at the Seattle Waterfront.*

This isn't a restaurant anchored to a dock. It's an $8 million dinner cruise ship styled like an early twentieth century river cruiser and built especially for on-the-water dining. Unlike many dinner cruises that offer pre-prepared entrées, the Argosy vessel has three full-scale galleys and several dining areas. The firm works with several Seattle restaurants, including Elliott's Oyster House and the Metropolitan Grill, to feature a Northwestern regional menu with several entrées available. Launched in the spring of 2000, the dinner ship offers two to three-hour cruises around Elliott Bay and Puget Sound.

2 THE BEST BARBECUE: R & L Home of Good Bar-B-Q ● *1816 Yesler Way; (206) 322-0271. No alcohol. Lunch through dinner Tuesday-Saturday; closed Sunday-Monday. No credit cards; $ to $$. GETTING THERE: This savory place is about a mile east of downtown between 18th and 19th avenues. To reach it, simply head out Yesler Way from the Pioneer Square area.*

The wonderful smell of spicy barbecue will reach your nose before the attractive fieldstone storefront reaches your eyes. The inside is simple and prim, with a few booths and tables and a jukebox that's been out of order so long it's being used as a potted plant stand. Folks don't come here for the décor; they come for the best barbecue in town. Specify mild, medium or hot when you order barbecued pork ribs, babyback ribs, sliced beef, chicken or hot links or any combination. You can get 'em by the plateful, by the pound, or between slices of bread. Other fare includes classic Deep South collard or mustard greens, blackeyed peas and rice or red beans and rice, with sweet potato pie for dessert.

3 THE BEST DIM SUM: Top Gun ● *668 S. King St.; (206) 623-6606. Chinese; wine and beer. Dim sum served daily 10 to 3; regular fare served through late evening. MC/VISA; $$. GETTING THERE: It's in the International District, near the corner of Seventh Avenue South.*

No, Tom Cruse didn't eat here; that restaurant scene was at Kansas City Barbecue in San Diego. This café's name is a Hong Kong term having nothing to do with hotshot jet pilots. What *is* hotshot is the *dim sum*. It's rated by most local food critics as the best in town, although China Gate at 516 Seventh Avenue (624-1730) is a close rival. For those unlettered in Chinese culinary ways, *dim sum* translates as "little hearts," and these are bit-sized morsels of creative cookery. Traditionally—and at Top Gun—they're served from carts wheeled around the restaurant. Point to what smells or looks good—whether or not you know what it is—and it's placed on your table. *Dim sum* is particularly fun for large groups, since each plate contains very small servings and you can try a startling variety without spending too much. At meal's end, the server totes your bill by counting the stack of little empty plates. Top Gun's *dim sum* offerings are quite creative, including squid sticks, steamed bean curd cut from sheet rolls, deep fried crab claws, shrimp toast, and minced shrimp and pork dumplings. Aw, go ahead— try the braised chicken feet!

4 **THE BEST PIZZA PARLOR: Mad Pizza** • *Outlets in the Fremont area on North 36th Street between Fremont Place and Fremont Avenue North, (206) 632-5453; in Madison Park at 4021 E. Madison St., (206) 329-7037; and in First Hill at 1314 Madison St., (206) 322-7447. (WEB SITE: www.madpizza.com) Wine and beer. Lunch through late evening daily; MC/VISA; $$.*

If you like pizza with an attitude, head for one of these lively, upbeat little places where nothing except the food is taken seriously. Our favorite is the Fremont neighborhood outlet, a tiny space with a kind of cheerful Gothic Hades décor—burnt orange walls and a kinchy medieval mural that seems to suggest a pizza delivery to Satan's lair. The pizza is simply the best in town, with a wonderfully crunchy crust, spicy tomato and cheese base, and spilling over with interesting toppings. Our favorite is Prozac Pie with serious chunks of Italian sausage, pepperoni, salami, black olives and sweet onions. Other choices include MADiterranean with pesto sauce, capers, salami, green peppers, red onions and basil; Smokin' Chicken with marinated barbecued chicken, garlic ricotta sauce, roasted red bell peppers and feta; and Rastaman, with Jamaican jerk chicken, pesto, yellow peppers and Roma tomatoes. Mad also offers several vegetarian pizzas for those who somehow can't abide pepperoni and salami. You also can create your own pizza-on-demand from a long list of ingredients.

5 **THE BEST SANDWICH PLACES: At Pike Place Market** • *Three Girls Bakery, 1514 Pike Place, (206) 622-1045; and Sisters Café, 1530 Post Alley, (206) 623-6723. No alcohol at either. Breakfast through late afternoon at both. MC/VISA at Three Girls; no credit cards at Sisters; $.*

This is a double listing because the best sandwiches in town are built by two Pike Place Market cafés that are within a few hundred feet of one another. Neither is in the main market. Three Girls is across the way in the Sanitary Public Market and Sisters Café is just to the north in Post Alley. Three Girls serves creative American sandwiches, offering a variety of breads with a variety of fillings. Breads include caraway seed, bagels and Kaiser rolls, and within them you can install assorted cheeses, chicken salad, corned beef, ham, hummus, meatloaf, liverwurst and beyond. In addition to a small counter and table sitting area, it has a take-out window offering cookies, cakes and other bakery goods. Sisters Café might be called a European version of Three Girls. Its sandwiches are mostly continental, such as black forest ham with artichoke hearts and fontina cheese, chicken breast with tomatoes, feta cheese and baked eggplant—and so goes a rather long list. It also offers several salads.

6 THE BEST SUNDAY BRUNCH: Campagne • *1600 Post Alley at Pine (the Inn at the Market); (206) 728-CAFE. French and American regional; full bar service. Brunch served from 8 to 3. (Also see listing in Chapter Three under "The ten very best restaurants.) Major credit cards; $$$. GETTING THERE: The Inn at the Market is just northeast of Pike Place Market, and the restaurant is on the lower side, opposite the entrance to Post Alley.*

Seattle's best Sunday brunch isn't one of those multiple choice affairs served from a steam table. It's offered as individual entrées in the cozy confines of one of the city's best restaurants. And what entrées they are! A partial list includes a Lyonnaise breakfast of dried sausage and fresh fruit; omelet Cape Corse with herbs and Parmesan cheese, served in a Corsican seafood compote; poached eggs with a caramelized onion, salt cod and potato hash; scrambled eggs with herbs; pan roasted Spencer steak served with fries; and sautéed filet of trout. For light fare, you can choose yogurt granola or cinnamon-honey brioche. Among bread choices are demi baguettes served with French butter and rosemary raisin toast. Room for dessert? Try the fruit sorbet, chocolate torte with berries, or crème caramel. And to accompany this repast, champagne or a champagne cocktail.

7 THE MOST COLORFUL CAFÉ: Wolfgang Puck • *1221 First Ave.; (206) 621-9653. American-Asian nouveau; full bar service. Lunch and dinner daily. Major credit cards; $$$. GETTING THERE: It's catty-corner from the Seattle Art Museum, downtown at the corner of First and University.*

That puckish celebrity chef from Los Angeles decided to get downright silly when he created a Seattle version of his café. While those in L.A., San Francisco and even glittery Las Vegas are rather stylish, this one looks like a set for a Mardi Gras food fight. It's emblazoned with geometric patches of ceramic tile, color-swirled glass sculptures and surrealistic murals. Difficult to be taken seriously, the place appears to appeal mostly to tourists. The menu is typical Puck—Cajun blackened catfish, pepper tuna steak charred rare, curiously spiced rotisserie lamb and barbecue glazed chicken.

8 THE MOST HISTORIC RESTAURANT: Merchants Café
● *109 Yesler Way; (206) 624-1515. American; wine and beer. Breakfast through early dinner daily. MC/VISA, AMEX; $ to $$. GETTING THERE: This venerable café is in the Pioneer Square area between First Avenue and Occidental Mall.*

Is Merchants Café, dating from 1890, Seattle's oldest restaurant? Well, sort of. It was operated by the founding family in this location until it closed in 1964. It reopened in 1972, and can boast of being "the oldest café on the West Coast operating in its original building." But never mind the historic hair-splitting. While not a culinary treasure, it's an historic one, with pressed tin ceilings and many original furnishings, including a thirty-foot bar that came around Cape Horn. Check out the cozy downstairs dining room, which originally was at street level until Pioneer Square's streets were elevated. The menu is simple—omelets for breakfast, assorted sandwiches and daily specials for lunch and dinner. Perhaps the most interesting menu items are the appetizers, such as boiled peel-and-eat tiger prawns, smoked chicken wings done in house and black bean nachos. The Merchant also has a sidewalk espresso bar with a few outdoor tables.

9 THE MOST STYLISH RESTAURANT: Roy's ● *In the Westin Seattle at 1900 Fifth Ave.; (206) 256-ROYS. "Euro-Asian"; full bar service. Breakfast through dinner daily, with a weekend brunch. Major credit cards; $$$. GETTING THERE: Roy's is on the lobby floor of the Westin, which is at Fifth Avenue and Stewart Street, in downtown Seattle's north end.*

Honolulu's noted chef Roy Yamaguchi has created a strangely dazzling setting for his Seattle restaurant, with severe geometric patterns offset by swirling splashes of color. Slender drop lamps descend from the high ceiling and modern art work graces the walls. The changing menu of "Euro-Asian" fare is mostly a mix of Japanese and Polynesian, with some European accents. It's a Pacific Rim melange of fowl, fresh seafood and meats, often prepared with curiously fruity sauces.

10 THE WILDEST LOOKING RESTAURANT: Planet Hollywood ● *1500 Sixth Ave.; (206) 287-0001. More or less American; full bar service. Lunch through dinner daily. Major credit cards; $$. GETTING THERE: This strange place, which probably never should have left Hollywood, is downtown between Pike and Pine streets.*

Planets Hollywood are cropping up all over America, selling—particularly to the teen-to-early-twenties set—bizarre décor and ordinary food. The Seattle version has a Northwest theme, with a cartoon character totem and a generic Boeing aircraft suspended over the restaurant, which occupies a pit beneath street level. It has the usual giant TV screens, framed sports regalia and production stills of assorted horror movies. For us older folks, this wacky setting and a booming stereo system probably will not work up an appetite for the ordinary 'burgers, pastas and pizzas. But be a good sport; stop by for a drink and enjoy the really strange look of the place.

Sunnyside Up: The Ten Best Breakfast Cafés

Wake up and smell the caffé latte! An early-to-rise city, Seattle abounds with restaurants featuring hearty breakfasts. And of course most of them serve designer coffees. In order to qualify for our list, an establishment must start serving at least by 8 a.m. and feature a good selection of wake-up fare. Many of them serve breakfast items well into the day; one of them—Beth's Café—offers waffles at midnight.

1 ATHENIAN INN • *1517 Pike Place Market; (206) 624-7166. Mostly seafood; full bar service. Daily except Sunday, early morning to early evening. Major credit cards; $$. GETTING THERE: It's at street level in the main market building.*

We mentioned in Chapter Two that Pike Place Market was a great place to start your day. The Athenian, one of the few market cafés serving early breakfast, is our favorite place to do so. Arrive at 6:30 or after for hearty American fare or some interesting international dishes. The menu offers scrambled eggs with tomatoes and Mexican peppers and ham, Scottish kippers, grilled pork, shad roe with bacon, hominy and grilled pork and a traditional pirate's dish of creamed dried beef called *biltong*. (When I was in the Marine Corps, it was served on toast and I can't repeat its name here.) Our favorite is a curious India-English concoction called *kedgeree*—smoked fish with rice, slice boiled eggs, capers and curry, served with a toasted English muffin. What's Athenian about the Athenian? Only its heritage; it was established in Seattle in 1903 by three Greek brothers and moved to the market in 1909.

2 ATLAS FOODS • *In University Village at 2820 E. University Ave.; (206) 522-6025. American eclectic; full bar service. Lunch through late dinner daily; breakfast served from 8 to 3. MC/VISA; $ to $$. GETTING THERE: To reach University Village, take I-5 north, go briefly east* *on Freeway 520, then exit north onto Montlake Boulevard, which goes through the heart of the University of Washington campus. Take a double left turn onto 25th Avenue NE, continue north briefly and the shopping center is on your right. Atlas Food is across the central mall from Barnes & Noble.*

This modern and spacious café with an open kitchen and comfy booths is a good place to start your day if you're in the University of Washington neighborhood. The daily menu dances from one corner of America to the next and it's reflected in the breakfast fare. Try the cowboy corned beef hash with peppers and onions, Kentucky corn cakes, burrito Sierra Madre with spiced *papas* and *poblanas* or the Mississippi Blue Highway biscuits and gravy. Atlas also serves the usual range of flapjacks, omelettes and fruit plates. Order a caffé latte and it arrives in a huge mug that requires two hands for sipping. The Atlas lunch and dinner menus change thematically with the seasons, or at the whim of its co-owners Jeremy Hardy and Peter Levy, who operate several other Seattle restaurants under their CHOW banner. When we last passed, the Atlas theme was Mississippi Blue Highway with fare such as smoked chili, blackeyed pea stew and Delta catfish.

3 **BETH'S CAFÉ** • *7311 Aurora Ave. North; (206) 782-5588. American; open 24 hours. MC/VISA; $. GETTING THERE: It's simple, if a bit out of the way. Head north on Aurora to the Green Lake area then, just as you clear the center traffic divider on Aurora, turn left onto Wanona and look for a place to park. Beth's is on the west side, half a block back. There's parking in the rear.*

There's no good reason to drive nearly five miles from downtown for Beth's ordinary—although very ample and inexpensive—breakfasts. However, if you happen to be staying along Aurora's motel row, hanging out at Green Lake Park or planning an early trip to the Woodland Park Zoo, the café isn't far away. With all the ambiance of an old truck stop, it's a longtime favorite of locals, who can get a twelve-egg omelet (so large that it arrives in a pizza pan) any hour of the day. The breakfasts seem designed for truckers—ample portions of ham and eggs, steak and eggs, biscuits and gravy, ribeye steak and eggs served with great heaps of hash browns, plus the usual waffles, flapjacks and French toast. Omelettes are a specialty here.

4 **BLUE STAR CAFÉ AND PUB** • *4512 Stone Way; (206) 548-0345. Full bar service. Breakfast through dinner daily; $$. GETTING THERE: This breakfast star is in the Wallingford neighborhood north of Lake Union. From downtown, go north on Aurora (Highway 99), cross the Lake Washington Ship Canal then exit onto Bridge Way North. Take a half left onto Stone Way and go about eight blocks north; Blue Star is between 45th and 46th.*

This lively, upbeat café housed in old brick serves hearty and sometimes creative breakfasts. It's worth a pause for its Bohemian-Yuppie décor with a crowd to match. On sunny weekend mornings, they pack the place and spill out onto sidewalk tables. Among breakfast offerings are French coast, pancakes, hobo eggs with ham or bacon or sausage, Laguna scramble with mushrooms, eggs Monterey with salsa, Smoky Mountain scramble with smoked sausage and pepperjack cheese, plus crisp waffles that arrive alone or with ham, bacon or pecan toppings.

5 *THE 5 SPOT CAFÉ* • *1502 Queen Anne Ave. North; (206) 285-SPOT. American regional; full bar service. Breakfast through late dinner daily; breakfast served until midafternoon. MC/VISA; $$. GETTING THERE: This spot can be spotted atop Queen Anne Hill, at the corner of West Gayler Street. From downtown, follow First Avenue uphill since Queen Anne is one-way coming down, then shift over to Queen Anne on Roy Street, after it becomes two-way.*

Can a café change its spots? This one does, four times a year, featuring regional food and décor from "five spots" in America—the Northwest, Southwest, New England and South, plus an "American hybrid" mix. We stopped by when the theme was "I Left My Heart in San Francisco". As authors of three San Francisco guidebooks, we can confirm that the food and SFO look were authentic. Owners dispatch the chef and manager to the chosen locales to check out regional food and décor. So of course, a recorded Tony Bennett was singing that song as we arrived, followed by several Johnny Mathis numbers. Why Mathis? He grew up in San Francisco, although he found his fame elsewhere. Those guys did their homework!

Although 5 Spot features interesting regional fare, we go there mostly for breakfast. The menu offers interesting omelettes and standards such as biscuits and gravy, *huevos rancheros* and griddle cakes, plus whatever's currently regional. (If you aren't familiar with a Joe's Special, you didn't leave your heart in San Francisco.) Our favorite, generally on the menu no matter what the theme, is Red Flannel Hash, a corned beef hash with diced cooked beets. It tastes better than it sounds.

6 *HI-SPOT CAFÉ* • *1410 34th Ave.; (206) 325-7905. Eclectic; wine and beer. Breakfast 8 to 2:30 daily, lunch Monday-Friday and dinner Tuesday-Saturday. MC/VISA; $$. GETTING THERE: It's in the Madrona neighborhood about two miles northeast of downtown. Take James Street from the lower downtown area under I-5; it curves to the right and blends into Cherry Street. After a bit more than a mile, go north about five blocks on 34th; the restaurant is between Union and Pike.*

This spot is a cozy little café on a tree-lined street in the intimate Madrona neighborhood. The look is deliberately charming, with milk glass drop lamps and framed prints on pale walls. Its eclectic menu is reflected in creative breakfast offerings—tofu scramble, French brioche toast with almond butter, breakfast burritos, and the rather busy "Mexi-fries,"—a spicy scramble of potatoes, sautéed onions, carrots, chili peppers, zucchini, tomatoes, olives and green chiles. For something more conventional, try the buttermilk pancakes with real maple syrup. Even the drinks reflect the deliberate trendiness of this place—designer root beer by Thomas Kemper, Africola from Germany and—for the adults—mimosa.

7 *JITTERBUG* • *2114 North 45th.; (206) 547-6313. Eclectic menu with Mediterranean accents; wine and beer. Morning through late evening daily; "blunch" served from 8 to 3:30; $$. GETTING THERE: It's in the Wallingford area north of Lake Union, near the corner of Bagley Avenue North. From downtown, go north on Aurora (Highway 99), cross the Washington Ship Canal then exit onto Bridge Way North. Take a half left onto Stone Way North, follow it to North 45th Street and go right (east) to Bagley.*

This jumping place in a mixed-ethnic Wallingford neighborhood serves quite creative breakfasts. Examples are gingerbread waffles, *huevos rancheros,* thick sourdough bread slices fried in custard, and avocado and squash omelet with pepperjack cheese. Our favorite is the "Italian Farmhouse Rumble," with a mix of chicken sausage links, sundried tomatoes and scallions. The more conventional buttermilk pancakes, ham and sausage also are available. But who wants to be conventional in this upbeat place? The lunch and dinner menus are interesting as well, changing frequently as they hop around the world from Savannah to Barcelona. There's also Liver Pawte and Dogiva Bon Bons on the menu, but that's for your mutt. The café offers "canine cuisine" for diners with pets—served out on the sidewalk, of course.

8 *LARRY'S GREEN FRONT CAFÉ* • *209 First Ave. South; (206) 624-7665. American; full bar service. Breakfast through late evening daily. MC/VISA; $$. GETTING THERE: It's part of the "outdoor café row" along First Avenue in the Pioneer Square area, between Washington and Main streets.*

Most of Pioneer Square's many small cafés open later in the day, although Larry's greets early risers with hearty breakfasts of pancakes and waffles, assorted omelets, chicken fried steak and eggs, Italian sausage and eggs, and Hangtown Fry. What's Hangtown Fry? It's essentially an omelet with fried oysters, borrowed from the California Gold Rush. (Early settlers brought chickens west and there were plenty of oysters in San Francisco Bay.) Larry's is an appealing old place, installed in one of the brick storefronts of the Pioneer Square area. The bar opens early, in case you want to start your day with Hangtown Fry and a Bloody Mary.

9 *MACRINA BAKERY & CAFÉ • 2408 First Ave.; (206) 448-4032. Breakfast through late afternoon weekdays, brunch weekends. MC/VISA; $. GETTING THERE: It's between Battery and Bell.*

This cozy European style bakery is noted city-wide—and nationally—for its creative and full-flavored breads, the work of owner Leslie Mackie. The faithful flock here for an amazing variety of whole grain breads and savory pastry items such as hazelnut pinwheels, assorted cheesecakes, lemon tarts, lemon sour coffee cake and fruit and oat bars. In addition to bakery goods, Leslie offers at least one creative breakfast entrée, such as chanterelle and goat cheese omelet with shallots, plus in-house granola and fruit bowls, accompanied by specialty coffees. The bakery-café has a few tables inside and out.

10 *VARSITY INN • 1801 N. 34th St., (206) 547-2161. No alcohol. Breakfast through lunch daily; breakfast served all day. MC/VISA; $. Non-smoking. GETTING THERE: The Varsity is in Wallingford near Gas Works Park. There's a second café at 2300 NE 65th St., in the Ravenna area; (206) 525-2701.*

This long, skinny restaurant with a 1950s diner look is popular with Wallingford locals, particularly on a Sunday morning. Your wait—usually short—will be worth it if you like breakfast variety. They aren't creative, although they're ample and quite inexpensive. Among your choices are the usual assortments of omelets, thick French toast, quite crispy waffles, flapjacks, eggs Benedict, steak and eggs, minced ham and eggs, eggs Florentine, and sausage and eggs, plus the usual cereals and breakfast breads. The décor is cleverly simple—Varsity logo drop lamps and potted ivy dangling over the long rows of booths.

FOOD AL FRESCO: THE TEN BEST OUTDOOR CAFÉS

Because of its often drizzly weather, some of Seattle's "outdoor cafés" are indoors, which may sound like a self-canceling phrase. They're on pedestrian promenades of covered malls and we've picked two of them—Gordon Biersch and Desert Fire—for our list of favorites. The rest are out there in the sunshine—or the rain. Many of the city's *al freco* dining spots are in the Pioneer Square area and we've included three of them in our list.

1 *MAGGIE BLUFFS MARINA GRILL • At Elliott Bay Marina at 2601 W. Marina Place; (206) 283-8322. American; full bar service. Lunch through dinner weekdays, breakfast through dinner weekends.*

Major credit cards; $$. GETTING THERE: Take Elliott Avenue about two miles northwest from downtown, cross the Garfield Street-Magnolia Bridge and take the Elliott Bay Marina/Smith Cove Park exit.

This attractive café sitting under the highly regarded Palisade (Chapter Three, page 71) has several outdoor tables offering one of Seattle's finest views, earning it the top spot on our list of *al fresco* dining spots. The vistas are of the city skyline and Elliott Bay, filtered through the masts of Elliott Bay Marina. It's very popular on sunny weekends, so expect a wait for an outdoor table. If you must retreat to the interior, it has a has a pleasant nautically wood paneled look, and window tables offer the same fine view. Menu offerings include spicy Creole chicken, grilled seafood, skewered teriyaki salmon, plus assorted salads, chowders, chiles and fish 'n' chips. A specialty is spicy red bean soup.

2 BRIAZZ • *Corner of Fifth Avenue and Union Street downtown. Also Grand Briazz in University Village shopping center, just north of the University of Washington campus. Light fare; wine and beer. Morning through early evening daily; $.*

To call Briazz a restaurant is an overstatement; it's a small walkup-takeout popular with downtown working folks. However, it is indeed an *al fresco* dining venue, with more tables outside than in, tucked along the sidewalks of both Fifth Avenue and Union Street. The much larger Grand Briazz in University Village has an abundance of outdoor tables. The fare is appropriate for quick bites—salads, sandwiches, soups, sweets and designer coffees. Don't believe the company slogan that this is a "new concept in gourmet" eating; the food is okay but not gourmet. And if you plan to hike about the city or retreat to a quiet corner, Briazz will fix you a box lunch.

3 THE CENTRAL • *207 First Ave.; (206) 622-0209. American; full bar service. Lunch through dinner daily. MC/VISA; $$. GETTING THERE: It's part of the "outdoor café row" along First Avenue in the Pioneer Square area, between Washington and Main streets.*

Is it an outdoor café, an historic pub or a nightclub? Certainly. By day and early evening, the Central is an appealing outdoor café, serving hearties such as meatloaf, pasta, ribs and assorted sandwiches. It's one of three places with outdoor tables in this block of First Avenue—pleasant spots for enjoying lunch or early dinner and watching the passing tourist parade. It's also one of Seattle's oldest pubs and restaurants, dating from 1892. And on most nights, it becomes a hotspot for live entertainment, with a modest cover charge. And any time of the day or night, it's an appealing old pub, with a classic polished wood bar and mirrored, arched backbar.

4 *DESERT FIRE* ● *In Pacific Place at 600 Pine St.; (206) 405-3400. Southwest menu; full bar service. Lunch and dinner daily. Major credit cards; $$ to $$$. GETTING THERE: It's on the fourth floor of Pacific Place downtown; the shopping center is rimmed by Pine Street, Olive Way and Sixth and Seventh avenues.*

It's easy to pretend that you're outdoors when you relax in the dining patio of Desert Fire, since a dramatic fan-shaped glass roof lets the sunshine in, while keeping the famous Seattle rain out. Planter boxes and hanging baskets add to the *al fresco* illusion. The interior is exceptionally attractive, featuring a Santa Fe modern look with peeled log ceilings, *faux* adobe brick walls and pueblo Indian artifacts. The menu fits the architectural mood, featuring *carne asada* (spicy marinaded sirloin), Yucatan chicken breasts with *achiote* marinade, and *paella* which is a mix of Spanish rice, fish, shrimp, lobster tails, roast chicken and chorizo.

5 *GORDON BIERSCH BREWERY-RESTAURANT* ● *In Pacific Place at 600 Pine St.; (206) 405-4205. Eclectic menu; full bar service. Lunch and dinner daily. Major credit cards; $$ to $$$. GETTING THERE: It's beside Desert Fire; see above.*

Like Desert Fire, Gordon Biersch has several tables on the fourth floor walkway of Pacific Place, beneath that imposing glass atrium roof. The "sidewalk" section of this popular brewpub even has live plants to enhance the outdoor impression. The fare is spicy to match the firm's assertive brews; choices range from herb rötisserie chicken and linguine with garlic roasted prawns to pizzas, Louisiana style stews and peppery stir fries. We've also picked G-B as one of Seattle's best brewpubs; see Chapter Eight, page 142.

6 *J&M CAFÉ AND CARDROOM* ● *201 First Ave. South; (206) 292-0663. American; full bar service. Lunch through dinner daily. Major credit cards; $. GETTING THERE: It's part of the "outdoor café row" along First Avenue in Pioneer Square, between Washington and Main streets.*

You like history with your outdoor dining? This place was established in 1889 as Jamison & Moffett and moved to this location in 1902. It's appealing as a sidewalk café because its outdoor tables wrap around the corners of First Avenue and Washington Street, affording lots of opportunities to people-watch Pioneer Square tourists. The fare isn't at all creative although it is inexpensive, with just about everything under $10. "Everything" consists of 'burgers, fish and chips, Cajun chicken fettuccine, linguine, sandwiches and daily specials.

7 **LARRY'S GREEN FRONT CAFÉ** • *209 First Ave. South; (206) 624-7665. American; full bar service. Breakfast through dinner daily. MC/VISA; $$. GETTING THERE: It's part of the "outdoor café row" along First Avenue in the Pioneer Square area, between Washington and Main streets.*

Like J&M and next-door Central Saloon, the Green Front is lodged in one of Pioneer Square's century-old brickfronts. It's a good breakfast spot and it makes that list above. The sidewalk patio is the most appealing part of this place, since the indoor café is rather spartan. Partake of simple fare such as chicken fried steak, assorted sandwiches, salads and daily "Blue Plate Specials." This isn't gourmet dining; the Green Front serves essential American grub, to be wolfed down in a pleasant sidewalk setting.

8 **MARION COURT** • *Third Avenue at Marion Street. Various hours for the cafés; mostly breakfast through midafternoon. GETTING THERE: The courtyard is in the southern part of downtown, not far from Pike Place Market.*

This isn't an outdoor café; it's an attractively landscaped courtyard rimmed by several takeouts, handy for a quick breakfast or lunch. Select your fare and adjourn to one of several tables on the courtyard, which is sheltered from busy downtown traffic. Choices include Taco Del Mar, Espresso Europa, Happy Teriyaki, The Frankfurter, Pasta Ya Gotcha, Gyro's Place, Mario's Pizza and Quizno's baked submarine sandwiches. The second-story Marion Court Café serves assorted breakfast and lunch fare, with tables indoors and out, overlooking the courtyard.

9 **TERRACE GARDEN** • *At Cavanaugh's on Fifth Avenue, 1415 W. Fifth Ave.; (206) 971-8000. American; full bar service. Breakfast through dinner daily. Major credit cards; $$$. GETTING THERE: The restaurant is off the lobby floor of the downtown Cavanaugh hotel, between Union and Pike.*

While most "outdoor" cafés in downtown Seattle are inside shopping malls, Terrace Garden braves the elements, offering the city's largest *al fresco* dining terrace. It's suspended over the street with views of surrounding highrises and a thin slice of Elliott Bay. Potted plants lend a bit of atmosphere and heat lamps warm things up on cool days. Of course the restaurant also has a large indoor area. The outdoor deck is more often used for lunches and cocktails than for dinner service. The menu offers an interesting mix, ranging from chicken Parmesan and apple pork chops to assorted seafoods.

10 *ZÍ PANÍ BREADS & CAFÉ* ● *1815 N. 45th St.; (206) 548-9012. (WEB SITE: www.zipani.com) American; no alcohol. Breakfast through evening daily; $ to $$. GETTING THERE: This particular Zí Paní is at 45th and Wallingford Avenue North, above Lake Union. From downtown, go north on Aurora (Highway 99), cross the Washington Ship Canal then exit onto Bridge Way North. Take a half left onto Stone Way North, follow it to North 45th Street and go right (east); it's on the corner of Wallingford Avenue.*

While this isn't a full-fledged restaurant, it's a very appealing place for *al fresco* dining, offering a large hedge-lined brick patio with umbrella tables. It's a good spot for people-watching in the upbeat Wallingford area, with its ethnic mix of cafés, bistros and small shops. There are tables inside as well. This is one of several cafés Zí Paní in the Seattle area. Offerings include bagel and *focaccia* bread sandwiches, hearty salads, zesty soups, a full line of bakery goods and Torrefazione Italia coffees. Bagels are a specialty, made in-house.

Vista VITTLES: THE TEN BEST VIEW RESTAURANTS

A city in such a pretty setting has an abundance of view restaurants. Many are along the Elliott Bay waterfront; others offer vistas across marinas. One—surprisingly—is in a huge outdoor store. Our clear winner on a clear day is Seattle's favorite tourist restaurant. The food may be pricey but you can't beat the view, particularly when the scenery seems to rotate while you're sitting still.

1 *THE SPACE NEEDLE RESTAURANT* ● *In Seattle Center; second level of the Space Needle observation tower; (800) 937-9582 or (206) 443-2100. American and continental; full bar service. Lunch Monday-Saturday and Sunday brunch; dinner nightly. Major credit cards; $$$$. Meal prices include Space Needle ascent.*

With its 500-foot perch above the heart of the city and its slowly revolving seating area, the Space Needle is easily the best view restaurant in the city. It spins at .6 mph, requiring nearly an hour to make a complete revolution, so eat slowly. Prices are as lofty as the restaurant, with entrées ranging into the high $30s. Is it worth it? A favorite sport of local food critics is to make fun of this popular tourist spot—or to ignore it entirely. Give the Needle a chance, folks! A newly dressed up and more innovative menu offers some rather interesting entrées, such as rack of lamb with dijon-garlic crust, herb-roasted chicken, veal chops and filet mignon.

2 **ATHENIAN INN** • *1517 Pike Place Market; (206) 624-7166. Mostly seafood; full bar service. Daily except Sunday, early morning to early evening. Major credit cards; $$. GETTING THERE: It's at street level in the main building at Pike Place Market.*

Many out-of-towners' first view of this view restaurant—and forgive the play on words—was in a scene from the film *Sleepless in Seattle* with Tom Hanks. However, the movie didn't create the legend; this pleasantly austere seafood house has been here for nearly a century. The view across Elliott Bay—from its two-tiered dining area—is simply grand and the fare is—well—simple. Don't come for lightly done fish in raspberry sauce, and don't come too late. The Athenian has an extensive seafood menu, but the kitchen closes around 6 p.m. Do come early; it's a popular breakfast place, topping our "Sunnyside up" list.

3 **CHANDLER'S CRABHOUSE AND FRESH FISH MARKET** • *901 Fairview Ave.; (206) 223-2722. American, mostly seafood; full bar service. Lunch Monday-Saturday and Sunday brunch; dinner nightly. Major credit cards; $$$. GETTING THERE: It's in Chandler's Cove on the southeast shore of Lake Union. From downtown, take Virginia Street northeast, go north on Fairview, then northeast along the lakeshore.*

This popular seafood parlor offers splendid views of Lake Union from the floor-to-ceiling windows of its semi-octagonal dining room. And when the elusive Seattle sun chooses to shine, you can dine on the dock outside for completely unfettered vistas. Faithful Seattle patrons come here for fine seafood as well as the pretty view. Although the kitchen features a few *nouveau* gimmicks, the best offerings are fresh fish and shellfish, simply prepared. If you like your shellfish really fresh, pick a seat at the raw bar near the entrance. And if you want to prepare your own fish at home or in your motel's kitchenette, Chandler's has a fresh seafood market.

4 **FISHERMAN'S RESTAURANT AND BAR** • *Pier 57 in Bay Pavilion; (206) 623-3500. American, mostly seafood; full bar service. Mid-morning through dinner daily. Major credit cards; $$ to $$$. GETTING THERE: It's just off Alaskan Way at the Seattle waterfront, south of Pike Place Market.*

Although this waterfront place attracts more tourists than locals and almost no local food critics, we've had decent meals here. The views are just grand, since this three-level restaurant sits on a pier extending into Elliott Bay. The best vistas are from the second level, which is the cocktail lounge, so you'll have to contend with second hand smoke here. The Fisherman's look is predictably nautical, with the usual brass and polished woods. The kitchen specializes in mesquite grilled fish, and it offers as few pastas and fish and meat combinations. If you've brought a big appetite, try the "Fisherman's Feast" for two or more, with chowder, salad, sourdough bread and an entrée.

5 *LOWELL'S* • *1519 Pike Place Market; (206) 622-2036. American; full bar service. Breakfast through early evening daily. Major credit cards; $ to $$. GETTING THERE: It's on the ground floor of the main Pike Place Market building.*

We often start a Seattle day at this somewhat scruffy place, sipping a caffé latte at the first floor espresso bar and watching the morning sun light up Elliott Bay. A market institution since 1908, Lowell's is a handy and inexpensive breakfast through early dinner stop. It offers mostly seafood fare such as salmon, clam chowder, prawns, calamari and fish and chips. It hasn't won any dining awards and most local gastronomy guides snub the place. However, the food is quite palatable and reasonably priced. Place your order at the busy counter and adjourn to one of three bare-bones dining rooms, all with bay views. Only the middle level remains open for dinner and—until Washington reforms its smoking laws—you'll have to inhale secondhand smoke from the adjacent bar.

6 *MAXIMILIEN IN THE MARKET* • *81-A Pike Place Market; (206) 682-7270. French and other continental; full bar service. Lunch and dinner Tuesday-Sunday and Sunday brunch. Major credit cards; $$$. GETTING THERE: The restaurant is in the rear of the main market building.*

When one thinks of a Pike Place view restaurant, seafood comes to mind. However, this long-established café is frankly French. Dark woods, beamed ceilings and black lacquered tables with white nappery suggest a pleasant French bistro setting; only the vista of Elliott Bay says it's tucked into a corridor of the market. Apparently influenced by the setting, the kitchen offers several seafood dishes. Fish stew is a specialty and the menu also features baked salmon with onions and capers, and *coquilles St. Jacques*. Other traditional French fare includes baked escargot, duck *confit*, and rabbit braised with dijon mustard and cream sauce. If you seek lunch with a view, try some of the unusual sandwiches such as chicken and brie or steamed mussels.

7 *McCORMICK & SCHMICK'S HARBORSIDE* • *1200 Westlake Ave. North; (206) 270-9052. American, mostly seafood; full bar service. Lunch and dinner daily. Major credit cards; $$ to $$$. GETTING THERE: This seafood haven is on Lake Union in the AGC Building. Follow Westlake Avenue north from downtown along the west shore of the lake and turn into the parking area at the AGC Marina.*

McCormick & Schmick's other two locations are in the downtown area with views mostly of busy sidewalks. However, the newest location offers grand vistas of Lake Union and the hilly Fremont-Wallingford neighborhood across the pond. The main dining room is on the second floor of the AGC building; ask for a table on the right side, where your vista also will include a generous slice of downtown skyline. The menu is typical of McCormick and Schmick's, with several fresh seafood selections, a serious choice of shellfish and a few chickens, steaks and chops for balance.

8 *RAY'S BOATHOUSE* • *6049 Seaview Ave. NW; (206) 789-4130. (WEB SITE: www.rays.com) American, mostly seafood; full bar service. Lunch and dinner daily. Major credit cards; $$ to $$$. GETTING THERE: The Boathouse is just south of Shilshole Marina in northwest Seattle. Head northwest from downtown on Elliott Avenue and then north on 15th Avenue West. Cross the Ballard Bridge and go west, following signs to Chittenden Locks. Continue past the locks on NW 54th Street, which swings north to become Seaview Avenue.*

Sitting on a dock on lower Shilshole Bay at the entrance to Salmon Bay, Ray's offers grand views—north to Shilshole Marina, west to the Olympic Peninsula and the Olympic Mountains, and south across Salmon Bay to the headlands of Discovery Park. The restaurant occupies two levels and the view is particularly impressive from Ray's Café upstairs and from its outdoor deck. A local fixture for three decades, Ray's also makes our list of Ten Best seafood restaurants; see Chapter Three, page 75.

9 *SALTY'S ON ALKI* • *1936 Harbor Ave. SW; (206) 937-1600. (WEB SITE: www.saltys.com; E-MAIL: alki@saltys.com) American, mostly seafood; full bar service. Lunch Monday-Saturday, Sunday brunch, dinner nightly. Major credit cards; $$$ to $$$$. GETTING THERE: It's in West Seattle near Duwamish Head. Take Marginal Way south, then go west on Spokane Street or the West Seattle Freeway, then fork to the right on Harbor Avenue SW.*

Salty's offers one of the finest aquatic dining views in Seattle. Canted window walls provide a grand panorama of the city skyline across Elliott Bay, from the Space Needle through the downtown highrises to Safeco Field. Of course, the place has a proper nautical look, although we aren't wild about the exterior décor with its rusty fish sculptures and broken concrete pilings with the rebar showing. They seem left over from a demolition project. Salty's views don't come cheap. Prices of entrées reach into the $30s, and they range from grilled salmon, Maine lobster, cioppino and mixed seafood grill to chicken breast and a few steaks. For more on Salty's, see Chapter Three, page 75.

10 **WORLD WRAPPS** • *Second floor of the REI building at 222 Yale Ave. North; (206) 223-1944. International fare; no alcohol. Open during store hours—weekdays 10 to 9, Saturday 9 to 7 and Sunday 11 to 6; $. GETTING THERE: REI is at the corner of Yale and John Street. Head east from downtown on Denny way and—just short of I-5— turn left on Minor Avenue, go a block to John and turn right.*

Whazziz? A fast food takeout is one of the ten best view restaurants in Seattle? Certainly, and it's also the least expensive. World Wrapps is a fast food franchise that offers international fare clad in wheat tortillas. While most outlets are in malls or small stalls, the one on the second floor of the REI outdoor store offers fine views of the Seattle skyline through large picture windows, or from an outdoor deck. The fare ranges from chicken Parmesan and *paella* to Thai chicken and spicy Southwest shrimp. These are essentially chopped up fillings, either wrapped into tortillas or served in bowls. You can't get tequila with your tequila lime shrimp, but you can get soft drinks or fruit smoothies.

THE BEST FISH & CHIPS PLACES

Fish and chips are to Seattle what cheeseburgers and fries are to most other cities. Dozens of small takeouts and virtually every seafood parlor serves them. Of course, any serious restaurant kitchen can properly prepare this fare. However, this is not a repast to be taken seriously. We limited our investigation to small take outs, for this is intended to be a casual meal, preferably eaten at an outdoor table and possibly shared with the seagulls. Our fish of choice—when available—was halibut. They are listed not in alphabetical order, but in the order of our ratings. And the winnah is:

1 **LITTLE CHINOOK'S** • *Fishermen's Terminal at 1900 W. Nickerson St.; (206) 283-4665. Lunch and dinner weekdays and brunch through dinner weekends. Major credit cards. GETTING THERE: Take Elliott Avenue northwest from downtown, blend onto 15th Avenue West and take the West Emerson exit just before 15th crosses the Ballard Bridge. Little Chinook's is on the east end of the building that houses Chinook's seafood restaurant.*

This is our runaway winner for the best fish and chips in Seattle and maybe the entire Northwest. Our halibut was so fresh and succulent that it was almost sweet, and it was perfectly deep-fried in a seasoned batter. The fries also were seasoned and the meal was accompanied by a little cup of coleslaw. Not only were the portions generous, with three thick wedges of fish atop a pile of fries, but the prices are among the cheapest of our ten candidates. Little Chinook's choices are cod, halibut, prawns, clam strips or a combination thereof. It's one of the few places that offers malt vinegar, a required accompaniment of fish and chips in England and Australia. You can eat inside or adjourn to the adjacent dock and dine with a nice view of the huge Fishermen's Terminal fishing fleet.

2 **ALKI SPUD FISH & CHIPS** • *2666 Alki Ave. SW; (206) 938-0606. Lunch through dinner daily. MC/VISA. GETTING THERE: Take the West Seattle Freeway or Spokane Street across the tip of Harbor Island and follow Harbor Avenue around Duwamish Point. The route becomes Alki Avenue and takeout is near the corner of 60th Avenue SW.*

Our second place winner, a little takeout across from Alki Beach Park, has been serving fish and chips since 1935. Choices are halibut, prawns, clam strips, oysters or scallops or chicken strips. Our four pieces of halibut had a crisp, light crust and a tasty, moist interior. The fries were the best of any of our candidates—thick cut, skins on and fried in seasoned oil. We like the seating choices at Spud's—all providing views of Puget Sound, the Olympics and on a really clear day, Mount Baker. You can sit upstairs or downstairs in the small takeout or carry your booty across the street to Alki Beach Park, where a couple of picnic tables and a low seawall provide seating. Ignore the pleading looks of the seagulls; offer them a single scrap and you'll create a feeding frenzy that may not be appreciated by nearby diners.

3 **LOCKSPOT CAFÉ** • *3005 NW 54th. (at the entrance to Hiram Chittenden Locks); (206) 789-4865. Lunch through evening weekdays and breakfast through evening weekends. Major credit cards. GETTING THERE: Head northwest from downtown on Elliott Avenue and then north on 15th Avenue West. Cross the Ballard Bridge and go west, following signs to Chittenden Locks.*

The Lockspot, which has been around since 1917, calls its fish and chips "world famous." That's an overstatement, although they're quite good. The Lockspot and Anthony's (below) finished in a virtual tie for third. The Lockspot gained a slight edge because it offers halibut and chips which—when we last checked—Anthony's did not. Otherwise, the quality was virtually identical. Your Lockspot choices are cod, halibut, clams, prawns or oysters. Our halibut arrived perfectly cooked, moist and flaky inside, with a nice, crisp crust. The fries were semishoestring, tasty and served in huge portions. You can dine indoors or on picnic style tables adjacent to a takeout window.

4 **ANTHONY'S FISH-BAR** • *2201 Alaskan Way; (206) 448-6688. Late morning through evening. Major credit cards. GETTING THERE: The Fish-Bar is on the street level of Anthony's Pier 66 on the north waterfront, off Alaskan Way at the foot of Bell Street.*

This take-out features very flaky, moist cod with a thin yet crisp coating. Although Anthony's doesn't offer halibut, you can get chips with cod, clam strips or prawns. Our cod was nearly as tasty as the Lockspot's halibut, although the servings aren't quite as ample. Fries are shoestring and properly crisp. If you elect soft drinks or ice tea over wine or beer, you can have unlimited refills. The Fish-Bar has more of a fast-food atmosphere, with paper or plastic containers, although you can't beat the location—right on the waterfront with indoor and outdoor tables offering views of the skyline and Elliott Bay.

5 TOTEM HOUSE SEAFOOD & CHOWDER • 3058 NW
54th; (206) 784-2300. Late morning through early evening. MC/VISA. GETTING THERE: It's at the corner of 32nd Avenue NW, opposite the entrance to Hiram Chittenden Locks. From downtown, head northwest on Elliott Avenue and then north on 15th Avenue West. Cross the Ballard Bridge and go west, following signs to Chittenden Locks.

At the Totem, styled as a kind of overdone Salish longhouse, your deep-fried halibut arrives as one large filet, which is probably equivalent to three normal pieces. Ours was very nicely done, moist in the middle and crisp around the edges, clad in a crunchy batter. The fries were skins-on and quite good, although a bit too salty for our taste. Fish and chip choices include the aforementioned halibut plus cod, salmon nuggets, prawns, clam strips, oysters, chicken or combinations. You can dine inside this small takeout or at picnic tables at streetside, opposite the Chittenden Locks and gardens.

6 LOWELL'S • 1519 Pike Place Market; (206) 622-2036. Morning through early evening daily. Major credit cards. GETTING THERE: It's on the street-level floor of the main market building.

Lowell's fish and chips, a dollar or more higher than most of the others we tested, are issued from the del-style takeout on the ground floor of this three-level restaurant. From there, you can adjourn to adjacent dining tables and enjoy that great view for which this legendary café is famous. You have a single choice—cod in a "panco" batter, which consists of a tasty mix of flour, fine bread crumbs and egg. Lowell's chips are worth the higher cost, since you get three large fish fillets plus a small cup of coleslaw. Ours was properly cooked, with that crunchy panco crust and a moist, flaky interior. Lowell's might have scored higher except for its rather ordinary skinless shoestring fries.

7 STEAMERS SEAFOOD CAFÉS • Pier 59 in front of the Seattle Aquarium; Pier 56 adjacent to Elliott's Oyster House; and in the Center House at Seattle Center. Late morning to evening. MC/VISA.

The two takeouts on the waterfront and the one in the Center House food court offer cod, clams or prawns and chips. The basic order was the most expensive of the five we've selected, although portions were generous, with five fair-sized pieces of cod. However, the fillets are rather slim, so they tend to be rubbery around the edges, although ours was properly moist in the middle. We liked the crunchy beer batter crust; the fries, partially skins-on, also were quite good.

8 **SEA SHANTY** • *4135 University Way NE; (206) 632-6822. Early morning through dinner. GETTING THERE: Not near the sea, this shanty is in the University District, just northwest of the University of Washington campus. It's in the middle of a long block between NE 41st and 42nd streets.*

This tiny café offers cod or halibut and chips, along with a few other fried seafood dishes, chowder and hamburgers. Order one or two pieces of fish—depending on your appetite and wallet—and you'll get large fillets, deep-fried to order, accompanied by a generous pile of skins-on fries. Our halibut fillet was lightly done and quite tasty. The batter, while properly crisp, could have used more seasoning. A nice feature of this little place is that you can douse your fish with malt vinegar in the British/Australian manner. Which is a mild surprise, since the tiny café is Chinese-owned.

9 **JACK'S FISH AND CHIPS SPOT** • *1514 Pike Place Market St.; (206) 467-0514. Early morning through early evening. MC/VISA, AMEX. GETTING THERE: This fried fish takeout is behind Jack's Fish Spot and Crab Pot, a large fish market in the Sanitary Public Market, across from the main Pike Place Market building.*

Jack's fish choices are cod, halibut, prawns, oysters and scallops. While our three pieces of halibut were fresh, they were slightly overdone, which seems to be typical at fish places catering mostly to tourists. We had the same problem with Ivar's (below). The tarter sauce was prepackaged Krafts, a definite minus. The fries were generous and quite good—thick skins-on shoestrings. There are a few counter stools at the takeout, or you can seek out seating elsewhere inside Sanitary Public Market or outdoors in adjacent Post Alley. Incidentally, if you like shrimp and crab walk-way cocktails in the good old San Francisco Fisherman's Wharf tradition, Jack's is one of the few places in Seattle that offers them, and they're huge.

10 **IVAR'S FISH BAR** • *Pier 54 at 1001 Alaskan Way; (206) 624-6852. Late morning through evening. Major credit cards. GETTING THERE: Ivar's is on the waterfront, between Madison and Spring streets.*

Ivar's makes our "dead last but finished" category. The servings are generous, but the fish was overcooked even though we sent it back twice, requesting that it be lightly done. Perhaps the fry cook was just having an off day. This takeout in front of Ivar's Acres of Clams offers cod, clams, salmon and scampi with its chips. The fries are shoestring type and quite tasty, and of course you get the usual sauce for the fish and catsup for dipping your fries.

THE TEN BEST COFFEE STOPS

Not coffee shops; coffee *stops*—small stalls and cafés that dispense espresso, cappucino, mocha and Seattle's official drink, caffé latte. The city's coffee culture began in 1971 when three college buddies opened the first Starbucks opposite Pike Place Market. Coffee stops have since spread throughout the city—to street corner carts, sports stadiums, shopping malls and even service stations. And they have proliferated throughout the nation. Starbucks is now the number one purveyor of coffee in the country, with more than 2,000 outlets.

Other coffee roasters have joined the caffeine parade. Some larger firms seek to match Starbucks' success while small independents simply try to brew the best cup of espresso or latte in the city. Tully's, pursuing its motto of "In beans we trust," has become America's third largest coffee roaster and Seattle's Best is another major local outlet. How many coffee stops are there in Seattle? According to the city agency that licenses cafés, more than 250 independent coffee stands are operating, along with dozens of Starbucks, Tully's and Seattle's Best outlets. Counting coffee stops within department stores, supermarkets, service stations and such, the total number of the city's caffeine vendors may approach a thousand. Seattle's USWest Yellow Pages is one of the few directories in the nation with a special section for "Coffee & Tea—retail," and it covers nearly two pages.

Emerald City's coffee parlors are particularly busy during the evening rush hour. Many homeward-bound Seattlites have wisely replaced martinis with coffee as the beverage of choice.

One of our favorite Seattle pastimes is to sit at a coffee stop, latte in hand, and watch the city's passing parade. And these are our ten preferred places to sit:

1 CAFÉ STARBUCKS • *Pacific Place, 600 Pine St.; (206) 587-2423. Lunch through evening daily. GETTING THERE: This coffee café is on the third level of Pacific Place shopping mall, which is downtown, rimmed by Pine Street, Olive Way and Sixth and Seventh avenues.*

Our favorite coffee stop is not the original Starbucks at Pike Place Market; its the firm's most upscale outlet in the city's trendiest shopping mall. One of several cafés Starbuck around the city, this is a fashionable little place with modern art on its walls and an outdoor balcony hanging over the street. It serves an assortment of soups, sandwiches, salads and pastries and—in addition to designer coffees—a featured wine of the day.

A "tall Americano" isn't a basketball player

In Europe, the classic coffee drink is espresso, served in a tiny cup and so thick that a spoon will stand upright, unaided. Other types, such as cappuccino, mocha and latte, are coffees mixed with milk, whipped cream or chocolate. However, some health-conscious Seattlites have modified their coffee tastes to cut down on caffeine and calories. They're likely to order an "Americano," regular coffee brewed in an espresso machine, or a "Skinny," which is a latte made with non- fat milk.

To sound like a local Joe Cool when ordering your designer coffee, don't ask for a "small," "medium" or "large." The proper terminology is "short," "tall" and "grande".

2 *ALKI BAKERY* • *2738 Alki Ave. SW; (206) 935-1352. Early morning through late evening daily. GETTING THERE: Take the West Seattle Freeway or Spokane Street across the tip of Harbor Island and follow Harbor Avenue around Duwamish Point. The route becomes Alki Avenue and the restaurant is at the corner of 61st Avenue SW.*

This prim little place is more bakery than coffee stall. However, it earns a spot on our list because it offers the full range of specialty coffees and a better selection of baked goods than most coffee houses, plus sandwiches, salads and fruit smoothies. It's in the heart of a popular beach area and its sidewalk tables provide fine views beyond the beach and across Elliott Bay to Seattle. The coffee of choice is Torrefazione (difficult to say unless you're Italian), a blend that originated in *Milano.*

3 *BEANS & MACHINES* • *1121 First Ave.; (206) 625-1482. Early morning to late afternoon. GETTING THERE: This upscale coffee beanery is just above the waterfront, near Seneca Street.*

As the name implies, this is both a coffee stop and a specialty shop for espresso paraphernalia. You can buy espresso machines, designer stainless steel vacuum bottles for toting your latte about and—for that outdoor person who has everything—a caffeine fiend's backpack with four coffee containers attached. The shop also features contemporary kitchenware and wonderfully aromatic bags of coffee from which you can build your own blend. An ongoing video demonstrates how to make that perfect cup of caffé.

4 *CHAPTERS COFFEE HOUSE* • *1109 North 36th St.; (206) 633-1825. Early morning to late afternoon. GETTING THERE: It's in the Fremont area, between Stone Way and Woodland Park. From downtown, go north on Westlake Avenue (skirting the western edge of Lake*

Union), then cross the Fremont drawbridge. Continue two blocks north on Fremont Street, then go right onto North 36th for about five blocks.

Unlike the sleek chain outlets, this is what a coffee house *should* be—a pleasant little place tucked into a weathered old shingle-sided building. Patrons relax on comfortable antique furniture, light filters through a stained glass window and soft music plays somewhere in the background. The place issues the usual specialty coffees and some tasty pastries. And of course the coffee is "Troll Blend" in honor of the legendary Fremont Troll. Chapters is adjacent to Shorey's Bookstore, a Seattle institution since 1890, offering new, used and collectors books; (206) 633-2990.

5 SEATTLE'S BEST COFFEE BAR DOWNTOWN • 1321 Second Avenue between University and Union; (206) 233-0612. Early morning through mid-evening daily.

This is perhaps the most appealing of several Seattle's Best outlets, set back off Second Avenue in a handsome brick and stone building. It has several comfortably worn leather chairs with a pot-bellied stove, a coffee service counter, and tables inside and out. Upbeat music from a good sound system and an abundance of reading material invites one to linger and relax. At a "whole bean silo," you can get a takeout sack of your favorite coffee blend.

6 SEATTLE'S BEST AT PIKE PLACE • At the entrance to Post Alley off Pine Street; (206) 467-7700. Early morning through evening daily. GETTING THERE: This coffee stop is near Pike Place Market, across Pine Street from the Inn at the Market and Campagne restaurant.

Look for the neon coffee mug replicated on the cover of this book and you've found this really cute Seattle's Best outlet. It's designed as a classic 1950s diner, with red plastic and chrome-rimmed stools, red neon piping behind the serving counter and red ceramic tile trim throughout. Sippers can perch on those stools or sit at tables outside and watch the ebb and flow of Post Alley and Pike Place Market people traffic. In addition to the usual coffees by the cup, it features a good assortment of freshly roasted coffee and coffee making apparatus.

7 THE ORIGINAL STARBUCKS • 1912 Pike Place Market St.; (206) 448-8762. Early morning to mid-evening. GETTING THERE: It's across the street from the north wing of the main Pike Place Market building, about mid-block.

The oldest of the Starbucks coffee stalls is historically interesting and is thus included in our list. However, it's a rather small and unimposing place, with the usual coffees, fresh beans and a few specialty food items. We like its location because we can pick up a caffé latte and adjourn to Victor Steinbrueck Park at the nearby corner of Western Avenue and Virginia Street to watch the sunset. (The park, which starts as a green slope and then extends across a parking structure roof, is a favorite haunt of the homeless, so you may have to share one of the many picnic tables—but not your latte.)

8 TORREFAZIONE ITALIA IN PIONEER SQUARE • *On Occidental Mall; (206) 624-5773. Early morning to late afternoon. GETTING THERE: This coffee haven is just off Pioneer Square's Main Street.*

The main appeal of this designer Italian place is its location on Occidental Mall, where you can sit outside, somewhat removed from the rumble of nearby traffic. There are tables inside as well, and it features the usual coffees—the Torrefazione brand from Milan—plus bakery items and other light fare, espresso machines, whole beans and assorted blends. A focal point here is an elaborate stainless coffee roaster.

9 TULLY'S DOWNTOWN • *1401 Fourth Avenue at Union Street; (206) 625-0600. Early morning through evening daily.*

Rivaling the success of Starbucks, Tully's has become the nation's third largest coffee retailer and it has dozens of outlets in Seattle. Our favorite is Tully's "flagship" store at the corner of Fourth Avenue and Union, where we like to sit at a sidewalk table, caffé latte in hand, and watch the flow of pedestrians and traffic. It's an upbeat place inside and it frequently hosts live combos. Stacks of newspapers are available for those who just want to sit, sip and relax.

10 TULLY'S ON HARBOR STEPS • *1222 Post Alley on Harbor Steps at Western Avenue; (206) 624-6397. Daily, early morning to early evening. GETTING THERE: Harbor Steps is below First Avenue at the base of University Street, just above the waterfront. Tully's is on the lower level.*

There are two good reasons for stopping at this Tully's outlet: It's at the base of Harbor Steps, which is a very attractive terraced park and a great people-watching place; and it's just above Blazing Saddles bike rentals. In case you want to rent a bike (Chapter Two; page 58) this is a good place to fuel up on caffeine and carbs before you start out. It's also a convenient stop if you're visiting the Seattle Art Museum at the top of Harbor Steps or some of the waterfront attractions just below. This Tully's has tables both inside and out, with a good selection of bakery items, plus the full range of designer coffees by the cup or the bag.

I wasn't born in a log cabin, but my family moved into one as soon as they could afford it.
— **Melville D. Landon**

Chapter five
PROUD PAUPERS
A BUDGET GUIDE

This chapter is for folks on a budget, who are seeking out the *really* thrifty places to play, dine and sleep. Seattle is not an inexpensive city, with most downtown hotel rooms ranging from $100 to $200 a night and restaurant entrées crawling into toward the $30 mark. On the other hand, we've found rooms in town and in suburban motels for less than $60, and there's an abundance of inexpensive restaurants in Seattle, particularly ethnic cafés in the International District and some of the other neighborhoods.

FRUGAL FUN: THE TEN BEST FREE ATTRACTIONS
Emerald City offers an abundance of freebies, starting with Pike Place Market, the most popular spot in the city. Seattle's public parks are free, of course, and some of them are so interesting that they make our Ten Best list. And the very best free things in Seattle? All of that gorgeous scenery!

1 **PIKE PLACE MARKET** • *First Avenue at Pike Street; (206) 697-4879. Information booth/ticket agency (206) 682-7453. (WEB SITE: www.pikeplacemarket.org) Info booth open Tuesday-Sunday noon to 6; hours may be longer in summer.* **Walking tours** *of the market are sponsored by the Pike Place Merchants Association, Monday and Wednesday at 8:30 and 9:30 a.m., Friday at 2 p.m. and Sunday at 9:30 and 10:30. For reservations, call (206) 587-0351.*

It's the city's most popular visitor attraction, it offers great variety and it's free. Of course, you can spend money in the dozens of shops, produce stands, seafood stalls, art and craft stalls and cafés at Pike Place Market. However, it doesn't cost a nickel to stroll about, watching the crowds, joking with the fishmongers and browsing through the shops. Many produce and specialty food stalls even provide free samples. For more on this grand place, see Chapter Two, page 36.

2 **THE CENTER FOR WOODEN BOATS** • *1010 Valley St.; (206) 382-BOAT. (WEB SITE: www.cwb.org; E-MAIL: cwb@cwb.org) Open 11 to 6 daily from May through Labor Day and 11 to 5 Wednesday-Monday the rest of the year. Free. GETTING THERE: The facility is just east of the old Naval Reserve building at the southern tip of Lake Union. Take West Denny Way from downtown, then go north on Westlake and then east on Valley. The center is immediately east of Northwest Seaport (see below).*

The Center for Wooden Boats is something unique—and we use the word properly. It's a combination aquatic museum, boat-building center and in-the-water exhibit center. It's also one of the few museums in the world where you can rent the "exhibits." You can wander about, admire the nautical displays indoors and out and watch boat builders for free. There are fees for renting the classic old wooden boats that are on display. For more on this "hands on history museum," see Chapter Two, page 45.

3 **DAYBREAK STAR CULTURAL ARTS CENTER** • *In Discovery Park; (206) 285-4425. Gallery and gift shop open Monday-Saturday 10 to 5 and Sunday noon to 5; free. GETTING THERE: From downtown, follow Westlake, Nickerson and then Emerson past Fishermen's Terminal. Take a half right from Emerson onto Gilman Avenue West, a half left onto Government Way and follow it into Discovery Park, then follow "Daybreak Star" signs west.*

The Sacred Circle Gallery of American Indian Art in the Daybreak Star Cultural Arts Center is one of the few free museums in Seattle—and well worth the trip to Discovery Park. Its focal points are several huge pieces of native art, including *bas relief* traditional Haida and contemporary native carvings on the walls of this second floor gallery. Adjacent rooms have changing exhibits. For more on Daybreak Star, see Chapter Two, page 62.

4 DISCOVERY PARK • *Northwest of downtown on a bluff over-looking Puget Sound. Visitor center at 3801 W. Government Way; (206) 386-4236. Visitor center hours 8:30 to 5 daily; park hours 6 a.m. to 11 p.m. GETTING THERE: See Daybreak Star listing above.*

Of course all Seattle's public parks are gratis, although only a couple are worthy of our Ten Best Free Attractions list. Discovery Park, a former military post occupying a dramatic coastal bluff northwest of downtown, is the city's largest, covering 513 acres. Some sections of the park are virtual wilderness areas within view of the city; others offer grand views *of* that city. The park has a fine visitor center with exhibits on area history, flora and fauna, and an excellent native arts gallery (see above). Both of these are free. And you're free to use your feet or bikes to follow a series of hiking trails and bike paths throughout the park. For more, see Chapter Two, page 46.

5 FISHERMEN'S TERMINAL • *3919 18th Ave. West on Salmon Bay, just west of the Ballard Bridge; (206) 728-3395. GETTING THERE: Take Elliott Avenue northwest from downtown, blend onto 15th Avenue West and take West the Emerson exit just before 15th crosses the Ballard Bridge.*

For Seattle's hundreds of commercial fisherpersons, Fishermen's Terminal is a fine place to dock their boats and sell their catch. For visitors, it's a fine place for strolling the docks, admiring more than seven hundred fishing boats and enjoying great views across Lake Union. This is the West Coast's largest fishing terminal, which is no surprise, since Washington vessels harvest more than half the total U.S. catch. You can sample some of that catch—not free, of course—at Chinook's Restaurant and the inexpensive Little Chinook's. Both are described in the dining sections of this book. And for more on the terminal itself, see Chapter Two, page 112.

6 GREEN LAKE PARK • *In Seattle's Green Lake neighborhood. GETTING THERE: Follow I-5 north from downtown, take exit 170 north to Ravenna Boulevard, go left (northwest) under the freeway and the park is within a quarter of a mile.*

This is the second Seattle park that earns a spot on our Ten Best Free Attractions list. It's one of the city's most popular recreation areas, with a walking/running/biking trail that circles the lake, kiddie playground, motorless boat rentals, ball fields and a basketball court. Expect it to be crowded most weekends. The park's best appeal is its loop trail, with separate lanes for walkers and cyclists, and even a sandy path for serious runners who disdain asphalt. The park is described in more detail in Chapter Two, page 48; and the recreation trail makes our Ten Best Hike Routes list in Chapter Twelve, page 186.

7 HIRAM CHITTENDEN LOCKS AND CARL S. ENGLISH JR. BOTANICAL GARDENS • *3015 NW 54th St.; (206) 783-7059. Locks and gardens open 7 a.m. to 9 p.m.; visitor center open 11 to 5. GETTING THERE: Head northwest from downtown on Elliott Avenue and then north on 15th Avenue West. Cross the Ballard Bridge and go west, following signs to Chittenden Locks.*

It seems odd that a set of navigation locks separating Puget Sound from lakes Union and Washington is a major tourist draw. Yet folks by the dozens gather here each day to watch the aquatic rite of passage of fishing boats and pleasure craft between fresh and salt water. It costs nothing to look, and the locks are even free to boaters. If watching boats pass through narrow concrete channels isn't your idea of recreation, you can check out the salmon passing through the fish ladder or stroll through the botanical wonderland of Carl English Gardens, which also are free. For more on the locks and gardens, see Chapter Two, page 39.

8 KLONDIKE GOLD RUSH NATIONAL HISTORICAL PARK AND PIONEER SQUARE • *Historical Park interpretive center is at 117 Main Steet near Occidental Mall; (206) 553-7220. Daily 9 to 5; free. Guided tours of Pioneer Square available in summer. Gold rush history movies shown periodically.*

As we established earlier, Pioneer Square is *almost* where Seattle began. The first settlers came here to start their city after deciding that their first stop—Alki Point—was too wet and windy. A few decades later, thousands of goldseekers passed through here, waiting for ships to take them north to Alaska, from where they made rough overland trips to the diggin's in the Yukon Territory. Elements of this rush to riches are preserved in the excellent visitor center of the Klondike Gold Rush National Historical Park. From there, you can stroll among century-old brick buildings and landscaped parks. And if you want to spend money, Pioneer Square's many curio shops, boutiques, antique shops, cafés and pubs offer ample opportunity. Check the index for several other references to this area.

9 WATERFALL GARDEN PARK • *Main Street and Second Avenue in Pioneer Square. Free; open daily 6 a.m. to 5:45 p.m.*

Visitors learn to expect the unexpected in Seattle, such as a 22-foot waterfall tumbling within a small enclosed park. Not an official city park, Waterfall Garden is a gift to Seattle by the United Parcel Service, which was founded on this site in 1907. This tiny fenced-in park is lushly landscaped and a merry stream cascades over a jumble of boulders at the rate of 5,000 gallons a minute. Benches invite visitors to linger. See Chapter Two, page 65 for more detail.

10 YE OLDE CURIOSITY SHOP • *1001 Alaskan Way; (206) 682-5844. Daily 9 to 9; MC/VISA. GETTING THERE: This curiosity is at the waterfront on Pier 54, below the foot of Madison Street.*

This century-old curio shop is so interesting that the owners probably could charge admission. Most folks would pay to see a couple of mummies, a two-headed goat, an extensive collection of Inuit and other native art, a few shrunken heads and lots of stuffed critters. Of course, proprietors hope you'll pick up a T-shirt, a Space Needle thermometer or maybe even a John Wayne wall clock. It costs nothing to browse. See Chapter Two, page 49, for more on this curiosity, which is Seattle's oldest continually operating business.

THE TEN BEST CHEAP EATS

We define "cheap eats" as places where you can get a filling entrée and at least one side dish—soup or salad—for less than $7.50. We're talking about dinner, not a light lunch, so all of our selected places serve at least into the early evening. We do *not* include the mainstream franchise fast food joints, despite the fact that most of them can fill you up with greasy burgers and over-salted fries for well under our price ceiling. Eating at MacDonald's or Taco Bell isn't a dining experience; these places are more into marketing than providing healthy food for their customers. (We've never cared much for plastic dinosaurs or Beanie Babies with dinner.)

Most of our Ten Best selections are ethnic—particularly Asian. These folks comprise more than ten percent of Seattle's population and they probably operate a larger percentage of its restaurants. Emerald City has dozens of simple Chinese, Thai and Vietnamese cafés where you can get a filling meal within our price limit. Most are in the International District, where we found many of our selections. Since most Asian restaurants are family owned, they can save on labor costs to keep prices down; daughters help serve the customers before and after school while the sons sweat in the kitchen. Enjoy these places while you can; odds are that the daughters and sons will graduate from the University of Washington and become stockbrokers or computer whizzes, and then it's back to Big Macs.

1 MAE PIM THAI • *94 Columbia St.; (206) 624-2979. Thai; no alcohol. Lunch through early dinner Monday-Saturday. No credit cards. GETTING THERE: It's just up from the waterfront and west of Pioneer Square, between First and Post.*

Our number one choice is a tiny, prim place decorated mostly with rave reviews from local food critics. Curiously, all twenty-four of its entrées where the same price when we last dined here. They were under our $7.50 limit, even when we added a glass of Thai style iced tea. Its sweet, flowery taste helps tame the spiciness of the food. The small kitchen—open to the equally small dining room—prepares a surprising variety of tasty entrées and most arrive over seasoned rice, with a large side of perfectly crisp stir-fried veggies. Among the choices are sweet and sour chicken, garlic pork (one of our favorites), oyster beef, chicken and cashew, and spicy hot beef with curry paste and coconut milk. The café also has a large vegetarian selection. Everything is faultlessly fresh, and you can designate the degree of spiciness. (Unless you really like things hot, don't go much beyond medium.) With a pivotal position near downtown, Pioneer Square and the waterfront, it's one of the most convenient cheap eats in the city.

2 *ASSIMBA* • *2722 E. Cherry St.; (206) 322-1019. Ethiopian; wine and beer. Lunch and dinner nightly; closes early evening Sunday. GETTING THERE: Assimba is about two miles east of downtown, toward Lake Washington. Take James Street from the lower downtown area under I-5; it curves to the right and blends into Cherry Street. Follow it about a mile; the restaurant is near Martin Luther King Jr. Way.*

This older, well-kept predominately Black neighborhood offers two restaurants that are distinctive and inexpensive—Assimba and Catfish Corner. They're located side-by-side physically and—in this book—alphabetically. At Assimba, you can dine frugally and try something new—the spicy cuisine of Ethiopia. It's based on interesting blends of meat or chicken, lentils, greens and other vegetables. Typically, the fare served over *injera,* puffy bread disks that are used—like Greek pita—as scoops for the food. A group can order several dishes, which are intended to be shared Chinese-style, and stay well within the $7.50 per capita budget. Some examples are beef with onion, rosemary and green chiles; sautéed chicken stewed in a sauce with ginger, cardomen and nutmeg; and for vegetarians, split peas with onions and ginger in tumeric sauce. Assimba is a charming little place with African folk crafts, burgundy nappery and blonde furnishings.

3 *CATFISH CORNER* • *2726 E. Cherry St.; (206) 323-4330. Southern-style fried seafood; no alcohol. Lunch and dinner daily. No credit cards. GETTING THERE: It's at the corner of Martin Luther King Jr. Way; see Assimba above.*

This simple takeout offers an affordable and one-of-a-kind Seattle treat—farm raised catfish, plus several other very inexpensive fish dishes. The signature dish—which is below our budget limit—is a half-pound oven baked spicy Cajun style catfish. Other entrées within our price range are a half pound of buffalo fish; red snapper or prawns with fries; and hushpuppies or catfish bits with chips. For less than $10, you can get a complete catfish, red snapper or buffalo fish dinner that includes red beans and rice, cornbread muffins or hushpuppies, plus a choice of potato salad or coleslaw.

4 **EAST WIN RESTAURANT** • *516 S. Jackson St.; (206) 622-8801. Chinese; wine and beer. Lunch through dinner daily. MC/VISA. GETTING THERE: It's in the International District area between Fifth and Sixth avenues.*

Most small Chinese restaurants can serve you a single-course dishes for less than $7.50. However, East Win has full combination dinners in this price range. Among them are chicken chow mein, sweet and sour pork and fried rice; fried rice with barbecued pork and Mongolian beef; and sweet and sour pork, fried rice and Kung Pao chicken.

5 **GOURMET SAUSAGE COMPANY** • *212 S. Jackson St.; (206) 547-2413. American; wine and beer. Daily noon to evening. MC/VISA. GETTING THERE: It's in the Pioneer Square area, between Second and Third avenues.*

"Gourmet sausage" may be a self-canceling phrase, but this place features some of the cheapest non-Asian food in town. For well under our $7.50 limit, it features a nightly buffet that includes meatloaf, chicken, pork chops or sausages plus vegetables. Another dollar gets you a side order of green salad, potato salad, baked beans or macaroni and cheese. This austere and curiously versatile little place also sells Hawaiian shaved ice and those gourmet sausages.

6 **PHÓ BÁC** • *415 Seventh Ave. South, in the International District; (206) 621-0532. Vietnamese; no alcohol. Lunch through dinner daily. MC/VISA.*

Phó means basic food in Vietnamese and that's what you'll get at this simple little place for very little currency. You can choose from small plates or the more expensive large plates. However, "expensive" is a relative term here; the big dinners are well under our $7.50 limit. Selections, all with noodle soup bases, include round steak, meat balls, lean brisket, tripe or *tendon* (prawns) or combinations thereof. There are two other outlets in the city, at 1314 S. Jackson St., (206) 323-4378; and 2815 S. Hanford St., (206) 725-4418.

7 **PHÓ HOÀ** • *618 S. Weller Street in the International District, (206) 624-7189; and 4732 Rainier South, just southeast of that area. Vietnamese. Open daily, mid-morning to late evening. MC/VISA.*

These are Vietnamese noodle shops known for their hearty fare at modest prices. In addition to the signature noodle dishes, you can dine heartily for very little money on ample entrées such as grilled chicken and fried egg rolls, grilled pork chops, shredded roast pork, or pork chops with lemon grass.

8 PHÓ SAIGON TERIYAKI • *North 45th Street and Walling-ford Avenue North. Eclectic menu; no alcohol. Lunch through dinner daily. MC/VISA. GETTING THERE: This multi-ethnic place is in the Wallingford neighborhood north of Lake Union. From downtown, go north on Aurora (Highway 99), cross the Lake Washington Ship Canal, then exit onto Bridge Way North. Take a half left onto Stone Way North, follow it to North 45th Street and go right (east) several blocks to Wallingford Avenue.*

This diner comes in several ethnic flavors. This is perhaps the only place in town where you can eat cheap and try Japanese, Southeast Asian or Indian fare without leaving your seat. Although some of the dishes exceed our $7.50 limit, virtually everything is less than $10. And there are many dishes within our price guidelines. Among them are several teriyaki combinations, *bun phit nuong* (charred broiled pork with rice noodles), tandoori chicken and several vegetarian dishes. Phó Saigon is a rather attractive little place with hanging plants, green nappery and—appropriately—multi-ethnic prints.

9 RASA MALAYSIA • *7208 E. Green Lake Way North; (206) 523-8888. Malaysian; no alcohol. Dinner only. MC/VISA. GETTING THERE: It's in the Green Lake district opposite Green Lake Park. Follow I-5 north from downtown, take exit 170 north to Ravenna Boulevard, go left (northwest) under the freeway and the park is within a quarter of a mile. The restaurant is on your right, between Maple Leaf and 72nd.*

Claiming that it uses no MSG or animal fat, this austere and slightly scruffy diner offers several dinner combinations within our price limit. Selections include seafood noodles with sautéed vegetables, fried noodles with chicken and tomato garlic sauce, grilled boneless chicken with coconut milk and saffron rice, barbecued pork and *hoisin* chicken with rice and vegetables, and *mee Siam* which is rice noodles in peanut sauce with a choice of shrimp, chicken or barbecued pork. Among its drinks are fresh fruit juices, coffee and tea.

10 TACO DEL MAR • *At least nine Seattle locations and growing; check the Yellow Pages. Mexican; no alcohol. Lunch through dinner daily. No credit cards.*

These taco takeouts are the only franchise fast food outlets to make our Proud Paupers list. Unlike rival Taco Bell, they prepare everything to order. Even the fussy folks who submit Zagat Survey reviews nominated Taco Del Mar for inclusion. The "Del Mar" refers to the fact that their signature product is a cod fillet burrito, which is quite tasty. For well under our limit, you can get a huge burrito—fish or otherwise—plus a drink and interesting side order such as rice and beans, chips and salsa, or nachos with guacamole sauce.

THE TEN BEST CHEAP SLEEPS

Like most large cities, Seattle doesn't offer many inexpensive rooms, although we did find a few, either in the city or in nearby suburbs. As our criteria for budget lodging, we sought motels with high season rates of $60 or less per couple. We chose only those that were well-maintained and clean. Some of our selections are members of budget chains, or they're hostels or "Y" accommodations.

Seattle's motel row is north of downtown along Aurora Avenue (Highway 99), which was the main route through town until the advent of freeways. You'll find a fair selection of inexpensive motels out there, although you might check the rooms before committing yourself, since some are a bit on the scruffy side. Other nearby modest priced motels—although not necessarily under $60 per couple—are in Bellevue and south of Seattle along I-5 and Highway 99, in towns such as Tukwila, Kent, Federal Way and Seatac.

Of course, prices of our choices below may be above $60 by the time you arrive. Also, room availability at the lowest rates may be limited, so make reservations as early as possible. These are listed in alphabetical order.

1 AIRPORT PLAZA HOTEL • *18601 Pacific Hwy. South, Seatac, WA 98188; (206) 433-0400. MC/VISA. GETTING THERE: The hotel is near the airport across from the Doubletree Hotel.*

This simple hotel provides free airport pickup and a continental breakfast with its modestly priced rooms, which have TV and phones. Weekly rates are available.

2 AMERICAN BACKPACKERS HOSTEL • *126 Broadway Ave. East, Seattle, WA 98102; (206) 720-2965. GETTING THERE: It's in an alley near Broadway and East John Street in the Capitol Hill area just northeast of downtown.*

This basic hostel has few private rooms for couples and singles, plus four-person dorm rooms. Prices include a continental breakfast, and downtown pickup is provided.

3 COMMODORE MOTOR HOTEL • *2013 Second Ave. (near Virginia Street), Seattle, WA 98121; (800) 714-8868 or (206) 448-8868. Major credit cards.*

This 100-unit motel immediately north of the downtown area features color TV, a guest laundry and access to a "community microwave." Rooms are rather basic and they have either private or shared baths; weekly rates are available.

4 **EASTGATE MOTEL** • *14632 SE Eastgate Way, Bellevue, WA 98007; (800) 628-8578 or (425) 746-4100. Major credit cards. GETTING THERE: Go east from Seattle on I-90 and take 150th Avenue SE (exit 11) briefly north to Eastgate Way.*

This 29-unit motel in Bellevue not only has modest rates, it also provides a free continental breakfast. Rooms have phones and TV movies; some have refrigerators and microwaves.

5 **GREEN TORTOISE HOSTEL** • *1525 Second Ave., Seattle, WA 98101; (206) 322-1222. GETTING THERE: It's near the corner of Pine on the northern edge of downtown.*

Green Tortoise provides funky Sixties style bus service between Seattle and San Francisco and it also operates this hostel. It has dorm rooms with potties down the hall, plus some doubles with private baths. Both types are well under $50 per couple. The hostel is in a rather scruffy neighborhood although the facility itself is clean, secure and well managed.

6 **JET MOTEL PARK 'N FLY** • *17300 Pacific Hwy. South, Seatac, WA 98188; (800) 233-1501 or (206) 244-6255. Major credit cards. GETTING THERE: The motel is just east of Sea-Tac Airport between 170th and 176th.*

This small motel has fifty-one rooms with TV and phones. A Denny's restaurant is adjacent.

7 **MOORE HOTEL** • *1926 Second Ave., Seattle, WA 98101; (800) 421-5508 or (206) 448-4851. MC/VISA. GETTING THERE: The hotel is near the corner of Virginia Street just north downtown.*

A simply refurbished older hotel, the Moore has 135 rooms with private or share baths, plus TV and phones. Although its rooms are rather basic, the location is convenient—near both downtown and the Belltown area.

8 **SEATTLE HOSTEL INTERNATIONAL** • *84 Union St., Seattle, WA 98101; (206) 622-5443. (WEB SITE: www.washingtonhostels.org; E-MAIL: reserve@hiseattle.org) GETTING THERE: Go to the base of Union street just above the waterfront, then take a set of steps down to the hostel entrance near Post Alley.*

The hostel has basic dorm style accommodations for singles, plus some rooms for couples and families. Kitchen facilities are available.

9 *VINCENT'S BACKPACKERS GUEST HOUSE* ● *527 Malden Ave. East, Seattle, WA 98112; (206) 323-7849. GETTING THERE: It's in the Capitol Hill area, just south of Volunteer Park. Malden is a short street running parallel between 14th and 15th avenues.*

Converted from a large home, the guest house offers mostly dorm rooms for singles, although it does have a few private rooms for couples. Facilities include showers, communal kitchen facilities and a backyard with picnic tables.

10 *YMCA* ● *909 Fifth Ave., Seattle, WA 98101; (206) 461-4888. GETTING THERE: It's in the downtown area between Madison and Marion.*

The sturdy old "Y" has been refurbished and—while not fancy—it has comfortable and clean private rooms for couples, plus inexpensive dorm beds. (The dorms usually are reserved for American Youth Hostel members, although rooms are available to non-members.) Potties are down the hallway.

A great hotel is like a duck swimming—composed and serene above the water, but paddling like hell underneath.

— Hotel executive Tim Carlson

Chapter six

PILLOW TALK
LISTS OF THE BEST LODGINGS

Seattle is not an inexpensive city for pillows. Plan on $100 and well beyond for well-located hotels and motels. It does offer a plenitude of rooms, with nearly ten thousand in the city and twenty-five thousand in King County.

This book isn't intended to be a detailed lodging guide; an abundance of such publications is available. However, in keeping with our Ten Best theme, we have selected some of the city's finer hostelries—from it first class hotels to its coziest bed & breakfast inns. Since we've chosen the best, this obviously isn't a budget directory. For that, you must retreat to the previous chapter.

We use dollar-sign codes to indicate price ranges, based on summer rates: **$** = a standard two-person room for $99 or less; **$$** = $100 to $149; **$$$** = $150 to $199; and **$$$$** = $200 or more.

Note: For many more lodging choices, call the Seattle-King County Convention and Visitors Bureau's Seattle Hotel Hotline reservation service, offering access to more than fifty budget to luxury hotels. Dial

(800) 535-7071 or (206) 461-5882, weekdays 8:30 to 5 Pacific Coast time. Also, call (206) 461-5840 for the free *Seattle Lodging Guide*, listing more than 300 area hotels and motels.

THE TEN BEST HOTELS

Most of Seattle's finest lodgings are either in the downtown area or near the Elliott Bay waterfront. They range from sleek, modern highrises and handsomely renovated older hostelries to elegant boutique hotels.

1 FOUR SEASONS OLYMPIC HOTEL • *411 University St., Seattle, WA 98101; (800) 821-8106 or (206) 621-1700. (WEB SITE: www.fourseasons.com) Major credit cards; $$$$. GETTING THERE: The Olympic is downtown between Fourth and Fifth avenues.*

Fewer that twenty-five hotels in America and only one in the Northwest have earned AAA's ultimate accolade, the Five Diamond Award. The Olympic is a study in Italian Renaissance opulence, with marble floors accented by thick carpet insets, rich wood paneling, brass accents and period furnishings. The hotel's Arcade Shops offer fashionably overpriced men's and women's wear, a gallery of splendid art works and a shop featuring rare antiques. The 450 rooms are furnished with antique reproductions; some have spa tubs. Hotel amenities include a solarium spa, pool and saunas. Hungry? The **Georgian Room** makes or list of the "Ten very best restaurants" in see Chapter Three. Other dining venues here are the cheerful **Garden Court** with high arched windows, and the nautically cozy **Shuckers**.

2 ALEXIS HOTEL SEATTLE • *1007 First Ave., Seattle, WA 98104; (800) 426-7033 or (206) 624-4844. Major credit cards; $$$$. GETTING THERE: The Alexis is located just above the south waterfront at the foot of Madison Street.*

Old world charm and bright splashes of color blend nicely into this 109-room Four Diamond (AAA) and Four Star (Mobil) hotel. Its claim as a "work of art" is well founded, since the warm, clubby public rooms are accented with paintings and sculptures by Northwest artists. Room decor is eclectic, with contemporary and antique furnishings and matching patterned drapes and bedspreads. Amenities include evening wine tasting, a fitness room and spa. Some suites have two-person spa tubs or fireplaces. The **Painted Table** restaurant (Chapter Three, page 781) is particularly striking, with cascading fabric wall coverings and curved floral patterned banquettes. For something more subdued, adjourn to The Bookstore (Chapter Eight, page 146), the hotel's clubby cocktail lounge.

3 HOTEL EDGEWATER • *2411 Alaskan Way, Seattle, WA 98121; (800) 624-0670 or (206) 728-7000. (WEB SITE: www.noble-househotes.com) Rates include continental breakfast. Major credit cards; $$$. GETTING THERE: It's on Pier 67 at the north waterfront, at the base of Wall Street.*

Seattle's only waterfront hotel, built on a pier overlooking Elliott Bay, the Edgewater has a cheery knotty pine interior with nautical accents and Northwest Indian decor. Particularly appealing is a large sitting area with overstuffed furniture, two fireplaces and picture windows overlooking the waterfront. The **Restaurant** also has window-walls on the water; it serves Northwest cuisine; breakfast through dinner, with full bar service. This unusual pier-piling hotel has 237 units with TV movies, phones and fireplaces; most have mini-bars and/or room refrigerator and microwaves. Many have balconies overlooking the water. Amenities include a pool, spa, sauna, fitness room and free shuttle service to downtown Seattle. Some rooms are a bit small although they're nicely furnished, and those facing south offer grand views of Elliott Bay. Step out onto the balcony to catch a nice slice of the waterfront and downtown highrises. You can even drop a hook and line into the bay, if you thought to bring a fishing pole.

4 HOTEL MONACO SEATTLE • *1101 Fourth Ave., Seattle, WA 98101; (800) 945-2240 or (206) 621-1770. (WEB SITE: www.monaco-seattle.com) Major credit cards; $$$$. GETTING THERE: It's downtown at the corner of Spring Street.*

A lofty lobby with imposing three-tiered iron chandeliers, wrought iron gates, white stucco walls and murals of stylistic dolphins give this boutique hotel an old European seaport feel. Plush couches and a fireplace invite one to linger. Rooms are splashy, multicolored mixes of floral patterns and stripes and they offer a resident goldfish. (We named ours Finster.) Well, not actually residents. On request, they're placed in the room just before guests arrive. They lounge about in a 100-gallon tank between engagements. Amenities other than Finster include personal FAX machines, voice mail, CD players and modem outlets. Some suites in this 189-unit hotel have spa tubs and VCRs. The adjacent **Sazerac Restaurant** has quite a different personality, with an upbeat, whimsical New Orleans theme. It makes our list of one of Seattle's "Ten very best restaurants" in Chapter Three.

5 HOTEL VINTAGE PARK • *1100 Fifth Ave., Seattle, WA 98101; (800) 624-4433 or (206) 624-8000. Major credit cards; $$$. GETTING THERE: It's downtown between Spring and Seneca streets.*

Occupying a fine old brick building, the Vintage Park is the most appealing of Seattle's boutique hotels, with 126 rooms featuring a

Washington wine theme. The lobby is small and quite cozy, with a pair of plush burgundy couches opposite a floor-to-ceiling fireplace. Dark woods, polished wainscotting, beam ceilings and original oil paintings add touches of class. The hotel has earned AAA Four Diamond and Mobil Four Star ratings, and it was selected by Conde Nast Traveler readers as one of the top 500 hotels in the world. Just off the lobby, **Tulio** restaurant, done in a lighter and brighter decor than the hotel, offers Italian entrées, pizzas and calzones.

6 **INN AT THE MARKET** • *86 Pine St., Seattle, WA 98101; (800) 446-4484 or (206) 443-3600. (WEB SITE: www.innatthemarket.com) Major credit cards; $$$ to $$$$. GETTING THERE: The inn is just uphill from Pike Place Market at the corner of Pine Street and First Avenue.*

One's first impression of the inn is a rather austere lobby. However, that's merely the surface. Most of its appeal lies in its large, nicely furnished country French style rooms, its cozy landscaped brick courtyard and its location next door to Pike Place Market. It also offers fine dining at **Campagne,** one of the city's finest restaurants (Chapter Three, page 68) and more casual fare from **Bacco,** a cozy bistro. The inn's rooftop deck and many of its rooms offer nice views of Elliott Bay—great places for watching the sunset. The boutique hotel has

7 **SHERATON SEATTLE** • *535 Sixth Ave., Seattle, WA 98101; (800) 325-3535 or (206) 621-9000. Major credit cards; $$$$. GETTING THERE: The Sheraton is in the heart of downtown at Sixth Avenue and Pike Street.*

After a recent $7 million renovation, the AAA Four Diamond Sheraton is one of Seattle's most attractive full-service hotels. The lobby is particularly appealing, with an impressive collection of contemporary Northwest art that ranges from oils to collages to strikingly pretty glass works. This inviting space is done in beige tones with polished marble and brass accents. The hotel's 840 rooms and suites offer all the usual amenities, including TV movies, phones, mini-bars or refrigerators. Most provide views of the city and Elliott Bay. Tower Room guests are provided with a continental breakfast, afternoon tea and snacks and soft drinks. Hotel facilities include an indoor pool, sauna, spa, health club, two lounges and three restaurants, with food service from early breakfast to midnight. **Fullers Restaurant** makes or overall Ten Best restaurant list in Chapter Three, page 69.

8 **SORRENTO HOTEL** • *900 Madison St., Seattle, WA 98104; (800) 426-1265 or (206) 622-6400. (WEB SITE: www.hotelsorrento.com) Major credit cards; $$$$. GETTING THERE: It's at the corner of Madison Street and Terry Avenue, just above downtown in the*

First Hill neighborhood. Madison is one-way downhill, so go uphill on Spring Street, cross under the freeway and turn left on Terry.

In contrast to Seattle's smart new glass and steel hotels, the 76-room 1909 Hotel Sorrento is a grand Italianate retreat clothed in old brick and memories. However, it's as contemporary as the newer hotels, having undergone a complete renovation, and it carries a prestigious AAA Four Diamond award. Step through the Old World fountain courtyard entrance into the richly paneled hexagonal lobby with its overstuffed chairs, grand piano and fireplace. This is one of the city's more pleasant and clubby retreats and its **Hunt Club** is on our list of Ten Best restaurants in Chapter Three. The hotel celebrated its ninetieth anniversary in 1999 with a display of old menus and other mementos in a small vestibule off the lobby. It may still be there so take a peek into yesterday, when a multi-course Christmas banquet with Beluga caviar cost an entire $1.50. The hotel's amenities include afternoon tea service, a small exercise room and in-room FAX and voice mail.

9 *W SEATTLE* • *1112 Fourth Ave., Seattle, WA 98101; (877) W-HOTELS or (206) 264-6100. (WEB SITE: www.whotels.com) Major credit cards; $$$$. GETTING THERE: The hotel is downtown at the corner of Fourth Avenue and Seneca Street.*

Your first clue that this isn't a conventional hotel is the auto entry and garage, simply marked "Wheels." The W is an intriguing experiment by Starwood Hotels & Resorts in kinchy hotel design, targeting the upbeat and affluent young professional market. The look is *art moderne* with soft and furry pillows on severely cut mauve couches, splashes of modern art on the walls, a curved orange settee, a cubistic fireplace and a sleek curved lobby bar. Even the bathrooms carry this "art deco severe" theme with stainless steel fixtures, can lights and mauve walls. Amenities are designed to spoil those who can afford the $200-plus rates, including rooms with goose down comforters, Aveda bath products, a CD player with disc library and cordless speaker phones. W also has a fitness center and business center. The **Earth & Ocean** restaurant serves an eclectic mix of international fare.

10 *THE WESTIN SEATTLE* • *1900 Fifth Ave., Seattle, WA 98101; (800) WESTIN-1 or (206) 728-1000. (WEB SITE: www.westin.com) Major credit cards; $$$$. GETTING THERE: The hotel is at Fifth Avenue and Stewart Street, in downtown Seattle's north end.*

With a pair of cylindrical towers as its focal point, the Westin is one of Seattle's most opulent hotels. Amenities include a large indoor pool, sun deck and spa, three restaurants and a gift shop. While the low-ceiling lobby isn't imposing, it's elegantly attired, with stylish decor, plush seating and a particularly handsome lobby bar. Modern rooms feature all the usual amenities, including TV movies and honor bars. Some have spa tubs and virtually all offer views of the city and Elliott Bay. The Westin has a heated indoor pool, spa and a small health club. Its restaurants are **Roy's,** with a severely modern look and a European-Asian-Polynesian menu fashioned by noted chef Roy Yamaguchi (see Chapter Four); and **Nikko,** with classic Japanese decor, a *Nippon-moderne* menu and sashimi bar (Chapter Three, page 79).

THE TEN BEST BED & BREAKFAST INNS

Victorian and turn-of-the-century American mansions provide great habitats for bed & breakfast inns, and Seattle has an abundance of these. Most of the city's B&Bs are in older and well-kept neighborhoods, particularly Capitol Hill just south of Volunteer Park and Queen Anne Hill northwest of the downtown area.

1 HILL HOUSE BED & BREAKFAST • *1113 E. John St., Seattle, WA 98102; (800) 720-7161 or (206) 720-7161. (WEB SITE: www.seattlebnb.com; E-MAIL: hillhouse@seattlebnb.com) Seven rooms with five private and two shared baths; full breakfast. Major credit cards; $ to $$. GETTING THERE: Hill House is in the Capitol Hill area just south of Volunteer Park. Take Olive Way northeast from downtown and blend onto John Street. The inn is between Broadway and 12th Avenue East.*

This elegant 1903 Victorian is Seattle's finest B&B, dressed in antiques and original works of art, accented with lace curtains and vases of fresh flowers. Individually decorated rooms feature oriental carpets, down comforters, handmade soaps and terry robes; four have phones and TV sets. The inn is noted particularly for its elaborate cooked-to-order breakfasts served on fine china in the nicely appointed dining room. A backyard deck shaded by a large weeping willow is an inviting place to take the air.

2 THE BACON MANSION BED & BREAKFAST • *959 Broadway East, Seattle, WA 98102; (800) 240-1864 or (206) 329-1864. (WEB SITE: www.site-works.com/bacon; E-MAIL: bacon-bandb@aol.com) Ten rooms; eight with private and two with shared baths; extended continental breakfast. Major credit cards; $$ to $$$. GETTING THERE: The mansion is in the Capitol Hill area just below Volunteer Park. Take Olive Way or the I-5 Olive Way exit northeast to Broadway, follow it north five blocks, then fork right onto Tenth Avenue. Go two blocks to Prospect and turn left to return to Broadway.*

This grand Edwardian style Tudor, listed on the National Register of Historic Places, has eight rooms in the main mansion with private baths, and two in a carriage house with a share bath. Furnishings are a mix of antique and contemporary American, with features such as TV, modem ports and phones with voicemail. The large Capitol Suite has a fireplace and it offers a view Seattle Center and the Space Needle. The inn's amenities include a fountain patio, rose garden, formal dining room and well-stocked library.

3 CHAMBERED NAUTILUS BED & BREAKFAST INN •
5005 22nd Ave. NE, Seattle, WA 98105; (800) 545-8459 or (206) 522-2536. (WEB SITE: www.chamberednautilus.com; E-MAIL: chamberednautilus@msn.com) Six units with phones and private baths; full breakfast. MC/VISA, AMEX; $$. GETTING THERE: The inn is just north of the University of Washington campus. Take the 50th Street exit east from I-5, go left onto 20th NE, right onto 54th Street, then right again onto 22nd Avenue.

This grand, square-shouldered 1915 Georgian style home occupies a hill above the university campus, with views of the Cascades. Rooms are furnished with American and English antiques; some have fireplaces and four have porches overlooking landscaped grounds. The inviting living room has a fireplace and well-stocked bookshelves.

4 CHELSEA STATION BED & BREAKFAST INN • *4915 Linden Ave. North, Seattle, WA 98103; (206) 547-6077. (WEB SITE: www.bandbseattle.com; E-MAIL: info@bandbseattle.com) Nine units with private phones and baths; full breakfast. Major credit cards; $$ to $$$. GETTING THERE: The inn is near North 50th Street; take exit 169 west from I-5 or the Woodland Park Zoo exit from Aurora Avenue North.*

This restored two-story 1927 brick Federal colonial style former apartment building sits across from Woodland Park and Zoo, a short walk to Green Lake Park. The inn is decorated in 1920s arts and crafts style with Craftsman furniture. A guest kitchen is available. Some suites have sitting areas with views of the Cascades, Woodland Park and nearby rose gardens.

5 GASLIGHT INN & HOWELL STREET SUITES • *1727 15th Ave., Seattle, WA 98122; (206) 325-3654. (WEB SITE: www.gaslight-inn.com; E-MAIL: innkeepr@gaslight-inn.com) Fifteen rooms and suites; some private and some share baths; continental breakfast. MC/VISA, AMEX; $ to $$. GETTING THERE: The Gaslight is in the Capitol Hill area. Go northeast from downtown on Madison Street (or take exit 165 onto Madison), turn left (north) onto Fifteenth and follow it three blocks to Howell Street.*

Fashioned from a late nineteenth century home, Gaslight Inn offers attractive, comfortable and individually decorated rooms, with early American, mission or modern furnishings. Some units have fireplaces, decks and/or views. A heated seasonal pool is available. The next-door

Howell Street Suites—designed more for business travelers—are furnished with refrigerators, microwaves, coffeemakers, honor bars and phones.

6 **MILDRED'S BED & BREAKFAST** • *1202 15th Ave. East, Seattle, WA 98112; (206) 325-6072. (WEB SITE: www.mildredsbnb.com; E-MAIL: mildredsbb@foxinternet) Four rooms with private baths; full breakfast. MC/VISA, AMEX; $$ to $$$. GETTING THERE: The inn is located in the Capitol Hill area opposite Volunteer Park, at 15th Avenue and Highland Drive. Take Olive Way northeast from downtown (or the Olive Way I-5 exit), then go left onto 15th and follow it about a mile to Highland.*

This twin-turreted 1890 Victorian sits just across the street from one of Seattle's most attractive parks. It's furnished with Victorian antiques, accented by plush red carpets, natural woods and lace curtains. All rooms have TV/VCRs, hair dryers and writing desks. Breakfast is served in a fashionable dining room, and guests have access to a small refrigerator, phone and reading material in a comfortable sitting area.

7 **MV CHALLENGER BED & BREAKFAST** • *1001 Fairview Ave. North, Seattle, WA 98109; (206) 340-1201. (WEB SITE: www.challengerboat.com) Five private and three share baths; full breakfast. Major credit cards; $ to $$$. GETTING THERE: It's north of downtown on Lake Union; take Fairview Avenue north and then northeast along the lake.*

This unusual "boat & breakfast" has great views of Lake Union since it sits at dockside. The *Challenger* is a converted 1944 tugboat with old style nautical decor, including portholes in the rooms. Most cabins have TV/VCRs and some have refrigerators. Largest unit is the Master's Cabin, with a separate sitting room. Ample breakfasts are served in an old fashioned galley and deck chairs invite topside lounging.

8 **QUEEN ANNE HILL BED & BREAKFAST** • *1835 Seventh Ave. West, Seattle, WA 98119; (206) 284-9779. (WEB SITE: www.seattlebandbs.com; E-MAIL: qabedbrk@aol.com) Five units; some private and some share baths; continental breakfast. MC/VISA; $ to $$. GETTING THERE: From downtown, go north on First Avenue North, left onto Roy Street and right onto Queen Anne. Go uphill several blocks then turn left onto Galer, right onto Seventh Avenue West and follow it three blocks to Howe Street.*

This handsome three-story, shingle-sided "saltbox" Victorian is in a quiet Queen Anne Hill residential area, offering views of Elliott Bay, Puget Sound and the Olympics. Rooms are furnished with American antiques and the inn is decorated with art and collectibles. A large garden surrounds the home.

9 *SALISBURY HOUSE* • *750 Sixteenth Ave. East (Aloha Street), Seattle, WA 98112; (206) 328-8682. (WEB SITE: www.salisburyhouse.com; E-MAIL: sleep@salisburyhouse.com) Five units with private baths; full breakfast. Major credit cards; $ to $$. GETTING THERE: It's in the north Capitol Hill area, at the corner of East Aloha, two blocks south of Volunteer Park. Take Olive Way or Madison Street northeast from downtown, go north on Fifteenth Avenue, then go right on Aloha to Sixteenth.*

This 1904 mansion with a mixed Victorian and American "prairie style" architecture is surrounded by landscaped grounds. Rooms are furnished with American and English country antiques and reproductions. Amenities include a sun porch, hot tub, library room with a fireplace and a self-service refrigerator. A wrap-around porch invites sunny day relaxing.

10 *THE SHAFER-BAILLIE MANSION* • *907 14th Ave. East, Seattle, WA 98112; (206) 322-4654. (WEB SITE: www.shaferbaillie.com; E-MAIL: smansion@sprynet.com) Thirteen units; ten with private baths; continental breakfast. MC/VISA; $$ to $$$. GETTING THERE: The mansion is in the Capitol Hill area just below Volunteer Park, near the corner of Aloha. Take Olive Way or Madison Street northeast from downtown, go north on Fifteenth Avenue, then left on Aloha to Fourteenth.*

Shafer-Baillie is a large English manor style mansion on Seattle's "Millionaires' Row" in the Capitol Hill area. The elegant 15,000-square foot home is furnished with antiques. Rooms feature linen padded walls, chandeliers and wall sconces. All guest rooms have TVs and refrigerators.

All the world's a stage,
And all the men and women merely players.
They have their exits and entrances,
And one man in his time plays many parts.
— **William Shakespeare**

Chapter seven

NIGHTSIDE
CULTURE, CLUBS AND CINEMAS

Nightlife is alive and thriving in Seattle. The city offers a full range of after hours pursuits, including a world-respected symphony with a stunning new performance hall, an opera, ballet and several live professional theaters. The Puget Sound area ranks third behind New York and Chicago in the number of professional drama groups.

Getting ticketed ● Pacific Northwest Ticket Service (232-0150) and Ticketmaster Northwest (292-ARTS) are Seattle's major agencies for theater, concert and sports tickets. Both have credit card charge-by-phone service. For unsold half-priced day-of-the-play tickets, stop by the Ticket/Ticket booths at Pike Place Market, Pine Street and First Avenue; and Broadway Market at 401 Broadway Ave. East; (206) 324-2744.

For a complete review of the local entertainment scene, including dramas, music, dance, movie theaters, art exhibits and book reviews, check out the *ARTS* section of the combined *Sunday Seattle Times* and *Post-Intelligencer*.

THE TEN BEST PERFORMING ARTS GROUPS

Much of Seattle's performing arts scene is focused in the dramatic **Benaroya Symphony Hall** built in the heart of downtown in 1998. It's a dramatic blend of rectangles and chubby cylinders, cascading downhill from Third to Second avenue, between University and Union. This $120 million complex has an acoustically-tuned 2,500-seat main auditorium and a 540-seat recital hall. Even if you have a tin ear, it's worth a visit for its architecture and dramatic works of art. Note particularly the stunning glass sculpture, "Crystal Cascade" in the hall's University and Third Avenue corner; see Chapter Thirteen, page 203. The symphony hall's doors generally are open and tours are available. Stop by the information center at 1203 Second Avenue (open weekdays 10 to 6), or call (206) 515-9494.

Seattle Center also is a serious cultural venue, home to the **Opera House,** the **Bagley Wright Theater** and **Intiman Playhouse.** The old Coliseum—now **KeyArena**—also occupies the Seattle Center grounds; it's home to the Supersonics basketball team. Before it was renovated, the Coliseum leaked so badly that the Sonics suffered the embarrassment of having the only game in the history of the NBA called on account of rain.

The beautifully refurbished **Paramount Theater** at 911 Pine Street downtown books traveling Broadway dramas and musicals and leading entertainers. Remodeled at a cost of $30 million, the lavishly coiffed theater is definitely worth a look. Call (206) 443-1744 for the theater itself and Ticketmaster at (206) 292-ARTS for shows. (WEB SITE: www.theparamount.com)

1 SEATTLE SYMPHONY • *Benaroya Hall, 200 University St.; (206) 215-4747. (WEB SITE: www.seattlesymphony.org)*

The symphony has been entertaining Northwest music lovers for nearly a century. With its striking new home in Benaroya Hall and its eclectic mix of programs, it's our favorite performing arts group. The symphony has a September to mid-June season of a hundred or more concerts, offering everything from classics to pops to intimate recitals to children's music to chamber music. The internationally rated orchestra has been nominated for Grammy awards ten times and it has produced several dozen CDs.

2 A CONTEMPORARY THEATRE • *700 Union St.; (206) 292-7676. (WEB SITE: www.acttheatre.org)*

Despite its name (which was contrived to spell ACT), this group reaches beyond contemporary drama to do an occasional classic. An example is its annual holiday presentation of A *Christmas Carol,* although it's a rather stylized version. ACT's versatile theater complex has three different stages.

3 EMPTY SPACE THEATRE • *3509 Fremont Ave. North; (206) 547-7500. (WEB SITE: www.seattlesquare.com/emptysdpace)*

This theater's spaces aren't that empty. Locally popular and feeling right at home in the sometimes zany Fremont neighborhood, the group offers everything from American classics to wacky comedies and melodramas.

4 5TH AVENUE THEATRE • *1308 Fifth Ave.; (206) 625-1900. (WEB SITE: www.5thavenuetheatre.org)*

This group is on the opposite side of the theatrical pendulum from Empty Space, presenting flowery Broadway musicals. The group hosts touring shows and occasionally presents original musicals.

5 INTIMAN THEATRE • *Intiman Playhouse at Seattle Center; (206) 269-1901. (WEB SITE: www.seattlesquare.com/intiman)*

Ranking with 5th Avenue and Seattle Repertory as one of the city's top three professional drama groups, Intiman presents a May through November season of classic and contemporary dramas. It once took its *Kentucky Cycle* drama to Broadway and came away with a Pulitzer prize.

6 NORTHWEST CHAMBER ORCHESTRA • *Performs at Benaroya Recital Hall, 200 University St.; (206) 343-0445.*

For nearly three decades, this fine group has entertained Northwest audiences with seventeenth to twentieth century classics. It presents more than a dozen concerts a year, at the Benaroya's small Recital Hall and elsewhere, including a "Music in the Park" series in Volunteer Park.

7 ON THE BOARDS • *100 W. Roy Street at First Avenue West; (206) 217-9888. (WEB SITE: www.ontheboards.org)*

This versatile organization presents a cultural mix that includes ethnic folk dance troupes, contemporary musical artists and experimental drama. The group draws from a talent pool of local writers, composers and performers, plus internationally known stars such as Rob Brown and Meredith Monk. Two performances spaces are utilized for this busy mix—a main showcase seating up to 500 and an intimate 100-seat studio theater.

8 *PACIFIC NORTHWEST BALLET* • *Performs at the Opera House in Seattle Center; (206) 292-2787. (WEB SITE: www.pnb.org)*

Regarded as one of the top regional ballet troupes in the nation, PNB presents at least five traditional or contemporary ballets each year. Its rendition of the *Nutcracker* is a Seattle holiday classic.

9 *SEATTLE OPERA* • *Performs at the Opera House in Seattle Center; (206) 389-7676. (WEB SITE: www.seattleopera.org)*

Book well in advance if you want to attend one of Seattle Opera's splendid performances, which generally sell out. The highly regarded company is one of the few in the world that presents—every four years—the complete cycle of Wagner's *Ring of the Nibelung*. The opera draws international stars for its five full-scale regular performances, which range from classic to contemporary.

10 *SEATTLE REPERTORY THEATRE* • *Performs at the Bagley Wright Theatre in Seattle Center; (206) 443-2222. (WEB SITE: www.seattlerep.org)*

In true repertory fashion, this group mixes its performers in an interesting variety of dramas, from durable classics to leading-edge *avant garde* experimental theater. The "Rep" is noted for its elaborate sets and ambitious productions. Hitting the boards from October to May, it's the oldest of Seattle's major professional drama groups, established in 1963.

PLAY IT AGAIN, JIMI: THE TEN BEST NIGHTSPOTS

Seattle suffers the distinction of being the birthplace of Grunge music in the early 1990s, with notable groups such as Nirvana and Pearl Jam. Grunge is a kind of acid rock that leaves a sour taste in the ear canals of most folks over thirty. Emerald City also has generated generous portions of more mainstream rock and pops. It was the launching pad for such notables as Ray Charles, Quincy Jones and Jimi Hendrix, although these folks achieved most of their fame elsewhere. Hendrix has been enshrined—along with American popular music in general—at the Experience Music Project; see Chapter Two, page 38.

With music in its soul, the city abounds with live sounds, emitting from dozens of clubs. Offerings range from jazz and swing to pops and rock, plus a couple of comedy clubs. Much of this action is focused in the Pioneer Square area and Belltown, and many of our selections are from these neighborhoods. With so many choices available, we've attempted to offer a balance of music types.

Not all of the places listed below offer live music every night, so call ahead before you go to find out who—if anyone—is performing. We've listed our selections in alphabetical order, with no particular favorites, since one person's music is another person's noise.

1 **BOHEMIAN CAFÉ** • *111 Yesler Way; (206) 447-1514. Open nightly except Monday; major credit cards. GETTING THERE: This bit of Bohemia is in the Pioneer Square area, between First and Occidental.*

Housed in old brick, the Bohemian offers a light dinner menu of Caribbean style fare, as well as live entertainment most nights. This two-level club features mostly folk music, blues and occasional jazz groups.

2 **COMEDY UNDERGROUND** • *222 S. Main St.; (206) 628-0303. (WEB SITE: www.comedyunderground.com) Shows nightly; major credit cards. GETTING THERE: This comic club is part of the Swannie's Sports Bar and Restaurant in the Pioneer Square area, between Second and Third avenues south.*

You can dine or catch a TV ballgame at Swannie's and then adjourn to the basement comedy club for a few yucks. Talent ranges from hungry local humorists to rising stars that are passing through town. It can be crowded on weekends so find out who's at the mike and get there early.

3 **CROCODILE CAFÉ** • *2200 Second Ave.; (206) 441-5611. (WEB SITE: www.thecrocodile.com) Open noonish through late evening Tuesday-Saturday; MC/VISA. GETTING THERE: This lively 'croc is in Belltown, at the corner of Second Avenue and Blanchard.*

Don't be intimidated by the funky look. Although it once focused primarily on Grunge groups such as Nirvana and Pearl Jam, this popular club now offers Seattle's best music mix, from classic rock to folk to blues and an occasional touch of jazz. It often attracts national artists; expect the cover charge to escalate when they're in town. The Croc also has a restaurant serving mostly pastas and sandwiches, and a cocktail lounge separate from the club venue.

4 **DIMITRIOU'S JAZZ ALLEY** • *2033 Sixth Ave.; (206) 441-9729. (WEB SITE: www.jazzalley.org) Dinner nightly; live entertainment Tuesday-Sunday; MC/VISA, AMEX. GETTING THERE: Despite the Sixth Avenue address, the entrance is indeed in an alley, off Lenora Street, between Sixth and Fifth.*

This is Seattle's classiest jazz club, with a seriously lighted bandstand and seating on two levels. Best seats in the house are along a balcony suspended over the main floor. The handsome club and restaurant, which corners on Sixth and Lenora, has two-story window walls, although there isn't much to see out there. Inside, it's quite a different matter. Owner John Dimitriou has earned a national reputation for booking some of America's finest jazz talent, from Eartha Kitt to the hottest new CD stars. Expect to pay handsomely for the leading acts.

5 **EL GAUCHO'S PAMPAS ROOM** • *90 Wall St.; (206) 728-1140. (WEB SITE: www.elgaucho.com) Entertainment Friday and Saturday only; major credit cards. GETTING THERE: The Pampas Room shares a building with El Gaucho Restaurant, in Belltown at the corner of Wall Street and First Avenue.*

Seattle's sleekest nightclub offers live jazz and music for well-dressed dancers on weekends. You can get dinner from 6 p.m., and music for dancing begins later in the evening. The Pampas Room is below El Gaucho's restaurant (dinner nightly), although the club entrance is on Wall, while the restaurant is reached via the Wall Street Inn on First Avenue.

6 **FENIX & FENIX UNDERGROUND** • *315 Second Ave. South; (206) 467-1111. Entertainment most nights; major credit cards. GETTING THERE: This dual club is in the southern part of the Pioneer Square area.*

The two clubs Fenix offer a versatile lineup of live entertainment. Main floor music generally appeals to an older crowd, featuring big bands and yesterday combos. The younger folks are drawn to the cellar, where they're likely to encounter everything from heavy rock and rap to jazz, blues and reggae. There's also—hold your breath—a cigar bar and pool hall on the premises.

7 **THE NEW ORLEANS** • *114 First Avenue; (206) 622-2563. Entertainment most nights, lunch and dinner daily; MC/VISA. GETTING THERE: It's in the Pioneer Square area between Yesler Way and Washington Street.*

One of the Square's liveliest spots, New Orleans presents live jazz and blues groups in a large showroom whose walls are papered with photos of present and past performers. It also makes our list as Seattle's best Cajun/Creole café in Chapter Three. The kitchen issues tasty portions of red beans and rice, pork ribs, seafood *étouffée*, jambalaya and filé gumbo.

8 **OWL 'N' THISTLE IRISH PUB AND RESTAURANT** • *808 Post Ave.; (206) 621-7777. (WEB: www.teleport.com/~dgs1300owlthistle.html) Open nightly; MC/VISA, DISC. GETTING THERE: This Irish establishment is northwest of Pioneer Square, in narrow Post Avenue* *(sometimes called Post Alley). Post is between First Avenue and Western Avenue, and the pub is midway between Columbia and Marion streets.*

A small storefront entrance widens into a large Irish pub with three large, brick-walled rooms. One offers mostly Celtic music several nights a week; another is a café featuring shepherd's pie, fish and chips and Guinness beef stew. A third is a comfortable but smoky old pool room with weathered brick walls and warm woods.

9 SPEAKEASY CAFÉ • *2304 Second Ave.; (206) 781-7081. Noonish through late evening daily. GETTING THERE: It's in Belltown, near Bell Street.*

No, not that kind of Speakeasy. This Belltown hangout is as close as Seattle gets to a San Francisco style coffee house. It features poetry and prose readings, small acting ensembles, art exhibits and assorted other earthy amusements. It's also an internet-ready café, popular with alternative lifestyle computer nerds.

10 TULA'S RESTAURANT • *2214 Second Ave.; (206) 443-4221. Live entertainment most nights; dinner nightly and late breakfast on weekends. Major credit cards. GETTING THERE: Tula resides in Belltown, between Blanchard and Bell streets, adjacent to Crocodile Café.*

You can mix your music with Italian, American and Mediterranean food in this appealing little club, decorated with photos of jazz artists. Tula books mostly local talent ranging from jazz bands and vocalists to rhythm and blues groups. There's live music most nights, usually with a modest cover charge. Between shows, relax to quite recorded jazz and blues.

THE TEN BEST PLACES TO CATCH A FLICK

Most of the cinemas in Seattle—as in the rest of the country—are multi-screen affairs. Many of these are in shopping centers, both downtown and in the 'burbs. However, preservationists have saved many of the city's older moviehouses—the kinds of places where we use to catch Saturday matinees. Some show current films, while others focus on independent productions, movie classics and foreign films.

1 CINEPLEX ODEON • *Seventh Avenue and Pike streets downtown; (206) 223-9600.*

Head for this large Meridien theater complex with its lofty, modern glass-walled lobby if you seek a good movie selection. One of the largest in Seattle, it has sixteen screens. Although some are only slightly bigger than bed sheets, it has couple of larger theaters with wall-rattling sound systems reserved for epic wide screen productions.

2 **CINERAMA THEATER** • *Lenora between Fourth and Fifth avenues; (206) 443-0808. GETTING THERE: It's just north of the downtown area, on the edge of Belltown.*

Remember Cinerama, one of the first wide screen movie systems? One of the original Cinerama theaters is still here, although it no longer shows tummy-lurching documentaries with rollercoaster rides. Its wide screen—one of the largest in the city—now focuses on current first run films. This is a good place to catch those big production movies. A nice feature of this movie house is that it provides earphones for people with hearing loss.

3 **CITY CENTRE CINEMA** • *In the City Centre shopping complex at 1420 Fifth Ave.; (206) 622-6465. GETTING THERE: The theater is on the third level of City Centre; the mall is rimmed by Fifth and Sixth avenues and Pike and Union streets.*

Large screens with excellent sound systems draw movie patrons to Cineplex Odeon's stylish City Centre Cinema. It presents first-run major films. We like the Cinema because it has two large auditoriums with good sized screens.

4 **EGYPTIAN THEATER** • *805 E. Pine St.; (206) 32-EGYPT. GETTING THERE: Head northeast from downtown on Pike (to avoid Pine's one-way grid), cross over I-5, then shift over to Pine; the theater is between Harvard Avenue and Broadway.*

Although a bit scruffy, this theater offers an interesting blend of limited production, offbeat, artistic, foreign and classic films. It hosts the annual Lesbian & Gay Film Festival in late October and it has other theme festivals throughout the year. Neither cutesy art deco nor modern, it occupies a sturdy old brick building with Egyptian trim on the façade and murals inside the lobby. The snack bar—appropriately—is called Café Cairo. This square-shouldered structure was built in 1915 as a Masonic temple, then it suffered the indignity of being a wrestling arena before its conversion into a theater.

5 **FREMONT OUTDOOR CINEMA** • *600 N. 34th St.; (206) 282-5706. In the Fremont neighborhood, in a parking lot at North 34th Street and Evanston Avenue North. GETTING THERE: From downtown, take Fourth Avenue or Westlake Avenue (skirting the western shore of Lake Union), then cross the Fremont Bridge over the Lake Washington Ship Canal. Go left for two blocks on 34th to Evanston.*

This isn't one of those old fashioned drive-ins where you hook a speaker to your car window and stare through your windshield at a huge billboard of a screen. This is a parking lot by day and an outdoor movie place at night. Patrons bring their own seats and watch films projected onto the white-painted wall of a building. There's even a simulated scalloped curtain painted on the structure—a cute touch. This is the sort of thing you'd expect in this kinchy neighborhood, which happens to be located precisely in the center of the universe; see other Fremont references in the index.

6 *GRAND ILLUSIONS CINEMA* • *1403 NE 50th St.; (206) 523-3935. GETTING THERE: The theater is near the corner of University Way NE in the U-District, northwest of the University of Washington campus.*

This charmingly funky theater in an old pitched-roof cottage is the U-District's art house. It shows foreign films and American independent productions. Grand Illusions also features offbeat fare such as 1930s black and white mysteries, early classics and documentaries, plus occasional thematic film festivals. Neighborhood night owls like to roost here for films that are shown in the wee hours.

7 *GUILD THEATER* • *2115 N. 45th St.; (206) 633-3353. GETTING THERE: It's in the Wallingford area north of Lake Union, near the corner of Bagley Avenue North. From downtown, go north on Aurora (Highway 99), cross the Washington Ship Canal then exit onto Bridge Way North. Take a half left onto Stone Way North, follow it to North 45th Street and go right (east) to Bagley.*

This is an absolute gem of a classic art deco theater, with a traditional neon-clad wedged marquee and sidewalk box office. It shows current films and you have a choice of two screens—the Pink Theater and the Blue Theater.

8 *PACIFIC PLACE CINEMA* • *In Pacific Place shopping complex downtown at 600 Pine Street; (206) 652-2404. GETTING THERE: Pacific Place is rimmed by Pine Street, Olive Way and Sixth and Seventh avenues.*

This eleven-screen theater occupies the top floor of the trendy Pacific Place shopping center. In contrast to the rest of the center's sleekly modern look, the Cinema has an unusual peeled log and raw wood facade. It shows current releases.

9 *UPTOWN THEATER* • *511 Queen Anne Ave. North; (206)285-1022. GETTING THERE: It's in the lower Queen Anne Hill neighborhood between Mercer and west Republican.*

Uptown is the most appealing of Seattle's several surviving art deco theaters. Note its traditional wedge-shaped marquee with blinking light bulbs and pink neon piping, and its sidewalk ticket window. The finishing touch is an ancient—and still working—Cretors popcorn popper in the small lobby. The theater's four screens show current films.

10 VARSITY THEATER • *4329 University Way NE; (206) 632-3131. GETTING THERE: The theater is in the University District between NE 43rd and NE 45th streets.*

Another of Seattle's old art deco theaters, the Varsity has the traditional wedge marquee and sidewalk ticket window. Appropriate to its U-District location, it offers an interesting mix of foreign films, American independent productions (offbeat and otherwise), and artistic documentaries. This is where you go for *The Rocky Horror Picture Show* or an interesting film animation festival. The theater often focuses on the works of specific producers or directors.

Once during Prohibition I was forced to live for days on nothing but food and water.

— W.C. Fields

Chapter eight

PUB CRAWLING
THE BEST PLACES TO SIT AND SIP SUDS

Can a city that's so serious about designer coffees also be a great drinking town? Seattle doesn't rival New York, Chicago or San Francisco for great saloons. For one thing, archaic drinking laws require a legal definition between a "tavern" which can serve only beer and wine, and a cocktail lounge—generally linked to a restaurant—that can serve the hard stuff as well. Liquor by the bottle is available only through state stores and they close on the Sabbath.

This is not to infer that Seattlites limit their imbibing to caffé latte. Emerald City does have a few grand drinking establishments—places where W.C. Fields would feel right at home. The Pacific Northwest leads the nation in per capita beer consumption, and Seattle also has some really fine brewpubs. Washington is America's third largest producer of wine and any decent cocktail lounge has a good selection of wines by the glass. As for the hard stuff, the most popular mixed drink in town is the martini. At least one bar—Von's Martini-Manhattan Memorial (see below) devotes itself to crafting the perfect martini, mixed at the patron's table.

THE TEN BEST WATERING HOLES

My idea of the ideal watering hole is a pleasant, cheerful and relaxing space where drinking is more of a social exchange than a melancholy ritual. While I'm fond of weathered old saloons with a dusty patina of history, I prefer more upbeat establishments. As for my wife and co-author Betty, she says hanging around bars is a waste of time. However, bars are part of a city's character and fabric. So I indulge in a bit of pub crawling when we research these city guides, while she's off in pursuit of interesting museums. These are my Seattle favorites:

1 BELLTOWN PUB ● *2322 First Ave.; (206) 728-4311. Lunch through late evening daily. GETTING THERE: Our favorite pub is between Bell and Battery, in Belltown north of the downtown area.*

This is the consummate Seattle watering hole—a cozy, relatively quiet Belltown retreat shrouded in old brick. Patrons can sit at the long bar and sip from an assortment of Northwest and other micro-brows, or choose from an excellent wine selection. High-backed wooden booths—so high that a seated Michael Jordan would be hidden from view—provide personal retreats for discussing private matters. A few sidewalk tables invite those who want to watch—and be watched by—the passing Belltown pedestrian parade. The pub's décor is rustically smart—lots of raw brick and dark woods, brass rails, drop lamps over the bar and a weathered rowing scull hanging inverted from the high ceiling. A small menu of regional fare tempts those who come for a power lunch or a Belltown dinner.

2 BIG TIME BREWERY & ALE HOUSE ● *4133 NE University Way; (206) 545-4509. GETTING THERE: It's in the University District just northwest of the University of Washington campus, in the middle of a long block between NE 41st and NE 42nd streets.*

On any given evening—particularly from fall through spring—a good percentage of the 35,000-plus students from the nearby University of Washington gather in this cheerfully noisy place to quaff beer, swap term paper notes and discuss the agonies of bio-chem. It's a large, appealingly weathered pub with distressed wooden tables, plank wood floors and high wainscotting. Hundreds of beer bottles—presumably emptied by patrons—line a high plate rail. Big Time brews its own beers and regulars are drawn to assertive varieties that are heavy on malt and tangy with the nip of hops. There's plenty space for evening standing room only crowds, and those seeking a little isolation can retreat to sheltered wooden booths in a back room. A walkup window dispenses nachos, sandwiches, pizzas and such. A major plus—this is a smoke-free drinking establishment.

3 *DAD WATSONS RESTAURANT & BREWERY* • *3601 Fremont Ave. North; (206) 632-6505. (WEB SITE: www.mcmenamins.com) Lunch through dinner daily. GETTING THERE: It's in the Fremont neighborhood just west of Lake Union's north shore. To get there from downtown, go north on Westlake Avenue (skirting the western edge of Lake Union), then cross the Fremont drawbridge and continue a few blocks; the pub is at Fremont and North 36th Street.*

Dad's is the best of several good pubs in the laid back Fremont District—a handsome old style space of dark woods and beam ceilings. Appropriate to the area, it's decorated with a kinchy assortment of odds and ends. The main bar, shaped like a question mark, is rimmed by a wrought iron rail and the rest of the room is filled with tables bathed in lamplight. In this pleasing atmosphere, you can sip microbrews such as Hammerhead (lots of malt and hops), Terminator Stout (Guinness with an attitude), wheat beer, and a curiosity called Ruby, with a touch of raspberries. Dad also offers a full range of other beers, wine and hard stuff. The café serves an assortment of 'burgers, sandwiches, pastas, a few things Mexican and an interesting chicken and sausage gumbo.

4 *ELEPHANT AND CASTLE PUB & RESTAURANT* • *At Cavanaugh's on Fifth Avenue, 1415 W. Fifth Ave.; (206) 971-8000. GETTING THERE: The pub is one the lower floor of this downtown hotel, between Pike and Union.*

Although Cavanaugh's has a rather austere glass box modern look, it offers a rather convincing looking olde English pub. It's adorned with pressed tin ceilings, brick walls, dark wood trim, wrought iron and leaded glass. It has a long, two-sided bar for those who prefer to perch on stools, and quite corners for those who want to be alone. On warm summer afternoons, sippers can adjourn to an attractive terraced outdoor patio. For serious suds sippers, the Elephant and Castle has fifteen beers on tap, including Guinness, of course.

5 *GORDON BIERSCH BREWERY-RESTAURANT* • *In Pacific Place at 600 Pine St.; (206) 405-4205. Eclectic menu. Lunch and dinner daily. Major credit cards. GETTING THERE: This popular pub is on the fourth floor of Pacific Place downtown. The shopping center is rimmed by Pine Street, Olive Way and Sixth and Seventh avenues.*

Started in the San Francisco Bay Area, Gordon Biersch has spread its upscale brewpub outlets to several major cities. The Seattle version has the requisite stainless steel brewing vats and exposed heating ducts, giving it a kind of industrial-modern look. It serves in-house brews by the glass or by mini-glass samplers, and it has cocktails and a good wine list. The food is eclectic and spicy to match the firm's hearty brews. We particularly like its savory and peppy stirfry dishes, ideal companions to an assertive beer. With outdoor tables beneath a dramatic glass atrium, it also makes our *al fresco* dining list in Chapter Four, page 96.

6 J&M CAFÉ AND CARDROOM • *201 First St.; (206) 292-0663. GETTING THERE: It's part of the "outdoor café row" along First Avenue in Pioneer Square, between Washington and Main streets.*

Like many historic Pioneer Square pubs, J&M is more café than watering hole these days. However, it does have quite a splendid nineteenth century bar, with a mirrored triple-arched backbar. The place offers the essentials of a good pub, with a pool table and cardroom in back, where serious drinkers can retreat from the tourists who come for hamburgers and Cajun chicken fettuccine. J&M has a sidewalk patio out front, so it also makes our list of Ten Best *al fresco* cafés in Chapter Four. This is one of Seattle's oldest drinking establishments, founded in 1889 as Jamison & Moffett. It has been serving booze from this spot since 1902.

7 PALISADE • *At Elliott Bay Marina, 2601 W. Marina Place; (206) 285-1000. Lunch through late evening daily. Major credit cards. GETTING THERE: Take Elliott Avenue about two miles northwest from downtown, cross the Garfield Street-Magnolia Bridge and take the Elliott Bay Marina/Smith Cove Park exit.*

One of Seattle's Ten Best restaurants (Chapter Three) also has one of its ten best bars. Palisade's cocktail lounge is a gorgeous space, with a modernistic curving main bar and comfy tables above—whazzis?—a tidepool? No, you haven't had too many martinis. A saltwater stream with live fish trickles between the bar and the dining area. Views from the Palisade are stunning—through the masts of Elliott Bay Marina to the downtown skyline and—on a good day—Mount Rainier. The best views are from the terraced dining area, although the elevated cocktail lounge provides proper vistas as well.

8 PIONEER SQUARE SALOON • *73 Yesler Way; (206) 628-6444. GETTING THERE: This drinking establishment is part of the Pioneer Hotel at the corner of Yesler Way and Western Avenue.*

If you like the essence of history and plenty of room to drink, head for this cavernous saloon in Seattle's Pioneer Square area. It has that yesterday look with an ornate main bar and lofty back bar, brick walls with wainscotting, milk glass fixtures and lazily turning fans dangling from a lofty ceiling. The bar rambles through several rooms, some looking rather Berkeleyian, with bentwood chairs and modern art on the walls. You can shoot a quiet game of pool in one of these small rooms, or sip your suds in the open air at a sidewalk patio.

9 *VIRGINIA INN* • *1937 First Ave.; (206) 728-1937. Lunch through late evening. GETTING THERE: It's at the corner of First Avenue and Virginia Street, between Belltown and Pike Place Market.*

Not an inn, this Virginian is an upbeat and smoke-free pub tucked beneath bay windows of a Victorian style waterfront building that could have been barged in from San Francisco. The SFO feeling persists in its old brick walls draped with local art, its polished main bar and its lively after-five white collar, hungry artist and messenger biker crowd. So *this* is where downtowners gather if they don't dig coffee bars! It's a serious drinking establishment, with a dozen specialty brews on tap, good wines by the glass, several single malt Scotches and small batch bourbons. Appealing to the faithful with frequent special events and good bar food, it's one of Seattle's liveliest spots.

10 *VON'S MARTINI-MANHATTAN MEMORIAL* • *619 Pine at Seventh Avenue downtown; (206) 621-8667. It's part of the large Vons Grand City Café complex.*

Seeking the perfect dry martini? Head for this large and cheerful cocktail lounge opposite Pacific Place shopping center, which claims to serve the city's best. Each martini is built and shaken right at tableside and served in the classic deep wedge-shaped glass, not in one of those shallow saucer things. It's an appealing place, with that proper Manhattan feel of wooden booths and weathered tables. The "Memorial" is busily decorated with airplane models, bicycles, footballs and sundry curios. Most of these objects are tacked to the ceiling, so you can study the décor as you tilt back a possibly perfect martini.

THE TEN BEST "PERSONALITY BARS"

What's a personality bar? It's a watering hole with special character, such as a particular theme, style or attitude. These are listed in no particular order.

1 *THE BEST BREWPUB: Pyramid Alehouse* • *1201 First Ave. South; (206) 682-3377. Beer and wine only. Lunch through late evening daily. Brewery tours weekdays at 2 and 4, and weekends 1, 2 and 4. Major credit cards. GETTING THERE: It's south of Pioneer Square at the corner of First and Royal Brougham Way, opposite Safeco Field.*

Although the name may suggest a cozy bistro, Seattle's best brewpub is a large drinking establishment occupying two floors of a handsome old warehouse building. The interior look is classic industrial, with heavy beams holding up lofty ceilings, rough-hewn brick walls and ranks of gleaming copper and stainless steel brewing vats. We like to sit at the long, curving copper-topped bar, trying to choose from twenty different brews. These are hearty beers typical of microbreweries, with names such as Wheaten Ale, Apricot Ale (rather fruity and strange), Best Brown and Iron Tub Porter. Our favorite is DPA (Draught Pale Ale), with a character similar to a soft Guinness Stout. This is as much a restaurant as a brewpub, with an open kitchen and seating on two levels. The menu offers the usual steaks, chops and chickens, plus a good assortment of pizzas and other spicy fare suited to beer quaffing. Pyramid has a strong following among sports fans for an obvious reason: It's just a short walk from the playfields of Seattle's Mariners and Seahawks.

2 THE COOLEST BAR: W Hotel lounge • *In the W Seattle Hotel at 1112 Fourth Ave.; (206) 264-6100. (WEB SITE: www.whotels.com) GETTING THERE: The hotel is downtown at the corner of Fourth Avenue and Seneca Street.*

The "W" hotels are an experiment in *art moderne*, designed to appeal to upwardly mobile business types. The look is exemplified in this stylish lobby lounge with a gently curving marble topped bar, glass-shelved backbar and severely modern yet comfortable furnishings in plush purple, black, beige and yellow. It serves designer coffees by day and cocktails and light fare in the evening. The bar and hotel target affluent intellectuals; patrons can play a game of tic-tac-toe or chess on built-in boards, or pull the latest art, photography or design book from nearby library shelves.

3 THE BEST IRISH PUB: Murphy's • *1928 N. 45th St.; (206) 634-2110. GETTING THERE: It's at the corner of Meridian in the Wallingford area.*

This is Seattle's consummate Irish drinking establishment, with Celtic paraphernalia and Guinness Stout signs on dark wood walls. High ceilings with lazily turning fans, a cheery fireplace (fake but cheery) and an elaborately carved wooden bar create an inviting place for sipping a pint o' Courage or Harp Lager. Wash it down with beer battered fish and chips or shepherds pie. With its cross-paneled exterior walls and Celtic crests set in leaded glass windows, it could as well be standing on a Dublin street corner.

4 THE BEST LOBBY BAR: Sheraton Seattle • *535 Sixth Ave.; (206) 621-9000. GETTING THERE: The Sheraton is in the heart of downtown at Sixth Avenue and Pike Street.*

This large, slightly sunken cocktail lounge occupies a key intersection in the Sheraton's modern lobby, near the Seafood Gallery and Oyster Bar and adjacent to the highly regarded Fuller's restaurant. With comfortable seats around the large rectangular bar and tables on the outer rim, it's a good place to meet, greet, sip and people-watch.

5 THE NOISIEST BAR: Tír Na Nóg • *801 First Ave.; (206)*
264-2700. GETTING THERE: This festival of noise is at First and Colum-
bia, near downtown and Pike Place Market.

Emerald City must have a large Irish population, for this Gaelic
watering hole is immensely popular, with noise levels often reaching
upper decibels. Its regular patrons—Irish by attitude if not by heritage—are joined by hoards of after-work office people from adjacent
highrises. Semi-enclosed booths provide some sanctuary from the
drinking din, and one can choose from several rooms in this oversized
place. It has typically deliberate Irish accouterments, from the Gaelic
paraphernalia on its dark paneled wood to its Guinness bar coasters. A
good bar menu wanders from traditional Irish cabbage rolls to more
contemporary grilled salmon and seafood pasta.

6 THE QUIETEST BAR: The Bookstore • *In the Alexis Hotel,*
1007 First Ave.; (206) 382-1506. GETTING THERE: This bookish drink-
ing establishment is on the Alexis lobby floor at First and Madison.

Not a book store but a bar with bookshelves, this quiet place is one
of the most appealing retreats in town. It has the feel of an elegant old
library with warm woods, touches of brass and—for those who want
to keep current—a large rack of magazines and newspapers. Although
it's a poplar after-work spot for the downtown crowd, the library atmosphere encourages quiet conversation, not the telling of raucous
party jokes. If you wish to linger through lunch or dinner, bar food is
available or you can have more elaborate fare sent in from the hotel's
highly esteemed Painted Table restaurant; see Chapter Three, page 71.

7 THE MOST HISTORIC BAR: The Central • *207 First Ave.;*
(206) 622-0209. GETTING THERE: It's part of the "outdoor café row"
along First Avenue in the Pioneer Square area, between Washington and
Main streets.

Although it's now more nightclub and café than pub, the Central is
Seattle's oldest drinking establishment. It was started in 1892 by one
Thomas Watson. The bar section is indeed a classic, made of polished
wood with a mirrored and multi-arched backbar. The Central features
live entertainment several nights a week with a cover charge. With a
good grub selection, it also makes our list as one of the city's Ten Best
outdoor dining venues; see Chapter Four, page 95.

8 THE SMOKIEST BAR: Blue Moon Tavern • *712 NE 45th*
St.; no phone. Lunch through late evening daily. GETTING THERE: It's
immediately east of the I-5 45th Street exit, between Seventh and Eighth
avenues northeast.

If you like history with your suds and you don't mind a blue haze of cigarette smoke, you may be drawn to this tattered old tavern on the western edge of the University District. Established in 1934, it once was the home of the U-District's beat generation and leftist literati. Poets Theodore Roethke, Carolyn Kizer and Richard Hugo, and novelist Tom Robbins once sipped suds out here. Although it's not far from the University of Washington campus, you won't see many students or even serious leftists these days. Most of the patrons are middle-aged puffers and quaffers who prop their elbows on the scarred bartop or slump comfortably in wooden booths, from which they rise occasionally to shoot a game of pool. Walls are still lined with books that appear to be left over from the bar's Bohemian era. The aged brick building survived a demolition threat following a public outcry a few years ago and bar owners won a long-term lease.

9 *THE BEST GLORIA STEINHAM MEMORIAL BAR: Hooters ● 901 Fairview Ave. North; (206) 625-0555. (WEB: www.hootersofamerica.com) Lunch and dinner daily. MC/VISA; $$. GETTING THERE: Hooters is in Chandler's Cove on the southeast shore of Lake Union. From downtown, go north on Fairview, then northeast along the lakeshore.*

"Delightfully tacky, yet unrefined," reads a sign at this harmlessly outrageous bar. Part of a national chain, Hooters is noted for nubile young waitresses wearing orange hotpants and scoop-neck T-shirts. Some years ago, the National Organization for Women tried to force the firm to hire male waitpersons. However, we were served by an attractive, amply endowed lass, not by a pouting male, so the lawsuit obviously didn't bear fruit. Hooters offers a long list of draft beers and wines by the glass, cocktails and simple pub grub such as hamburgers, seafood platters, salads and pastas. Predictably, it's a popular a sports bar, with the usual TV monitors hanging about. The overall décor consists mostly of the girls and their pin-up photos.

10 *THE BEST VIEW BAR: Top Lounge at the Space Needle ● Observation deck hours: summer 8 to midnight; the rest of the year 9 to midnight GETTING THERE: Seattle Center is just northwest of downtown, two blocks up from the waterfront, off Broad Street.*

There's no better view of Seattle than from the Space Needle, and the small lounge on the observation deck is a fine place to enjoy that vista with drink in hand. The lounge is a cozy little retreat with candle-lit tables, in pleasant contrast to the busy gift shop environment immediately outside the entrance. Unlike most sky bars whose prices increase with the altitude, the drinks here are reasonable. If you're hungry, you can order light fare such as quesadillas, crab cakes, buffalo wings, jalapeño poppers and such from a small bar menu.

Lottie went to the diggings!
With Lottie we must be just.
If she didn't shovel tailings—
Where did Lottie get her dust?
— Klondike mining camp jingle
about Seattle's Lottie Burns

Chapter nine

ROMANCE
AND OTHER PRIMAL URGES

Emerald City certainly had a romantic past, what with Ira Mercer's imported brides and those frisky ladies of old Pioneer Square and the Klondike Gold Rush.

Today, however, most folks don't regard Seattle as a particularly romantic or sensuous city. At least, not in the sense of Paris or San Francisco or sexy Las Vegas. (*Sleepless in Seattle* was a very romantic movie, although most of its passion occurred in New York.) Warm sun and bottles of good California or French wine kindle romance, not drizzling rain and cups of espresso. The city probably takes itself too seriously to be a sensual place, and there's nothing sexy about its aviation and computer industries. No one has ever written a romantic ballad about Seattle; no songwriter has left his heart there or called it "my kind of town."

On the other hand, the gorgeous scenery surrounding Emerald City can create romantic moods. Certainly, there are many restaurants with sexy views or candlelit tables, and sometimes both. And that drizzling rain? Unless you're Gene Kelley dancing in Paris, daytime rain isn't particularly romantic. At night, however, seek out a cozy fireplace with your partner and share a bottle of good Washington Merlot. Or simply peer out a window and watch the city's lights dance on wet streets. Don't say a word; just listen to the rain.

And save the coffee for morning.

THE TEN BEST PLACES TO SNUGGLE WITH YOUR SWEETIE

Is it difficult to find a place to be alone together in a big city? Not if that city is Seattle, with its many uncrowded parks, lonely waterfront vistas and even hidden corners of popular espresso cafés.

1 **SMITH COVE PARK** • *On the waterfront, just south of Elliott Bay Marina. GETTING THERE: Take Elliott Avenue about two miles northwest from downtown, cross the Garfield Street-Magnolia Bridge and take the Elliott Bay Marina exit. You'll see the entrance to the park on your left as you drive toward the marina parking area.*

This tiny park is our favorite Seattle snuggle spot because it has benches offering grand views of Puget Sound and Elliott Bay Marina, and it's rarely crowded. Although it's on the waterfront, it's not part of the busy shoreline biking/walking trail. The path into the park is a dead-end so most joggers and cyclists, seeing their error, make a polite retreat, leaving the two of you alone with the views and the seagulls. If you've brought your appetites as well as your sense of romance, two popular marina restaurants—the casual Maggie Bluffs with outdoor tables and the more stylish Palisade—are a short stroll away.

2 **THE BOOKSTORE** • *In the Alexis Hotel, 1007 First Ave.; (206) 382-1506. GETTING THERE: This bookish drinking establishment is on the lobby floor of the Alexis Hotel, at First and Madison, near Pike Place Market.*

This Bookstore is a cozy, dimly lit bar just off the lobby of the Alexis Hotel. A small nook on a landing above the bar is a great place to be alone with your sweetie. This intimate space has only a few tables, each lit by a votive candle. The bar's clubby library atmosphere seem to dictate that conversation remain hushed. There's plenty of reading material here—books and magazines abound on its library shelves. But you're with your lover; who has time to read?

3 **DIAGONAL AVENUE SOUTH PUBLIC SHORELINE ACCESS** • *South Seattle industrial area. GETTING THERE: Drive south about 2.5 miles from downtown Seattle on Alaskan Way, which becomes Marginal Way. The turnoff to the shoreline park is to the right, just beyond the West Seattle Freeway overpass.*

The name doesn't suggest much, and it certainly doesn't sound romantic. However, this is a charming little public park tucked among the container terminals of the south Seattle port area. The main park area has a few picnic tables and benches, and a short trail leads down to the shoreline of Duwamish Waterway. In this rarely visited spot, you can sit on a driftwood log, disturbed by no one except possibly an occasional passing kayaker. There's even a gnarled old apple tree along the short trail, in case you want to do the Adam and Eve thing. But do keep your clothes on.

4 *IN A ROLLS ROYCE LIMO* • *First Class Limousine; (206) 329-5395. (WEB SITE: http://psweb.com/limo)*

Six pages of ads in the Seattle Yellow Pages pitch limousine service, offering stretched-out luxury sedans with seating for as many as ten passengers. *Ten?* How about something just for the two of you? We liked First Class Limousine's offer of "Romantic Woo Woo Packages" for weddings, anniversaries and even proposals. The firm will chauffeur you two around in a Rolls Royce sedan with a CD player, TV/VCR and a moon roof—for gazing at the stars, of course.

5 *AGC MARINA* • *On Lake Union at 1200 Westlake Avenue North. GETTING THERE: Follow Westlake north from downtown along the west shore of Lake Union and turn into the AGC Marina parking area.*

If you stroll along the shoreline of AGC Marina between McCormick and Schmick's Harborside in the AGC building and the Argosy Cruises dock, you'll see two benches on the shoreline. They offer fine views across the marina's forest of masts. Most folks miss this spot because the benches are sheltered by pine trees—all the better to provide you with privacy as you sit and watch your mate watching the seaplanes and boats play on the lake.

6 *VINTAGE PARK HOTEL LOBBY* • *1100 Fifth Ave.; (206) 624-8000. GETTING THERE: It's in downtown Seattle between Spring and Seneca streets.*

Two plush burgundy couches, one with its back discreetly turned to the registration desk, sit opposite an imposing floor-to-ceiling fireplace in the Vintage Park's cozy, clubby lobby. It's a romantic place to sit and watch the fire flicker its reflections in your mate's eyes. Dark woods, polished wainscotting, beam ceilings and original oil paintings add touches of class to this intimate setting.

7 *SEATTLE'S BEST COFFEE AT PIKE PLACE* • *Corner of Pike Street and First Avenue near Pike Place Market; (206) 284-1303.*

Although this coffee bar is directly opposite the entrance to Pike Place Market, don't bring your sweetie here to watch the tourists from its sidewalk tables. Step inside and you'll find a cozy little landing above the main floor, with a few overstuffed chairs. With luck, you may be the only occupants of this small space, particularly if you give those who approach that "we want to be alone" look.

8 **WATERFALL GARDEN PARK** • *Main Street and Second Avenue in Pioneer Square. Free; open daily 6 a.m. to 5:45 p.m.*

Need a cozy retreat from busy Pioneer Square? Step into this walled sunken garden, where a 22-foot waterfall tumbles over a pile of boulders. You can sit cozily together on inviting benches or small tables and chairs, admiring the lush landscaping and listening to the falling water. Expect to share this popular little nature preserve with others. But don't worry; the rumble of the water will drown whatever's being whispered into your partner's ear. The park was given to the people of Seattle by a foundation funded by the United Parcel Service. Its founder, Jim Casey, started his messenger service on this site in 1907.

9 **WATERFRONT PARK** • *Just south of the Seattle Aquarium and Omnidome. GETTING THERE: Take any of several downtown streets to Alaskan Way; the park is below and just south of Pike Place Market.*

This large park with an interesting fountain of angular concrete chunks occupies a former pier. It provides nice views across Elliott Bay to the Olympic Range and uphill to the city's dramatic skyline. Several benches, concrete risers and picnic tables offer nice places for couples to sit and enjoy the view. Although the park is in the heart of the busy waterfront, it usually isn't crowded. It was undergoing renovation when we last passed, so the scarred and initial-carved picnic tables may be gone by the time you arrive, although the homeless folk who like to hang out probably will still be here. Be discreet and so will they. Incidentally, you'll have to do your snuggling early, since the park is closed from 11 p.m. until 6 a.m.

10 **JOSÉ RIZAL PARK** • *In the Beacon Hill district, southeast of downtown. GETTING THERE: Take Jackson Street east from the Pioneer Square area, cross under the I-5 freeway and go right (south) on 12th Avenue for about five blocks. Cross over the I-90 freeway, then turn right onto St. Charles Street in front of the Pacific Medical Center.*

If you want to snuggle with a view, there's no better city vantage point than from José Rizal Park, in front of the large Pacific Medical Center. A single bench between the park's picnic shelter and public restrooms offers a grand, uncluttered vista of Seattle—from the port district, Safeco Field and the new Mariners stadium, over the city skyline to the Space Needle and beyond to Elliott Bay and the distant Olympic Mountains. Should you wish to impress your partner with a picnic spread, one of the tables just outside a picnic shelter offers the same great vista.

So who's José? Rizal was a Filipino patriot and martyr who lived from 1861 to 1896. The adjacent Beacon Hill neighborhood has a large Filipino population, so the park was named in their hero's honor. Facilities include that picnic shelter, public restrooms, a small play area and a gaudily colored concrete and tile "triptych" erected by the Filipino community.

THE TEN MOST ROMANTIC RESTAURANTS

Seattle is a great dining town and it does not suffer a shortage of romantic restaurants. Whether you seek snuggly banquettes, stunning sunset views or intimate French restaurants, this can be your kind of town.

1 ROVER'S ● 2808 E. Madison St.; (206) 325-7442. (WEB SITE: www.rover-seattle.com) Wine and beer. Dinner Tuesday-Saturday; reservations required. Major credit cards; $$$$. GETTING THERE: Rover's is northeast of downtown near Lake Washington Park, in a courtyard off Madison near 28th Avenue. Follow Spring Street under the freeway (to avoid Madison's one-way grid), then shift over to Madison and follow it nearly two miles._

If you want to spoil your lover with a lavish festival of the culinary senses in sensually simple setting of gauzy curtains and white nappery, this is the place. Rover's is a disarmingly cute little cottage restaurant in a quiet courtyard. Plan an entire evening—indeed a quiet and re-laxed one—as you enjoy one of Chef Thierry Rautureau's *grand ménus de dégustation*. A typical evening's indulgence might include sturgeon caviar with scrambled eggs, Alaskan spot prawns, sturgeon with cara-melized turnips, a Pinot Noir sorbet and venison medallions with chanterelles and black peppercorn sauce. End all of this with a sinfully wonderful dessert. And on a warm summer Seattle night, all of this can be enjoyed in a hedge-enclosed courtyard. Rover's also is on our list of Seattle's "Ten very best restaurants" in Chapter Three.

2 AVENUE ONE ● 1921 First Ave.; (206) 441-6139. Eclectic; full bar service. Dinner nightly. Major credit cards; $$$. GETTING THERE: It's between Stuart and Virginia streets, about midway between Pike Place Market and Belltown._

This stylish 1930s *Paris chic* café has an intimate candle-lit dining area overlooking the waterfront. There are very few view tables in this section, so call early to reserve one for a romantic evening. The rest of the restaurant is pleasant as well, with thirties "beautiful people" murals, art deco wall sconces and an inviting copper-top bar. The menu wanders from America to Europe and the Mediterranean, offering entrées such as pan roasted monkfish, peppered and grilled tuna, Moroccan spiced salmon over *cous-cous*, and Alaskan scallops with mushrooms.

3 *BAHN THAI* ● *409 Roy St.; (206) 283-0444. Thai; full bar service. Lunch weekdays and dinner nightly. MC/VISA, DISC; $$. GETTING THERE: It's just behind Seattle Center between Fourth and Fifth avenues.*

From the outside, it's an old Carpenter style American cottage; from within, it's one of Seattle's most appealing and romantic Asian restaurants. While retaining the original home's interior arches, designers have created a gentle Thai retreat with carefully placed artifacts and art work, candle-lit tables and soft music. The food is excellent and remarkably inexpensive. The spiciness of Thai cooking can certainly put spice into your meal together, although gentler fare is available as well. Since the two of you like to share, choose from several moderately priced combination dinners. For more on the food, flip to Chapter Three, page 77.

4 *EL GAUCHO* ● *90 Wall St.; (206) 728-1140. (WEB SITE: www.elgaucho.com) Full bar service. Dinner nightly. Major credit cards. $$ to $$$. GETTING THERE: This cozily chic restaurant is Belltown at the corner of Wall Street and First Avenue.*

Although the name suggests something on the Argentine pampas, Seattle's El Gaucho is a dark, moody and sexy restaurant on the edge of Belltown. Snuggle with the special someone in a plush banquette in the dark wood dining room, sip your martinis and share châteaubriand. Or if you want to see lights flicker in your lover's eyes, order the skewered lamb tenderloin flamed in vodka at your table. But avoid the garlic bread; this is supposed to be a romantic evening. If it's Friday or Saturday, you can adjourn to the downstairs Pampas Club and dance the rest of the night away.

5 *FULLERS* ● *In the Sheraton Seattle, 1400 Sixth Ave.; (206) 447-5544. Northwest cuisine; full bar service. Lunch weekdays, dinner Monday-Saturday. Major credit cards; $$$ to $$$$. GETTING THERE: Fullers is on the lobby level of the Sheraton, which is at Sixth and Pike.*

Cozy octagonal booths, each with tiny drop lamps and individual works of art on the walls, create one of Emerald City's most intimate dining retreats. The restaurant is done in soothing shades of beige; white nappery and fine crystal grace its tables. With attentive and discreet service and a nationally recognized kitchen, this is an ideal venue for quiet escape with that significant other. The menu, which changes frequently, may feature artful presentations such as oven-roasted chicken with baby fennel and mustard, lamb chops with herb polenta or duck confit with rice noodles and shiitake mushrooms. Fullers also makes our "Ten very best restaurant" list in Chapter Three, page 69.

6 *GEORGIAN ROOM* • *In the Four Seasons Olympic Hotel at 411 University St.; (206) 621-7889. (WEB SITE: www.fourseasons.com) American regional; full bar service. Dinner Monday-Saturday. Major credit cards; $$$$. GETTING THERE: The Olympic is downtown between Fourth and Fifth avenues.*

You'll take romance? Take him or her to this gorgeous dining haven off the main lobby of Seattle's most elegant hotel. The setting is perfect for a romantic evening—beaded chandeliers, intimate table lamps, pink nappery, attentive yet unobtrusive service and—somewhere in the background—a tinkling piano. Settle yourselves into one of the plush banquettes for two and prepare for a leisurely—and expensive—evening. The Four Season Olympic has earned the Northwest's only AAA Five Diamond Award and the Georgian Room has earned four diamonds. If you're a suitor, perhaps this is the place to present a diamond to her. For Georgian Room menu details, see the "Ten very best restaurants" listing in Chapter Three, page 70.

7 *THE HUNT CLUB* • *In the Sorrento Hotel at 900 Madison St.; (206) 343-6156. (WEB SITE: www.hotelsorrento.com) Northwest regional; full bar service. Lunch weekdays, brunch weekends and dinner nightly. Major credit cards; $$$$. GETTING THERE: The Sorrento is at the corner of Madison Street and Terry Avenue, just above downtown in the First Hill neighborhood. Madison is one-way downhill, so go uphill on Spring Street, cross under the freeway and turn left on Terry.*

The Old World dark wood elegance of the Hunt Club provides a suitable setting for a romantic evening. The room is a bit on the clubby side, although the subdued lighting and candle-lit tables will contribute to the proper mood. Before or after your meal, share smooth martinis or a wee dram of port in the cozy Fireside Room adjacent. While the atmosphere is old Europe, the fare is contemporary American, with entrées such as salmon with artichokes and leeks, and roasted breast of duckling with glazed endive. For more on this opulent restaurant, turn to Chapter Three, page 70.

8 *THE PAINTED TABLE* • *In the Alexis Hotel, 92 Madison St. (206) 624-3646. Northwest nouveau; full bar service. Breakfast and dinner daily, lunch weekdays. Major credit cards; $$$$. GETTING THERE: This elegant table is off the lobby of the Alexis, which sits at First and Madison Street downtown, near Pike Place Market.*

Slip into something sexy the next time the two of you decide to go out to dinner—such as the Painted Table. Dining rooms don't necessarily have to be dimly lit and subdued to create a romantic environment. The "Table" is a sensual space because it's so artistically gorgeous, with cozy and curved floral patterned booths, tapestry-draped walls and stimulating splashes of color. The food is gorgeous as well, with a focus on "elegantly simple" Northwest cuisine, using local herbs and vegetables and faultlessly fresh seafood. Asian and French accents add spice to the menu. For more on this bright yet romantic restaurant, see Chapter Three, page 71.

9 *PALISADE • At Elliott Bay Marina, 2601 W. Marina Place; (206) 285-1000. Northwest cuisine; full bar service. Lunch and dinner Monday-Saturday, and Sunday brunch. Major credit cards; $$$ to $$$$. GETTING THERE: Take Elliott Avenue about two miles northwest from downtown, cross the Garfield Street-Magnolia Bridge and take the Elliott Bay Marina/Smith Cove Park exit.*

You two can enjoy one of Seattle's most romantic moments with a sunset dinner at this dramatic "Polynesian modern" restaurant, with its window walls on the city. Make reservations early and specify one of the candle-lit window tables, where you can watch sun's last rays glitter across Elliott Bay, while masts in the marina become a silhouette forest and lights wink on sleepily in the distant skyline. And where's that soft piano music coming from? Look toward the lofty ceiling and you'll see a player-piano perched precariously on a false roof above the bar. If you want to pretend you've run away to a tropic island, get silly with a Polynesian drink, pluck the orchid from it and place it behind your lover's ear. See Chapter Three, page 71.

10 *THE SPACE NEEDLE RESTAURANT • In Seattle Center; second level of the Space Needle observation tower; (800) 937-9582 or (206) 443-2100. American and continental; full bar service. Lunch Monday-Saturday and Sunday brunch; dinner nightly. Major credit cards; $$$$; meal prices include Space Needle ascent.*

Whazzis? The city's most unabashed tourist diner—the required stop for every resident's visiting Auntie Maude—also is one its most romantic restaurants? Certainly. The next time the two of you feel the urge for an intimate evening out, make reservations for one of the Space Needle's candle-lit tables-for-two. Sundown is a grand time, when the lights are dimmed in the restaurant even as city lights begin twinkling below. Are you so dizzily with love that the room seems to be spinning? It is, at the rate of six-tenths of a mile an hour. It takes nearly an hour for a complete revolution, all the more time to enjoy staring at the city lights—and into one another's eyes. Romantic dining doesn't come cheap at these heights; expect prices to travel well into the $30 range. For more on the Needle, see Chapter Four, page 98.

The Ten Friskiest Diversions in Seattle

In a very public waterfront brawl, Bertha "the Adder" tore off all of "Seattle" Emily's clothes, then chased her naked victim through town, pelting her with rocks. (From Good Time Girls of the Alaska-Yukon Gold Rush by Lael Morgan, © 1998; published by Epicenter Press, Fairbanks and Seattle.)

This didn't happen recently and it didn't happen on the Seattle waterfront; it occurred around the turn of the last century in Dawson City, Yukon Territory, during the great Klondike Gold Rush. However, Emerald City was the gateway to that great rush to riches, outfitting eighty percent of the 60,000 men who headed north and sending many of its prostitutes to help them pass the time. Seattle was a wild lumbering town and fishing port, with its own share of bawdy houses and saloon brawls.

However, it's a considerably tamer city these days. Due in part to a recently-passed ordinance that describes what a nude dancer can do and how she can interact with the bald-headed row, it's one of America's more conservative large cities.

Vice cops, who "may enjoy their work too well," according to the alternative newspaper *The Stranger*, routinely enter nudie parlors in plainclothes to check out the dancers' performances. The new anti-porn law prohibits any kind of contact between dancers and johns. In fact, it even spells out the distance that a dancer must maintain—at least six feet. That *does* put a crimp in lap-dancing. In fact, many of the topless dancers now perform their art behind glass partitions.

Several blocks of First Avenue above the waterfront once was lined with porn shops and nude dance clubs; only a handful remain today. We found no naughty newspapers in streetside news racks, no pleasure palaces thinly disguised as massage parlors. Thus, compiling our list of ten naughty diversions—an easy task for our Ten Best guides for San Francisco, Las Vegas and even conservative San Diego—proved to be rather a challenge here.

To complete the list, we even had to resort to listing a major lingerie stores where very respectable folks can be found browsing among the see-through nighties. Our frisky choices are presented in no particular order.

1 RENT OR BUY A PORNO FILM OR SOMETHING INTERESTING IN LATEX • *Along First Avenue near Pike Place Market.*

Need a flick for your next bachelor party, or some spicy footage for fooling around with your wife or girlfriend? You'll find several shops near Pike Place Market. Among them are **Taboo Video** at 1012 First Avenue; the **Adult Entertainment Center** upstairs, half a block up

Pike Street from First Avenue; and the **Champ Theater Adult Superstore** at 1510 First near Pike Street. All three also offer sexually graphic books and magazines and curiously shaped latex products.

2 *OGGLE NUDIE DANCERS UNDER GLASS* • *The Lusty Lady at First near University opposite the Seattle Art Museum, and Champ Theater Adult Superstore at 1510 Pike near First.*

Both of these places entice frisky tourists and businessmen with signs advertising "live nude dancers." However, as noted above, they're separated by law from their lusty customers—sometimes by glass—. So these are essentially peep shows for lonely voyeurs. The Lusty Lady calls itself the "Testoster-Zone," and urges passersby to "have an erotic day." Champ is the largest adult outlet in town, with 101 video channels in addition to its —uh—performers.

3 *PERUSE THE PAGES OF AN ALTERNATIVE NEWSPAPER* • *The Stranger tabloid, published at 1525 Eleventh Avenue in Seattle. It calls itself "America's hometown newspaper."*

No stranger to vice, this thick adult-oriented publication covers Seattle's alternative life styles. It's definitely not an erotic tabloid, although it offers ads for phone sex, dating services and personals for straights and gays. Its editors like to exercise their First Amendment rights by printing four-letter words and publishing an occasional nude photo. The paper's editorial policy decries the conservative attitude of city officials and police, who have spoiled the local sex scene with their laws prohibiting entertainers from performing acts "which simulate sexual intercourse, masterb..."—well, you get the idea. However, the publication is not entirely preoccupied with sexual freedom. It comments on the local social and political scene, provides reviews of movies, art and cultural events and it has a useful calendar of these activities.

4 *GET YOUR SEX BY WIRE* • Want to hear naughty talk on the telephone? Several local companies offer phone sex conversation for a price, and you can find several of their ads in *The Stranger;* see above. These aren't toll-free; rates are as high as $2.49 a minute, although that's still cheaper and safer than seeking out ladies of the night, most of whom have been run out of town.

5 *GET A DATE BY WIRE OR EVEN E-MAIL* • Looking for a temporary or possibly permanent significant other? You'll find several dating service listed under that category in the Seattle USWest yellow pages. Some also list e-mail addresses. Or you can turn again to *The Stranger* tabloid, whose ads are less subtle.

6 *CATCH A SKINFLICK* • The largest Seattle porno theater— and one of the few—is Fantasies Unlimited Arcade downtown at the corner of Seventh Avenue and Westlake. Call (206) 682-0167 to see who's taking off what in which film.

7 *DRINK AND DINE AMONG LADIES DIVINE* • *Hooters, 901 Fairview Ave. North; (206) 625-0555. (WEB SITE: www.hooterso-famerica.com) Lunch and dinner daily. MC/VISA; $$. GETTING THERE: Hooters is in Chandler's Cove on the southeast shore of Lake Union. From downtown, take Virginia Street northeast, go north on Fairview, then northeast along the lakeshore.*

Sexuality and sexism are alive and well at Hooters, where bosomy ladies in orange T-shirts and cutoff shorts serve simple fare, good drinks and sweet smiles to a mostly male clientele. And that's all they serve; this national bar-and-restaurant chain offers only charm with its hamburgers, seafood platters, salads and pastas. The place is harmlessly outrageous, boasting that it is "delightfully tacky yet unrefined." The fare is typical sports bar, supported by a long list of beers and wines by the glass. The décor consists mostly of the girls and their pin-ups, calendars and logo items, plus TV sets tuned to the latest games.

8 *SHOP FOR SOMETHING SEXY AT VICTORIA'S SE-CRET* • *Southcenter Mall, (206) 241-8577; Bellevue Square, (425) 454-6415; Northgate Mall, (206) 368-7798; and downtown at 401 Pine St., (206) 623-6035.*

Unmentionables are quite mentionable these days, and Victoria's Secret has brought new levels of sensual dignity to scanty and sexy underthings. As the century turned, the firm unveiled a $10 million Millennium Miracle Bra and thong, studded with 2,000 diamonds and sapphires. The Millennium came and went with apparently no takers for the size 34B support bra, so it still may available if you really want to impress your lady love. And if her cups don't runneth over, the firm will alter it to fit. Don't have the capital for such an uplifting investment? You can buy her a regular Miracle Bra for about $20. Victoria offers a full line of other sexy underthings and outer things as well. Always with class and never in poor taste, the shops are the best places in town to buy something nice for your lady. The naughty comes later.

9 *SURPRISE SOMEONE WITH NAUGHTY PASTRY* • *The Erotic Bakery, 2323 North 45th St.; (206) 545-6969. Monday-Thursday 10 to 7, Friday-Saturday 10 to 8 and Sunday noon to 5; MC/VISA. GETTING THERE: It's in the Wallingford neighborhood at the corner of Sunnyside Avenue North.*

This isn't a bakery that shapes cakes and pastries into suggestive shapes. It's an adult shop offering a small case of adult bakery goods. This is the sort of place where baked buns take on a different meaning. A popular item is single-candle birthday cake and you can imagine what form candle takes. You also can dress up the birthday party with naughty paper plates and napkins. Other adult wares include adult movies, kinky greeting cards and the usual latex love toys.

10 CHECK OUT THE SINGLES SCENE • *Active Singles Life newspaper*, *available at news racks or by subscription: 15830 Ambaum Blvd. SW, Burien, WA 98166-3014.*

Single in Seattle? This tabloid is *not* one of those sex-laden adult newspapers. It's a monthly publication designed to get single folks together. It lists singles clubs, dances and events and it contains articles concerning relationships, internet dating and such. You can post a personal ad or respond to one—"Single white male seeks submissive female in need of discipline." Interested in a picture bride? Several display adds offer the opportunity to correspond with eager-to-marry ladies from Russia, Latin America, China, the Philippines and beyond. While relatively conservative, the newspaper does get a bit frisky, with articles on sybersex and ads seeking "erotic pen-pals." And what's that *www.findsex.com* listing?

"What is the use of a book," thought Alice, *"without pictures?"*
— **Lewis Carroll, from** *Alice's Adventures in Wonderland*

Chapter ten

POINTS OF VIEW
WHERE TO STARE AND SHOOT

Seattle enjoys one of the grandest settings of any city in the world, perched on the shores of Elliott Bay and rising into hills beyond, with the snowcapped peaks of the Olympic and Cascade ranges serving as its horizons.

It is a city of a thousand and one great views and certainly a great place for photography. However, the best vista points don't always produce the best photographs. Our slightly offset eyes provide us with three-dimensional vision and a near 180-degree angle of sight. A camera, unless it's equipped with a fisheye lens, has a much narrower field of view and the resulting photos are of course two dimensional.

Thus, we have compiled separate lists. We begin with the Ten Best Viewpoints in and about Seattle, and we then follow with the Ten Best Picture Spots. In between, we offer a quick course in scenic photography, so you can take home some good photos of Emerald City instead of just snapshots.

THE TEN BEST VIEWPOINTS

If Seattle has a "signature vista," it's the downtown skyline and Space Needle, rising about the waters of Elliott Bay. We begin with the best place to enjoy that view:

1 **THE BEST ELLIOT BAY-SKYLINE VIEW** • *From Duwamish Head, at any point along Harbor Avenue SW in West Seattle. GETTING THERE: Cross the tip of Harbor Island on the West Seattle Freeway or Spokane Street and go right onto Harbor Avenue.*

In a hilly city known for its views, none matches this fine vista from a place with an ugly name. Duwamish Head is a promontory in the community of West Seattle and the view from here across Elliott Bay takes in the entire sweep of the city—from Queen Anne Hill and the Space Needle through the downtown highrises to Safeco Field and the industrial port, and all of the beachfront in between

2 **THE BEST OVERALL VIEW** • *From the Space Needle in Seattle Center; (206) 443-2111. (WEB SITE: www.spaceneedle.com) Observation deck hours: summer 8 to midnight; the rest of the year 9 to midnight; $$. GETTING THERE: Seattle Center is just northwest of downtown, two blocks up from the waterfront on Broad Street. The Space Needle is easy to find; just look up.*

Pardon the pun, but you just can't top the Space Needle for the best overall view of Seattle, even though there are higher vantage points in the city. (The higher observation deck of Bank of America Tower also has a public viewing area; see Chapter Two, page 61.) You can circle the city completely at the Needle, either by walking around the indoor or outdoor observation deck or by sitting down at the revolving restaurant one level below. Graphics along the rim of the indoor deck tell you what you're seeing, identifying local landmarks and distant mountain peaks. One sign points out that Sydney, Australia, is 7,850 miles away but of course you can't quite see *that* far. However, on a good day, you can see the North Cascades and beyond, into Canada.

3 **THE BEST TIME TO VIEW MOUNT RAINIER** • *At sundown, from anywhere that offers an unobstructed vista.*

Majestic Mount Rainier quietly watches over Seattle, although folks can't always see the famous peak. Low clouds and foreground hills and buildings often block the view. When the sky and foreground are clear, enjoy your vision of "The Mountain" at sunset, when slanting rays paint the snow-streaked peak a soft pink while casting haunting shadows across its surface. The highest object in the region, Rainier catches the sun's last rays, continuing to glow long after twilight has fallen on the rest of the Puget Sound area. A particularly impressive view is from southbound I-5 as you leave the city—but keep your eyes on the road. The freeway seems headed directly toward the mountain's broad base.

4 **THE BEST VIEW OF ELLIOTT BAY & THE SKYLINE** ● *Victor Steinbrueck Park at the corner of Western Avenue and Virginia Street, just beyond the northern end of Pike Place Market.*

This waterfront park, which begins as a grassy slope and then becomes the roof of a parking structure, is a great place to view the skyline and bay, particularly at sundown. As daylight dims, the bay fades to slate gray, ships becomes silhouettes and downtown highrise windows catch glittery glints of light. Large orange cargo cranes at the nearby Port of Seattle—looking like mechanical creatures from a *Star Wars* movie—catch the last light of day. The concrete part of the park has several wooden and well scarred picnic tables, where you can sit with a cup of designer coffee from the original Starbucks (a block away at 1912 Pike Place Market Street) and watch this fading light show. The park is popular with the homeless, so you might have to share a table.

5 **BEST WIDE ANGLE VIEW OF DOWNTOWN** ● *From Gas Works Park on the north shore of Lake Union. GETTING THERE: Take Aurora Avenue (Highway 99) north from downtown, cross the Lake Washington Ship Canal and exit right onto Bridge Way North. Take the first half right onto North 38th Street, go right on Stone Way North, then swing to the left (east) onto Northlake Way.*

If you have good peripheral vision, you can stand at the shoreline tip of Gas Works Park and see a 180-degree sweep of Seattle, from the I-5 bridge and downtown highrises to the Space Needle, Aurora Bridge and Queen Anne Hill. And in the foreground, you can watch boats at play on Lake Union. This is a better vision than a photograph, since you'd need a fisheye lens to capture all of this on one piece of film.

6 **BEST VIEW OF THE OLYMPICS** ● *From a vista point near Daybreak Star Cultural Arts Center in Discovery Park. GETTING THERE: From downtown, follow Westlake, Nickerson and then Emerson past Fishermen's Terminal. Take a half right from Emerson onto Gilman Avenue West, a half left onto Government Way and follow it into the park. Once there, follow "Daybreak Star" signs west.*

Almost any spot in the greater Seattle area is a good place to see the Olympics—on a clear day. Our favorite is a small, often overlooked vista point reached by a short trail from the parking lot of the Daybreak Star Cultural Arts Center. We like it because you're on a high bluff above the water with nothing to impede your view of the Olympic Peninsula. Off to your right is the Shilshole Bay Marina with its zig-zag breakwater that suggests the mark of Zorro. On most days, you'll see pleasure boats at play in Puget Sound below.

7 **BEST VIEW FROM QUEEN ANNE HILL** • *From Kerry Park on West Highland Drive between Second and Third avenues. From downtown, follow First Avenue uphill to Roy Street, shift left onto Queen Anne Avenue North, continue uphill, then go left onto Highland.*

The sign reads: *Kerry Park was given to the City of Seattle in 1927 by Mr. and Mrs. Albert Sperry Kerry Sr., so that "all who stop here may enjoy this view."* And it certainly is a fine vista. Kerry Park is a tiny sliver of green created just for the views as the Kerrys intended. It provides a nice visual sweep of downtown, the waterfront, Elliott Bay and Mount Rainier beyond. Trees in the foreground are beginning to block the vista and city parks officials may one day be faced with a tortuous decision.

8 **BEST DOWNTOWN VIEW FROM A PUBLIC ROOFTOP** • *Bell Street Pier's Roof Plaza on the waterfront. GETTING THERE: From the foyer of the Bell Harbor International Conference (2211 Alaskan Way), take an elevator to the plaza level. From the foot of Bell Street at Elliott Avenue, stroll above Alaskan Way on a pedestrian overpass.*

Most visitors miss this rooftop "park" atop the Bell Street International Conference Center on Bell Street Pier (also called Pier 66). It provides grand views of the city skyline, a small marina and public boat landing below and the lower waterfront beyond. You'll find benches for sitting and swivel binoculars that you don't even have to feed coins. A pedestrian overpass leads above Alaskan Way to Elliott Avenue and Bell Street.

9 **BEST PLACE TO WATCH PLANES LAND** • *From the Museum of Flight's mockup "control tower" at Boeing Field, 9404 E. Marginal Way; (206) 764-5720. Daily 10 to 5 (Thursdays until 9). GETTING THERE: Head south from downtown on Alaskan Way, which becomes East Marginal Way and takes you to Boeing Field. Or take exit 158 from I-5 and follow signs.*

The mock-up control tower at the Museum of Flight provides an air traffic controller's view of Boeing Field. From this high point fused into the main museum building, you can watch aircraft takeoff and land, and hear the voices of air controllers guiding them in.

10 **BEST VIEW OF ELLIOTT BAY MARINA & BEYOND** • *From Eighth Avenue West on Queen Anne Hill. GETTING THERE: From the Seattle Center area, go north on First Avenue for about ten blocks, turn west (left) onto Prospect and follow it to Seventh Avenue*

*West. Take a brief half right to the intersection of Eighth Place and High-
land Drive, then continue west to Eighth Avenue.*

Most of the best views from Queen Anne Hill are taken by houses.
However, a section of Eighth Avenue is terraced above a steep slope
and a sidewalk rimmed by a decorative wall offers unobstructed vistas
to the west. This layered vision includes the Garfield Street-Magnolia
Bridge, Smith Cove, Elliott Bay Marina, the wooded homes of Magnolia Bluff, and across Puget Sound to the distant Olympics. Plant your
car near tiny Marshall Viewpoint Park (which doesn't offer the best
view) and begin strolling northwest along Eighth Place. It soon merges
into Eighth Avenue, from where you can enjoy splendid vistas westward. We include this section in one of our Ten Best walks in Chapter
Twelve, page 184.

Shooting seattle

Because photos are two-dimensional, good photographers use several techniques to give them depth. You can suggest dimension in a
scenic view by placing a tree limb or interesting street lamp in the
foreground, and perhaps something in the middleground. On the other
hand, if you're focusing on a single object, don't clutter your photo
with framing; let the viewer see only that subject.

Most outdoor scenes are predominately blue, green and brown, the
colors of the sky and the earth. With Seattle's abundance of water and
sometimes sunny skies, you'll get plenty of blue in your photos. To
brighten them, add colors from the warm side of the spectrum—reds,
yellows and oranges. Dress Auntie Maude in a bright yellow dress or
place a brilliant flower in the foreground of your photo, off to the side
where it won't interfere with the main subject.

When you photograph people, don't force them to squint into the
sun. Position them with the sun behind you but to the right or left so it
strikes them at an angle, accenting their features. Also, have your subjects interact with the setting instead of just staring morosely at the
camera or—worse—wearing a silly grin.

Light and shadow are key elements in photography, giving two-dimensional photos a feeling of shape and contour. Early morning and
late afternoon are the best times to shoot, when shadows are stronger,
bringing out detail in your subjects. This is particularly true for structural photos such as the highrise cluster of Seattle's skyline. At midday
when the sun is shining straight down, objects appear flat, washed out
and uninteresting. Further, in the late afternoon, the atmosphere at-
tains a subtle golden quality, giving warm tones to your pictures. If
clouds are drifting overhead, watch for the likelihood of a spectacular
sunset over Puget Sound, particularly from the waterfront.

While lofty perches such the Space Needle provide great visual
panoramas, they aren't necessarily the best places for shooting city
scenes. High places tend to flatten the view below. For more dramatic

skyline shots, find a low vantage point, such as the waterfront. An exception to this rule is at night, when aerial shots of city lights can be spectacular.

Aiming your canon: the ten best picture spots

You can get good results at these suggested picture spots with an adjustable camera (we're partial to Canons) or a simple point and shoot. You'll even get fair results with a disposable camera if you remember to hold the darn thing still; disposables have very slow shutter speeds. If you have an adjustable camera, a 28mm to 80mm zoom lens will greatly enhance your photo opportunities.

1 *THE BEST OVERALL SEATTLE SHOT ● From José Rizal Park opposite the Pacific Medical Center. GETTING THERE: Take Jackson Street east from the Pioneer Square area, cross under the I-5 freeway, go right (south) on 12th Avenue for about five blocks, cross over the I-90 freeway, then turn right onto St. Charles Street in front of the medical center.*

It's not even marked on some maps and it's missed by most visitors. However, small José Rizal Park offers the best overall photo angle of Seattle. No camera? This is a nice vista point as well, and a great place for a view picnic. It's all here—a panoramic sweep that takes in the port district, Safeco Field and the new Seahawks' stadium, the downtown skyline with historic Smith Tower looking rather dwarfed by newer highrises, the Space Needle, Elliott Bay and the distant Olympics. In the foreground, the curving merger of freeways 5 and 90 add depth to the photo. And all of this can be framed by the park's foreground foliage.

The best photo angle—and view—is from an open area between the restrooms and a picnic shelter. This should be a horizontal photo, using a wide angle to medium range telephoto lens, depending on how much of Seattle you seek to capture in a single click of your shutter. For more on the park, see Chapter Nine, page 151.

2 *THE BEST SEATTLE PANORAMIC SHOT ● At any point along Harbor Avenue in West Seattle. GETTING THERE: Cross the tip of Harbor Island on the West Seattle Freeway or Spokane Street and go right onto Harbor Avenue SW.*

This is the same vantage point that tops our list as Seattle's best view, above. If you have one of those gimmick panoramic cameras, it's a good place to put it to use, since you can capture the entire sweep of the city skyline across Elliott Bay, from Queen Anne Hill through the downtown area to the south port district. It's definitely a horizontal, with a wide to medium range lens. Shoot it at mid-morning for an interesting silhouette effect on the highrises, or toward sundown when slanting rays accent the skyline shadows. Then hang around until sunset for some nice city light shots.

3 THE BEST SKYLINE SHOT • *From the corner of Stewart and Pike Place Market streets.*

The photo angles—and views—of the city's skyline are from the waterfront, since the highrises stand boldly on terraced hills above Elliott Bay. Our favorite angle is from the corner of Stewart and Pike Place, just north of the main market entrance. Aim your camera above the Seattle Garden Center and you can catch a splash of foreground color, since its sidewalk overhang is filled with blooming flowers. This is a horizontal shot using a normal lens, best taken in late afternoon when slanting light casts nice accents on the buildings. It won't work in the morning because the buildings will be back-lighted.

4 BEST SHOT FROM THE MONORAIL • *From behind the driver's seat.*

If you want to have a little fun with a downtown Seattle shot, sit just behind the monorail operator's seat, camera at ready. As it cruises from Seattle Center toward downtown, you can get an interesting shot with the profile of the driver in the foreground, the curving track in the middle ground and a cluster of highrises beyond. You'll need a moderate wide angle—24 to 28mm—for the best effect. It's a nice afternoon shot, when enough sunlight pours into the Plexiglas driving compartment to balance the light outside. It works on an overcast day as well. Returning from downtown, you can use the same angle to frame the Space Needle through the windshield—but only for a moment as you approach Seattle Center and the Experience Music Project, so be watchful. You also can try some shots of that strange looking "Project" just before the Monorail enters passes through it. (The facility was built around the Monorail tracks, leaving a tunnel for the trains to go through.)

5 BEST SHOT OF THE SPACE NEEDLE • *From a lawn area behind Pacific Science Center just off Broad Street. The center is at Denny Way and Broad.*

If you walk around to the Broad Street side of the Pacific Science Center, you'll see a strange bright orange "assemblage" that looks like a welded together cluster of large water pipes. Using this as a splash of foreground color, you can frame the Space Needle between branches of trees for a nice combination shot. This is a vertical with a medium range lens.

6 *THE BEST SPACE NEEDLE & SKYLINE SHOT* • *Kerry Park on West Highland Drive between Second and Third avenues. GET-TING THERE: From downtown, follow First Avenue uphill to Roy Street, shift left onto Queen Anne Avenue North, continue uphill, then go left on Highland.*

Queen Anne Hill's best vista point (see above) also is the best place to get a combined shot of the Space Needle and the skyline. From most angles, the Needle and skyline aren't aligned. However, that famous tripod rises right in front of the city's skyscrapers from this vantage point. You can take a telephoto shot for a tight blend of spire and sky-scrapers, or use a medium range lens and include—on a clear day—Mount Rainier, which rises to the right of the skyline. For the latter shot, the best angle is from the eastern edge of Kerry Park. Standing on a bench there gets you above foreground trees.

7 *THE BEST "EYE OF THE NEEDLE" SHOT* • *Through the "Black Sun" sculpture in front of the Seattle Asian Art Museum in Volun-teer Park. GETTING THERE: Take Olive Way or Madison Street north-east, go left (north) on Fifteenth Avenue East, left again onto East Prospect Street at the edge of the park, and then turn right for the mu-seum.*

This is the eye of the needle in reverse. A sculpture resembling a badly formed donut, done in 1969 by Isamu Noguchi, sits on a con-crete base between the Seattle Asian Art Museum and a reservoir. If you're at least six feet tall (or have something or someone to stand on), you can frame the distance Space Needle within the hole of the donut for an interesting photo. Use a normal lens.

8 *BEST SHOT OF SEATTLE'S FISHING FLEET* • *Fisher-men's Terminal. GETTING THERE: Take Elliott Avenue northwest from downtown, blend onto 15th Avenue West and take West Emerson exit just before 15th crosses the Ballard Bridge.*

This is home to the West Coast's largest commercial fishing fleet with more than 700 boats. For a great shot of this great flotilla, walk to the end of one of the docks and shoot back toward the city. Your horizon will be the thickly wooded Queen Anne Hill and Magnolia Bluff, with homes tucked among the trees. This can be a vertical or horizontal, with a medium to telephoto lens, depending on the effect you want. The light is best in the late afternoon.

9 *THE BEST SHOT OF MOUNT RAINIER* • *From the Loop Trail in Discovery Park. GETTING THERE: From downtown, follow West-lake, Nickerson and then Emerson past Fishermen's Terminal. Take a* *half right from Emerson onto Gilman Avenue West, a half left onto Government Way and follow it into the park. You can pick up the Loop Trail at the visitor center.*

Mount Rainier rivals the Space Needle as the most photographed object in Western Washington. There are dozens of great photo angles in the Seattle area and our favorite is from the coastal bluffs of Discovery Park, off the Loop Trail. This shot requires a bit of effort—a hike of more than a mile from the visitor center. (For trail details, see Chapter Twelve, page 185.) After you've followed the Loop Trail to the bluffs on the park's southwestern edge, look back over your shoulder and you'll see that great mountain, rising above tree-shrouded homes terraced into Magnolia Bluff. A crescent bay below adds a nice foreground touch and you can frame your shot in nearby trees. Use a medium range telephoto to bring the mountain up close.

10 **THE BEST SHOT OF HOMES AFLOAT** • *From Lake Union off Fairview Avenue East. GETTING THERE: Take Fairview Avenue North from downtown and follow it northeast and then north along the Lake Union shoreline. Staying close to the lake, fork left onto Fairview Avenue East.*

Just like Tom Hanks in *Sleepless in Seattle*, scores of folks live in elaborate floating homes, mostly on the shores of Lake Union and Lake Washington. Understandably, they don't like to be gawked at by tourists; signs posted on many of their private piers proclaim "absolutely no soliciting, sightseeing or picture taking." However, there are a couple of places along the Fairview Avenue East floating home community where you can get non-intrusive photos. To get there, just keep wrapping around the east side of Lake Union on Fairview, which becomes a narrow lane opposite a floating home section between Newton and Lynn streets. Immediately south of the corner of Fairview and East Boston Street, you'll see a break in shoreside foliage where you can get a clear shot of a dockfull of houseboats, with the Aurora Bridge and Queen Anne Hill beyond. This is best as a horizontal shot, using a normal lens. Another nice view, with a similar format, offers a row of houseboats with the city skyline in the background. To reach it, continue along Fairview for a couple of blocks until you see tiny Lynn Street Park, with a couple of picnic tables. Stand atop one of these tables—providing it's not occupied—and you'll have sufficient clearance to get the Space Needle and several highrises above the rooflines of the floating homes. For a suggested walk through this area, see Chapter Twelve, page 185.

✧ ✧ ✧ ✧

Live within your income, even if you have to borrow money to do so.
— **Josh Billings**

Chapter eleven

CREDIT CARD CORRUPTION
SHOPPING UNTIL YOU'RE DROPPING

While Seattle has the usual ration of suburban malls—including some of the largest complexes in the entire Northwest—most of its finest shopping is downtown. The ongoing development of new shopping centers, both above ground and below, has reversed the suburban retail flight that many cities have suffered in recent decades.

With the development of such venues as Pacific Place, City Centre, Westlake Center and Rainier Square, Seattle rivals San Francisco as one of the most lively and appealing city centers west of the Rockies.

THE TEN BEST MALLS & SHOPPING AREAS

Most of our selections are malls and most Seattle malls—out of respect for winter weather—are covered. These are great places for spending rainy days.

1 *PACIFIC PLACE* • *600 Pine St.; (206) 405-2655. (WEB SITE: www.pacificplaceseattle.com) Most stores open Monday-Saturday 9:30 to 9 and Sunday 11 to 6. GETTING THERE: The complex is downtown, rimmed by Pine Street, Olive Way and Sixth and Seventh avenues.*

Need a $10,000 bauble for your significant other, some designer kitchenware or a solid brass light switch? Pacific Place is Seattle's most upscale shopping complex, featuring stores such as Tiffany, Williams-Sonoma, Ann Taylor and Cartier. Restoration Hardware is a kind of Sharper Image for homemakers, offering stylish decorator items, creative kitchenware and designer switchplates. The humbly-named Pottery Barn is in fact an upscale interior decorator store, and Pacific Place houses downtown's largest bookstore, a two-level Barnes and Noble. Dozens of boutiques and specialty shops occupy four levels, topped by an imposing fan-shaped skylight. The complex also is home to several trendy restaurants, including Il Fornaio, Gordon Biersch Brewery, Stars Bar and Café, and a handsome Southwest style café called Desert Fire.

2 *BELLEVUE SQUARE* • *NE Eighth Street and Bellevue Way NE, Bellevue; (206) 454-8096. Most stores open Monday-Saturday 9:30 to 9:30 and Sunday 11 to 7. GETTING THERE: Take the Evergreen Point Floating Bridge east to Bellevue, go south on I-405, then take NE Eighth St. (exit 13) west about half a mile.*

Bustling Bellevue, with a downtown core rivaling that of Seattle in style if not in height, has one of King County's most appealing shopping complexes. The covered, two-tiered Bellevue Square is a pleasing space with potted plants, atrium skylights and suspended walkways. A modernistic three-story clock tower above the information desk is a striking focal point. The mall has more than 200 shops and restaurants, anchored by the Bon Marché, JCPenny and Nordstrom. Nearly all of the center's parking is covered—something to keep in mind on a rainy day. The mall also is home to the **Bellevue Art Museum;** (206) 454-3322. When we last visited, its exhibits we were foolish examples of alleged modern art—things like a video of a hand squishing someone's face out of shape, and a mosaic of life-sized men's and women's restroom logos.

3 *CITY CENTRE* • *1420 Fifth Ave.; (206) 622-6465. (WEB SITE: www.seattlecitycentre.com) GETTING THERE: This shopping complex is downtown, rimmed by Fifth and Sixth avenues and Pike and Union streets.*

Decidedly upscale City Centre occupies three floors of the US Bank Centre building in the heart of downtown. It has only about twenty-five shops and restaurants and they're mostly high end places such as Barney's New York men's wear, Boutique Europa, Europa for Men, and Lawrence Anthony. Art works—stunning hand blown glass when we last visited—line corridors and balconies and some are for sale in the adjacent Foster-White Gallery. A large wedge of the complex is occupied by the wonderful FAO Schwarz toy store; see below. The stylish Palomino Café, a designer's vision of warm colors, hanging garlic garlands, glass sconces and potted palms, is spread about much of the Third floor; it serves Italian-Mediterranean fare for lunch and dinner. Also on that floor is City Centre Cinema, with two large screens; see Chapter Eight, page 137. City Centre's main entry off Fifth is particularly striking, with a zodiac globe suspended within a teardrop framework, hanging from the three- story atrium ceiling.

4 NORDSTROM • *Fifth and Pine downtown; (206) 628-2111. Monday-Saturday 9:30 to 9, Sunday 11 to 7.*

Although it's an individual store, Nordstrom's flagship is large enough to be a shopping center, with five floors covering nearly a full city block. In addition to a full range of merchandise, it offers valet parking service, a spa, a cocktail bar, café, sidewalk espresso bar and even a shoe shine stand. A pianist tinkles on a Steinway on the main floor, between jewelry and women's shoes. A skybridge connects Nordsrom to Pacific Place across Sixth Avenue. The Nordstrom chain was founded by John W. Nordstrom, a Klondike miner who used his gold diggin's to establish a shoe store in Seattle at the turn of the last century.

5 NORTHGATE MALL • *Northgate exit from I-5; (206) 362-4777. Most stores open Monday-Saturday 10 to 9:30 and Sunday 11 to 6. GETTING THERE: The mall is about seven miles north of downtown on the east side of I-5; take Northgate Way exit 173.*

Although it doesn't look its age—thanks to a recent facelift—Northgate was the first covered shopping mall in the country, established in 1950. Apparently, designers then felt that longer was better because this single-level mall is more than a quarter of a mile in length! This offers a couple of advantages. Because of its long-slender layout, it's easy to find your way around. And if rain prevents you from getting your daily workout, you can log several miles by striding mall's main corridor a few times. Northgate has the usual anchors—Bon Marché, JC Penny and Nordstrom, plus more than a hundred other shops and cafés. It also has one of the largest food courts in the Northwest, with a lengthy list of takeouts that includes Baskin- Robbins, Panda Express Chinese food, Sbarro Taco Time, Kid Valley hamburgers, Ivar's Seafood Bar, the Great Steak and Potato Company, Edo Japanese fare, Starbucks coffee and Taso's Euro Deli.

6 PIKE PLACE MARKET • *At the foot of Pike Street; (206) 697-4879. Information booth/ticket agency (206) 682-7453. (WEB SITE: www.pikeplacemarket.org) GETTING THERE: As if you didn't know by now, it's at the foot of Pike Street, between Virginia and Union streets.*

We've already praised Pike Place Market as Seattle's most interesting attraction in Chapter Two. It's also a fine place to shop, and we don't mean just for tomatoes and tourist curios. There is of course the great array of produce and fish stands although the latter are practical only if you have the means to cook a just-off-the-boat halibut. More appealing to visitors are the dozens of arts and craft stalls and three levels of assorted shops in the main marketplace. They include shops offering antiques and collectibles, used books and records, specialty foods and of course, lots of curios. More shops and cafés are in the Sanitary Public Market across the way and still more are in Post Alley, which angles uphill from the main market. Don't overlook the grand DeLaurenti Italian specialty store just south of the main market, which we praise below, under specialty stores. If you have the energy for the Pike Hillclimb, you'll find yet another group of shops terraced into the slope below the main market, between Alaskan Way and Western Avenue. While down there, don't miss the Iberian specialty store Spanish Table on Western, which we also list below.

7 RAINIER SQUARE • *A downtown block rimmed by Fourth and Fifth avenues and Union and University streets; (206) 628-5050. Various store hours.*

Not exactly a shopping center, Rainier Square is a merchants' association with a large assortment of shops, boutiques and cafés terraced along balconies, at ground level and beneath the streets. One subterranean section stretches a full city block, emerging at Union Square on Sixth Avenue near the Seattle Hilton. This corridor's walls are lined with historic photos and other exhibits; see "The Ten Best overlooked attractions" in Chapter Two, page 64.

8 SOUTHCENTER MALL • *Southcenter exit from I-5; (206) 246-7400. (WEB SITE: www.shopyourmall.com) Most stores open 10 to 9:30 Monday-Saturday and 11 to 7 Sunday. GETTING THERE: The mall is about eleven miles south of downtown on the east side of I-5; take exit 154-B to Southcenter Boulevard.*

One of Washington's largest enclosed malls, Southcenter has more than 150 shops and restaurants, anchored by JCPenny, Bon Marché, Sears and Mervyn's. Its wide corridors are lined with more than a score of specialty kiosks, and a large food court under a greenhouse roof offers fifteen fast food venues, serving everything from corn dogs to tacos. The facility is surrounded by smaller strip malls, free-standing stores and office complexes in the fast-growing Seattle suburb of Tuckwila-Renton. In fact, there are so many satellite businesses that a newcomer may find it difficult to locate the central mall. It fronts on Tukwila Parkway, rimmed Southcenter Parkway, Strader Boulevard and Andover Park West.

9 *UNIVERSITY VILLAGE* • *Just north of the University of Washington campus at 25th Avenue NE and NE 45th Street. Most stores open Monday-Saturday 9:30 to 9 and Sunday 11 to 6. GETTING THERE: The center is in northeast Seattle. Take I-5 north, go briefly east on Freeway 520, then exit north onto Montlake Boulevard, which goes through the heart of the University of Washington campus. Take a double left turn onto 25th Avenue NE, continue north briefly and the shopping center is on your right.*

Unlike most area malls, University Village is open to Seattle's sometimes blue skies. However, in deference to the sometimes drippy weather, some of the walkways are covered with attractive sail-like fabric tarps. This is a large and attractive complex with more than a hundred stores, shops and restaurants. Plazas and fountain courtyards offer inviting places to pause. Among its major stores are the largest Barnes & Noble on the West Coast; see below.

10 *WESTLAKE CENTER* • *Pine Street between Fourth and Fifth avenues downtown; (206) 467-3044. Most stores open weekdays 9:30 to 9, Saturday 9:30 to 8 and Sunday 11 to 6.*

In the heart of downtown Seattle, Westlake Center has more than seventy shops and cafés, on a main floor and terraced above on three balcony levels. It has a food court on the top level with an outdoor balcony, and direct access the monorail that runs between downtown and Seattle Center.

THE TEN BEST SPECIALTY STORES

Since these stores aren't related, not even by marriage or merger, they're listed in no particular order, except for REI, which is our favorite store of any sort and thus earns a top spot.

1 *THE BEST PLACE FOR OUTDOOR TYPES: REI* • *222 Yale Ave. North; (206) 223-1944. (WEB SITE: www.rei.com) Weekdays 10 to 9, Saturday 9 to 7 and Sunday 11 to 6. GETTING THERE: This outdoor mecca is at the corner of Yale and John Street. Head east from downtown on Denny way and—just short of I-5—turn left on Minor Avenue, go a block to John and turn right.*

Not only is REI the Northwest's largest outdoor store, it's Seattle's most imposing retail outlet, with a cascading waterfall and mini-woodland out front, and a 65-foot climbing structure inside a glass tower. The store's interior is imposing as well, done in natural woods with a huge fieldstone fireplace on the main floor and a comfortable lounge on the second deck. Are you into the great outdoors? This place has it all—camping, hiking, climbing, cycling, skiing and boating gear. Check out the latest kayaks, crawl into backpacking tents, test a mountain bike on a small track or hike a rocky mini-slope to get the feel of a pair of hiking books. You'll find departments for outdoor wear, books and magazines and even an art gallery. There's so much neat stuff here that—if you're an outdoor type—you almost hope there's something you need. If this largess works up an appetite, there's a World Wrapps café upstairs, offering light fare and imposing views of the Seattle skyline.

2 THE BEST PLACE TO BUY A PIECE OF WASHINGTON:
Made in Washington • *At Westlake Center on Pine Street between Fourth and Fifth avenues; (206) 623-9753. Weekdays 9 to 9, Saturday 9:30 to 8 and Sunday 11 to 6. Other stores are located elsewhere in the Puget Sound area.*

This is no tacky souvenir shop. Made in Washington features works by area artists, local specialty foods, smoked salmon gift packs and such. You can get free nibbles of the state's famous Aplets and Cotlets and buy boxes to take home.

3 THE BEST ANTIQUE SHOP: Pioneer Square Mall • *The corner of First Avenue, James Street and Yesler Way; (206) 624-1164. Monday-Saturday 10:30 to 5:30 and Sunday noon to 5. GETTING THERE: The mall is on the north side of Pioneer Square, near the wedge-like Pioneer Place park.*

We noted earlier in this book that the street level of Pioneer Square was elevated as a buffer against high tides and to improve drainage, and an elaborate labyrinth of rooms and corridors still exists beneath the streets. Pioneer Square Mall is tucked into this labyrinth, with eighty dealers in a dozen interlinked rooms covering more than 6,000 square feet. Even if you aren't an antiquer, you'll enjoy strolling this busy grotto of collectibles, browsing from one room to the next. You could almost get lost down here, although a friendly staffer will keep you on course.

4 THE BEST PLACE FOR ATHLETIC TYPES: Nike Town
• *1500 Sixth Ave.; (206) 447-6453. Weekdays 9:30 to 10, 9:30 to 7 Saturday and 11 to 6 Sunday. GETTING THERE: Nike Town is downtown, at the corner of Sixth Avenue and Pine Street.*

While not as elaborate as the flagship store in Portland, Seattle's version of Nike Town is still the best place in the state to buy sports gear. Spread over two floors, it's busy with sports videos, high tech design and mega-posters of leading jocks. You'll find mens, womens and kids departments for everything from basketball and soccer to conditioning regalia and golfing gear. And of course, there's an abundance of designer athletic shoes that made this Oregon firm famous.

5 *THE BEST BOOKSTORES • Elliott Bay Book Company (624-6600) and the University Village Barnes & Noble (517-4107). GETTING THERE: Elliott Bay is in Pioneer Square at 101 Main St., (corner of First Avenue). This Barnes and Noble is in the University Village shopping center just north of the University of Washington campus at 25th Avenue NE and NE 45th Street.*

We couldn't decide between these two, so we chose both. Elliott Bay is the best independent book store in Seattle, installed in an old brick building with three levels of new and used books, plus a cellar café. It's a fine place to find whatever's current, plus assorted used book treasures. We particularly like the Travel Loft with a fine selection of travel books. Elliott Bay is a great browsing place, particularly at the café where you can pull a used book from a shelve and read as you nosh. (Patrons are asked not to bring unpurchased books from other areas.)

University Village is home to the largest Barnes and Noble on the West Coast—a huge two-story facility with hundreds of thousands of titles, a comfortable café and a large CD and music department. It also is a place that lends itself to browsing, with lots of overstuffed chairs and an occasional couch. (Time for an ego-feeding frenzy: When we last checked, both stores carried a good selection of our Pine Cone Press titles.)

6 *THE BEST KIDS' STORE: FAO Schwarz • Sixth Avenue at Pine Street downtown; (206) 624-7711. Open daily; Major credit cards.*

You're greeted by a three-story tower of toys as you step into this kids wonderland. Say hello to the talking dinosaur, the conversational tree and a growling lion. Browse among hundreds of stuffed critters—some larger than their real-life counterparts. The toy selection ranges from old fashioned table games to the latest high tech gadgets. A pedestrian bridge across the mezzanine level is a keyboard; with a proper hop-skip-and-jump, you might be able to play "Chopsticks."

7 *THE BEST WINE SHOP: Seattle Cellars, Ltd. • 2505 Second Ave.; (206) 256-0850. Monday-Saturday 11 to 7. GETTING THERE: It's just north of the downtown area on the edge of Belltown.*

This is a serious place for wine lovers, with large selections from the Northwest, California and around the globe. Tastings are conducted every Thursday and at various other times, perhaps to herald the arrival of an interesting vintage. And if you're a wine collector lives in the area and find it impractical to dig a *chai* beneath your house, you can rent temperature and humidity controlled storage space.

8 **THE BEST SUPERMARKET CHAIN: QFC** • *Quality Food Stores main office is in Bellevue; (425) 455-3761.*

Most outlets of this Washington-based supermarket chain are *huge*—virtual self-contained shopping centers. In addition to large grocery departments, they generally have deli counters with take-out foods, sit-down cafés, bakeries, pharmacies and even bank outlets. With wide aisles and large selections, they're among the most appealing supermarkets we've encountered.

9 **THE BEST SPECIALTY FOOD STORE: DeLaurenti** • *1435 First Ave.; (206) 622-0141. GETTING THERE: It's in the south end of Pike Place Market.*

Now, *that's* Italian! This large, rambling market just south of Pike Place Market is one large celebration of Italian gastronomy. Wander its narrow aisles piled high with pastas, an amazing assortment of olive oils and prepared olives and specialty foods that you never knew existed. A huge deli complex features all sorts, sausages, cheeses, salads and freshly made pastas. You can get a proper caffé latte at a coffee bar and all sorts of diet-destroying savories at a large bakery. The complex also has a small café and a pizza takeout. A huge wine department features a good selection of Italian *vino*, plus hundreds of choices from the Northwest, California and the rest of the wine world.

10 **THE BEST IBERIAN SPECIALTY STORE: The Spanish Table** • *1427 Western Ave.; (206) 682-2827. Monday-Saturday 9:30 to 6 and Sunday 11 to 6. MC/VISA. GETTING THERE: This Iberian outlet is just below Pike Place Market.*

What on earth is an Iberian specialty store? Iberia is the peninsula occupied by Spain and Portugal and the "Table" is a two-level shop and café dedicated almost exclusively to its food, wines, tableware, music and culture. For a light snack, you can pick up a bowl of *gaspacho*, a Spanish-inspired salad or a chorizo and cheese sandwich and dine among the specialty foods on the upper level, or adjourn to an adjacent patio. The downstairs section is busy with more than 200 varieties of Portuguese and Spanish wines (including some great ports), Iberian music on CDs and tapes (from flamenco to that sorrowful *fado* sound), cookbooks, Spanish language books, specialty foods and the utensils with which to prepare them.

The only way to keep your health is to eat what you don't want, drink what you don't like and do what you'd rather not. — **Mark Twain**

Chapter twelve

GETTING PHYSICAL
THE BEST PLACES TO WORK OFF THAT MOCHA

Seattle is a rather hilly city, so some of our Ten Best walking routes tend to be hike routes. Even a stroll through downtown is rather vertical. On the other hand, most of our suggested bike routes are single-gear affairs because they tend to follow scenic waterfronts.

A couple of good reference books, from which we borrowed a few ideas for our walking and cycling routes are *Seattle City Walks* by Laura Karlinsey and published by Sasquatch Books; and *Short Bike Rides: Western Washington* by Judy Wagonfeld, published by Globe Pequot Press. Both are available at most Seattle area bookstores.

THE TEN BEST HIKE ROUTES

Our favorite Seattle walk begins at Pike Place Market and covers the waterfront—at least the area that appeals to visitors. Although much of Seattle is hilly, as we just noted above, this is a relatively level walk, with a gradual incline as you complete your loop back to the market.

1 PIKE PLACE TO PIONEER SQUARE ● *From Pike Place Market south along the waterfront to lower Pioneer Square and back. Mostly level with a gradual incline on the return leg, ending with a steep stair climb; about two miles. GETTING THERE: Start at Pike Place Market at the foot of Pike Street.*

This is a great Seattle sampler stroll, taking you through the labyrinthian Pike Place Market and then along its historic waterfront to Pioneer Square. There is much to see and many places to pause so plan most of a morning even though it's only about two miles. And we say "morning" because that's when you should begin—with breakfast at Pike Place Market. And get there early before our two favorite breakfast cafés, the Athenian and Lowell's fill up.

Begin your stroll at the Pike Place Market information booth. It won't be open in the morning (hours are noon to 6 Tuesday-Sunday), although you can pick up a free copy of the *Pike Place Market News* with a map in the centerfold. You'll find a stack beside the booth. From there, follow a set of bronze pig tracks to Rachel, the giant piggy bank that has become the market's mascot. Enter the main market building, turn right into the market's **North Arcade** and—if you need breakfast—stop at either the **Athenian** or **Lowell's**. Both offer Elliott Bay views and early breakfasts.

From there, continue along the market's north wing, past a friendly gauntlet of hawkers selling produce, fish, flowers and crafts. If you like things spicy, pause at **Mick's Peppourri,** where you can sample a variety of hot pepper and garlic jellies and garnishes. Continue through the North Arcade, passing a large garment and clothing section on your left and flower stalls on your right. You'll pop out the lower end, where artisans and crafts people display their wares on sidewalk stalls. (Being artistic types, many are late risers who don't generally start setting up until 8 or 9 a.m.)

From here, go left across the intersection of Virginia Street and Western Avenue at to **Victor Steinbrueck Park.** It starts as a grassy slope and then cleverly extends across the roof of a parking structure, where you'll get a fine view of Elliott Sound and—on a clear day—the distant Olympic Range. Walk back across Western Avenue and the rough brick Pike Place Market Street (they merge here) and stroll south beneath a sidewalk overhang, passing more shops, boutiques and international cafés opposite the main market. At mid-block—1912 Pike Place Market Street—you'll pass the city's oldest **Starbucks** outlet. When you reach the corner of Stewart Street, savory aromas may draw you into **Le Panier French Bakery.** Continue across Stewart, passing the lush botanical displays of the **Seattle Garden Center.**

Just across Pine on Pike Place Market Street, **Mee Fum Pastries** offers walk-away potstickers, steamed pork buns and such—handy fuel for your stroll. You'll shortly encounter a place with a somewhat disconcerting name—**Sanitary Public Market.** (We should hope!) Like Pike, it's busy with produce and fish stalls, curio shops and ethnic cafés. If you're still hungry or want to assemble a lunch to go, **Three Girls Bakery** in this market builds excellent sandwiches, with an amazing selection of fillings on a good variety of breads; (206) 622-1045.

As you draw abreast of the main Pike Place Market entrance, go into reverse for half a block and then take a half right into **Post Alley.** Generally less crowded and quieter than the rest of the market, it's busy with ethnic cafés, takeouts and streetside tables. As you emerge onto Pine Street, hang a left and re-enter Pike Place Market, this time focusing your exploration on the **South Arcade.** You'll encounter more produce and fish stands and three levels of shops.

You'll eventually emerge from the market's south end, where a series of steps called the **Pike Place Hillclimb** will lead you down toward the waterfront. When you reach Western Avenue, check out the **Spanish Table,** a combination café, shop and wine cellar featuring the products of Spain and Portugal; see Chapter Eleven, page 176, for more on this interesting place. Now hike uphill a block to the **Market Heritage Center,** an outdoor museum beneath an elevated crosswalk; displays focus on Pike Place Market's history and you'll find more detail in Chapter Two, page 64.

Having thoroughly seen the market and learned about its past, return to the Spanish Table, go down a final set of Pike Market Hill Climb steps and cross Alaskan Way to **Waterfront Park** and the **Seattle Aquarium** on Pier 59; see Chapter Nine, page 151, and Chapter Two, page 43. In getting there, you'll cross the **Waterfront Streetcar Line** and you'll want to ride its old fashioned trolleys up and down the waterfront; see Chapter Two, page 59. While exploring Waterfront Park with its angular concrete fountain and its benches and picnic tables offering fine Elliott Bay vistas, note the curiously bionic statue of **Christopher Columbus** on the park's south side, toward **Fishermans Restaurant.**

Although you'll enjoy fine views of Elliott Bay on this waterfront stroll, much of the vista back toward the skyline is blocked by the ugly two-deck Alaskan Way Viaduct. San Francisco and Portland got rid of their waterfront expressways; why can't Seattle do the same?

Continuing along the waterfront, you'll pass Pier 57 with its **Bay Pavilion,** a carny-type place with a large carousel, curio shops and restaurants. Just beyond, on Pier 56, is **Elliott's Oyster House,** one of the city's better seafood restaurants, and terminals for **Argosy** harbor and dinner cruises (Chapter Two, page 56) and the **Tillicum Village Salmon Bake** at **Blake Island State Park** (Chapter Two, page 58). Pier 54, the last in this string of tourist piers is home to **Ye Olde Curiosity Shop** (Chapter Two, page 49) and **Ivar's Acres of Clams** restaurant. A bit beyond, pier 50 to 52 are occupied by the **Washington State Ferry Terminal.** Pier 52, known historically as the Coleman Dock, built by James Coleman in 1882 as city's most modern ferry terminal. Burned and rebuilt a couple of times since, this two-dock complex is "home port" of the Washington State ferry system, where you can catch—afoot or in your vehicle—ferries that fan out across Puget Sound. We discuss them in some detail in Chapter One, page 16. At Pier 50, you're at the foot of Yesler Way and the lower end of **Pioneer Square,** which we explore in the next walk.

If you choose to return to your starting point instead of doing the square, take a stairway up to an elevated pedestrian ramp on the north side of the ferry terminal. It elevates you above Alaskan Way and Western Avenue and deposits you on First Avenue. Note the fun Seattle scenes done by school children, decorating the walls of this pedestrian crossing. As you approach First Avenue, you'll pass a tempting lunch stop—**Cilantro,** an inexpensive multi-Asian restaurant.

When you hit First Avenue, turn left (north) and begin working your way back to Pike Place Market. Although your shoreline walk was level, the return trip to the market is a gradual uphill climb. A block from Marion Street, you'll pass the elegant **Alexis Hotel** on your left at First Avenue and Madison. If you didn't do lunch at **Cilantro,** consider the hotel's **Bookstore** café and bar, with seats inside and on the sidewalk. A short distance beyond, near the corner of Seneca Street is **Beans & Machines,** a particularly appealing coffee stop that also features espresso-making equipment and designer kitchen gear.

Weary of this gradual incline along First Avenue? As you approach the **Seattle Art Museum** at First and University Street (Chapter Two, page 53), turn left beside the outlandishly decorated **Wolfgang Puck Café** and begin descending the landscaped concrete terraces of the **Harbor Steps.** You'll be accompanied by a fountain that alternately gurgles on one terrace, disappears beneath the concrete and then reemerges at a lower level. If you feel the need for caffeine speed, there's a **Tully's Coffee** stop on one of the lower terraces, with a few tables and chairs out front. Around the corner is **Blazing Saddles,** where you can rent bikes with "ride boards" to keep you from getting lost; see below on page 191 and in Chapter Two, page 58.

As you reach Western on the Harbor Steps, note the mural of a leaping orca on a wall of the historic **Seattle Steam Generating Plant.** You can take either Western Avenue or Alaskan Way back to Pike Place Market. If you stay on Alaskan Way, you can do the full **Pike Place Hillclimb,** 143 steps extending up to market level. It's a good way to work up an appetite for one of the market's several cafés. If you're not up to it, you'll find an elevator near the **Market Heritage Center** on Western Avenue, leading to a high pedestrian bridge.

2 .PIONEER SQUARE ● *Just south of downtown, roughly bordered by Alaskan Way, Jackson Street, Fourth Street and Yesler Way. This walk is less than a mile, mostly level with some slight inclines. GET-*

TING THERE: First Avenue leads into the heart of the square. Or, this walk can be done as an extension of the "Pike Place Market-Waterfront Stroll" above. To do so, continue along the waterfront past the Seattle Ferry Terminal to Pier 52 (Coleman Dock) instead of looping back to Pike Place Market.

Ready for a walk into history? We've discussed the significance of Henry Yesler's sawmill, Skid Road and Pioneer Square earlier in this book. Start this walk at the base of Yesler Way at Pier 50. Look up Yesler Way—under the ugly Alaskan Way Viaduct—and try to imagine this as a muddy "skid road" where logs from the hills above were skidded down to Yesler's Mill. In fact, you're standing near Henry Yesler's mill site, which was on a waterfront pier.

Half a block up Yesler Way, you'll encounter **Pioneer Square Hotel and Saloon** at Yesler and Western Avenue, a square-shouldered brick structure dating back more than a century. A block beyond is **Pioneer Place,** a small vee-shaped park wedged by First, Yesler and James Street. Although this area has been gentrified, some of the homeless are still here. In fact their numbers have increased of late, since several have fled here from the newly Yuppified Belltown on the north side of downtown. From here, walk three blocks south along First Avenue and you'll encounter most of the cafés, saloons and shops that attract visitors to this area. This is "sidewalk café row" with four old restaurants and saloons spilling onto the sidewalk.

Hang a left onto Main and go a block up to **Klondike Gold Rush National Historical Park**; see Chapter Two, page 44. This small interpretive center is Seattle's part of the historic park that also has elements in Skagway, Alaska, and Dawson City, Yukon Territory, where gold was discovered toward the end of the nineteenth century. Just beyond the interpretive center, the former Occidental Street running between First and Second avenues is now pleasantly landscaped and traffic-free **Occidental Mall.** At the corner of Occidental and Main, note the dramatic **Seattle Fallen Firefighter' Memorial**—four bronze figures of firemen in action. Before strolling the pedestrian way, walk a block uphill on Main to **Waterfall Garden Park,** an appealing little enclave built by United Parcel Service to mark the site of its founding; Chapter Two, page 65.

Return to Occidental Mall and go north. After a block, it expands into **Occidental Park,** site of summer concerts and other special functions. Continue another block to Yesler Way, turn right and hike a block uphill to **Smith Tower** at the corner of Yesler and Second Avenue. Built in 1914, this 500-foot brick skyrise was the tallest building west of the Mississippi until 1959. An elevator runs to an observation floor at the top for imposing city views; see Chapter Two, page 49. From the tower, follow Second Avenue Extension four blocks south to the bold and brick **Union Station,** which was being renovated at this writing into a shopping and dining complex. It may have been accomplished by the time you arrive.

Just beyond, you'll see the new **Safeco Field,** home of the Seattle Mariners baseball team, with its curious steel-girder sliding roof and—either under construction or finished by the time you arrive—the home of the **Seattle Seahawks** football team; it's due for completion in 2002. A block above Union Station at Fifth Avenue and Jackson is a regional transit station and terminal for the jolly old trolleys of the **Waterfront Streetcar** line. Catch one of the cars for a ride along the waterfront, or stroll down Jackson to Alaskan Way and go north to your starting point. Along the way you'll pass the **Washington Street Public Boat Landing** near the spot where Henry Yesler built his waterfront sawmill. It has a nineteenth century look with wrought iron grillwork and old fashioned park benches.

3 *NORTH WATERFRONT* • *Pike Place Market north to Elliott Bay Marina. Completely level; about six miles round trip.*

If you want to cover all of the waterfront, take this walk in addition to the Pike Place to Pioneer Square stroll. It's thrice as long and thus more ambitious. However, you'll be rewarded with great views, a fine new maritime museum and a neat place to have lunch with a view. This also can be done in reverse, starting at Elliott Bay Marina, which offers the advantage of free parking. Of course, this will require you to read the following paragraphs backward.

Head north from Pike Place Market, either staying close to the waterfront on a broad Alaskan Way sidewalk, or following a pedestrian/biking path alongside the **Waterfront Streetcar** tracks. After a few blocks, you'll encounter the **World Trade Center** and **Bell Street Pier,** home to the fine new **Odyssey Maritime Discovery Center**; see Chapter Two, page 52. For a grand waterfront and skyline view, step into the foyer of the Bell Street International Conference Center and take an elevator up to the Bell Street Pier Roof Plaza, a grand little urban park missed by most visitors.

Pressing onward, you'll pass the **Edgewater,** the only harborside hotel in Seattle and one of the few in America built onto a pier. Beyond that, at Pier 69, is the dock for the **Victoria Clipper** that offers high-speed cruises to Victoria and the San Juan Islands; see Chapter Two, page 56.

Historic Pier 70, the old **Ainsworth and Dunne Wharf** comes up next. It may or may not be a new waterfront shopping complex by the time you arrive. It's conversion to a mall a year behind schedule when we last strolled past. Across the street is the terminus of the **Waterfront Streetcar** and its old fashioned car barn. Alaskan Way curves away from the waterfront here to become eastbound Broad Street, headed into **Seattle Center.** You can follow it and visit the **Space Needle** and **Pacific Science Center,** although that's not the direction of our walking route. Walk through a parking lot beside the streetcar barn and you'll pick up the Elliott Bay Waterfront walking/biking trail as you enter the long and slender green strip of **Myr-tle Edwards Park.** The path has separate strips for bikes and walk-ers, cleverly marked "all wheels" and "all heels" in some areas. Watch on your left for a silly assemblage of huge stones and concrete slabs that's supposed to be a piece of public art; we insult it in more detail in Chapter Thirteen, page 214. Just beyond, Myrtle Edwards Park blends seamlessly into **Elliott Bay Park,** where you'll approach the towering **Seattle Grain Terminal.** A sign advises you that this massive facil-ity is capable of holding 4.2 million bushels of grain, and other statisti-cal trivia. A bit beyond is the **Elliott Bay Fishing Pier.** This small public dock is popular with local fisherfolk. If you want to drop in a line but don't have one, you can rent everything you need from **Happy Hooker Bait and Tackle Shop** in front of the pier. It also sells drinks and light snacks. Even if your luck is bad, you'll enjoy great views back at the city skyline, and there are shelters on the pier in case it rains.

The walking/biking path emerges from the north end of long and skinny Elliott Bay Park and does a 90-degree right turn to skirt the edge of **Smith Cove,** a deep inlet containing cargo piers 90 and 91. The route will take you onto West Galer Street, and you'll see a sign here indicating the **Pier 91 Bike Trail.** It curves around the perime-ter of a large port and industrial area, and we suggest it in our water-front bike trail below. However, it involves a mile-and-a-half detour through an area that's not very interesting, so it probably isn't worth the walk.

Instead, follow Galer to Elliott Avenue, go left briefly, then go left again onto the **Garfield Street-Magnolia Bridge.** This is a viaduct over the industrial area, with a nice wide sidewalk on the bay side. Look down to the pier as you cross the viaduct and you may see great ranks of Japanese-made cars, offloaded from ships and are awaiting distribution. Your sidewalk route drops down to 23rd Avenue West; do a left turn and stroll into **Elliott Bay Marina,** your turnaround point. As you walk toward the marina parking area, you'll pass the en-trance to cute little **Smith Cove Park** on your left. Since it's three miles from Elliott Bay Marina back to your starting point, you might want to take a lunch or at least an ice tea break at **Maggie Bluffs,** a casual café with indoor and outdoor tables that offer nice views through the marina to the city skyline; see Chapter Four, page 94. A bit more flossy and offering even better views is the second-floor **Pali-sade,** reviewed in Chapter Three, page 71.

4 **BEACON HILL** • *Beacon Avenue, from Columbian Way south to Barton Street. Mostly level with some gentle inclines; about six miles round trip. GETTING THERE: Head south from Seattle on I-5, take Co-lumbian Way exit and go south and then southeast to Beacon Avenue. (Columbian Way merges with 15th Avenue South for a few blocks.)*

Beacon Avenue follows a ridgeline through the Beacon Hill neighborhood southeast of Seattle, and a walking path meanders down its wide, landscaped median strip for three miles. Strolling along, isolated from traffic, you'll catch frequent glimpses of Boeing Field, Elliott Bay and the distant Olympic Mountains to the west and—on occasion—vistas of the snowcapped Cascades to the east.

To begin, drive to the intersection of Columbian Way and Beacon Avenue, where you'll find unlimited parking in the Beacon median strip. The path heads south from here, lazily curving from one side of the landscaped boulevard strip to the other. The route takes you through a pleasant tree-shaded middle class neighborhood. Your turnaround point is South Barton Street, where the center median ends and Beacon blends into 39th Avenue South.

This also works well as a bike route, and you can venture down cross streets for improved views of the Olympics, Boeing Field and the Cascades.

5 QUEEN ANNE HILL • *From Eighth Place West to West View Drive. About two miles round trip, mostly level, with one steep downgrade and—of course—an upgrade on the return. GETTING THERE: From the Seattle Center area, go north on First Avenue for about ten blocks, turn west (left) onto Prospect and follow it to Seventh Avenue West. Take a brief half right to the intersection of Eighth Place and Highland Drive.*

The lucky residents of Queen Anne Hill enjoy the best views, and their homes block the vistas from those of us strolling or driving through the area. However, sections of Seventh and Eighth avenues on Queen Anne's western bluff are terraced above steep slopes. Sections of sidewalk lined with decorative low walls provide nice places for enjoying the views while strolling past upscale homes.

Begin by parking at the busy merger of Highland Drive, Seventh Avenue West and Eighth Place West. On the east side of the intersection is Parson Memorial Garden, a lush botanical jungle of mixed trees, flowering bushes and trailing vines. Take time to stroll its cobblestone paths and perhaps pause on a shady bench. From here, cross Eighth Place to tiny Marshall Viewpoint Park, with more benches and some interesting mosaic patterns embedded in the concrete path. Now, head north on Eighth Place, enjoying layered vistas of the Garfield Street-Magnolia Bridge, Smith Cove, Elliott Bay Marina, Magnolia Bluff and across Puget Sound to the snowcapped Olympics.

The route soon merges into Eighth Avenue West, flanked by elegant homes with cascading front lawns on the right and that great Puget Sound view on the left. After about a third of a mile, the route swings to the right, briefly becoming West Blaine Street. Turn left onto Seventh Avenue and, after a block, you'll again pick up a terraced sidewalk offering fine vistas. After two blocks, go left and downhill on

Crockett Street, then turn right on Eleventh. Follow it a block north—you'll lose the view to a row of tightly packed cottages—then take a half right onto Sound View Terrace, where the vistas open up again. Continue a couple of more blocks to West View Drive, then turn around and return to your starting point.

6 *DISCOVERY PARK LOOP* • *From Discovery Park Visitor Center on Magnolia Bluff northeast of downtown. Just under three miles, mostly level with a few modest elevation changes. GETTING THERE: From downtown, go northwest about 1.5 miles on Elliott Avenue, then north another 1.5 on Fifteenth Avenue West. Turn left onto West Emerson near Fishermen's Terminal, go right onto Gilman Avenue West, fork left onto Government Way and follow it into the park. The visitor center comes up shortly, on your left.*

Seattle's largest park, occupying 513 acres of a former hilltop military installation, offers some of the city's finest hiking areas. The main Loop Trail winds through the heart of the park, with spur trails leading to breezy beaches and wooded glens. A map available for a small fee at the visitor center will keep you on course. Start your walk just behind the center, heading south on a slight upgrade through a thin stand of trees. You'll curve westward, pass the South Parking Lot, then emerge into a meadow area. Less than half a mile beyond, the trail follows a steep coastal bluff, offering fine views across Puget Sound to Bainbridge Island and the Olympic Peninsula. Look back over your shoulder and you'll catch vistas of Magnolia Bluff and distant Mount Rainier.

Shortly after you leave the bluff, you can fork to the left and follow a three-quarter-mile trail down to the beach and the West Point Lighthouse. Beyond the trail junction, the main route wraps around the edge of a military housing complex, and then enters a virtual rainforest of thick ferns and moss-clad trees. After a mile of this thick woodland, you'll cross under the main road and return to the visitor center.

7 *FLOATING HOMES STROLL* • *Fairview Avenue east on the eastern shore of Lake Union. This is a brief walk of about a mile, all level. GETTING THERE: Take Fairview Avenue north from downtown, then follow it northeast and then north along the eastern shore of Lake Union shoreline.*

As we noted in Chapter Ten (Ten Best photo angles), several dozen floating homes are tucked into enclaves along the shores of Lake Union and Lake Washington. Without being too intrusive—these folks don't like being regarded as tourist attractions—you can stroll along Fairview Avenue east and see a large flotilla of these houseboats. They come in all shapes and sizes and most are quite charming, with nautical decor, planter boxes on small decks and even a few potted trees. Virtually all of them have boats parked alongside. Some of these floating homes are quite elaborate; we noted one with a two-story atrium ceiling in the living room that must have offered grand views of the Seattle skyline across Lake Union. (If you'd like to enjoy the good life on the water, look for signs along Fairview Avenue advertising rentals.)

To begin your houseboat haven stroll, drive around Lake Union's eastern shore and turn from Fairview Avenue North onto Fairview Avenue East, which becomes a narrow lane. Park and walk north along Fairmont (trying not to look like a tourist.) You can peer down docks at dozens of these cute little floating homes; please respect the residents' privacy. After a couple of blocks, you'll encounter tiny Lynn Street Park at the foot of Lynn Street, where you can perch at a picnic tables and enjoy a clear view of several houseboats, with the city skyline in the background. Continuing northward, you'll see another postage stamp preserve called Roanoke Street Mini-park at Fairview and Roanoke. Vistas across Lake Union are quite pleasing and you'll encounter another cluster of houseboats just beyond this point.

Stroll uphill for about two blocks of Roanoke, go left onto Eastlake for another two blocks, and then left again on Hamlin Street to another section of Fairview. You'll find another small cluster of houseboats. There are mostly marinas and waterside industries beyond, so this is a logical turnaround point.

8 *GREEN LAKE LOOP* • *A 2.8-mile loop around Green Lake with an optional three-mile round trip extension on Ravenna Boulevard. Mostly level, with some hill climbing on Ravenna. GETTING THERE: Follow I-5 north from downtown, take exit 170 north to Ravenna Boulevard, go left (northwest) under the freeway and the park is within a quarter of a mile.*

Don't plan on a lonely stroll around Green Lake. It's one of the most popular public parks in the entire state, getting about a million visitors a year. It is a pleasant stroll, however, and it's fun to watch the passing parade of cyclists, rollerbladers and skaters. You won't tangle with the faster traffic, since there's a separate lane for cyclists and even a separate sandy path for walkers.

The first part of this walk doesn't require much instruction. Just find a place to park, cross through the park to the lake and keep walking until you return to your starting point. From here, you might enjoy strolling through the adjacent Green Lake neighborhood with its small cafés, espresso stops, shops and book stores. Most are along Green Lake Drive.

As an option, you can head southeast on Green Lake Drive and blend onto Ravenna Boulevard near NE 71st Street. This almost duplicates our University Village to Green Lake bike route below, except that this one ends in Ravenna Park. You'll start climbing uphill shortly after leaving Green Lake, and enter a fine old of neighborhood of elegant homes shaded by ancient trees. Note that there's a separate bike route on the boulevard's landscaped median. Several blocks after you pass under the I-5 freeway, as your route begins to level, you'll reach small **Cowen Park.** Go left from Ravenna Boulevard onto Cowen place (opposite the 1924 Park Vista apartment) and stroll into the park. You'll pick up a walking path and enter a ferny woodland that seems completely remote from the busy residential area. Following the path, you'll pick up Ravenna Creek and shortly enter **Ravenna Park.**

If you continue through this larger park, you'll eventually exit at Ravenna Boulevard, near NE 55th Street. You can loop back through the park or follow the nicely landscaped Ravenna Boulevard back to Green Lake.

9 *CAPITOL HILL • Volunteer Park to Broadway. Level with a few gentle grades; about three to six miles, depending on how far you walk along Broadway. GETTING THERE: The starting point is the Seattle Asian Art Museum in the park. To get there, take Olive Way or Madison Street northeast, go left (north) on Fifteenth Avenue East, left again onto East Prospect at the edge of the park, and then right to the museum.*

You can begin this walk indoors, by strolling among the fine exhibits of the **Seattle Asian Art Museum** if you haven't already done so. Then step outside and take a leisurely loop around an old reservoir in front of the museum. At the lower end, you'll get some nice views of downtown Seattle, although they're mostly blocked by trees.

Head north from the museum on the park loop road or adjacent forest paths to the Victorian style **Volunteer Park Conservatory,** styled after the Crystal Palace in London and recently given a new face-lift. Step inside and stroll through this tropical haven under glass, with a large orchid collection, thousands of flowering plants and tropical trees. From here, head east (right) following a road out of the park to East Galer Street. A block after you've left the park, turn north (left) onto 16th Avenue East and begin a leisurely ramble past some of Seattle's most opulent mansions.

Our walking route will basically wrap you around the northern end of the park. From 16th Avenue, jog a block west on East Garfield to 15th Avenue, then walk north to small **Louisa Boren Park,** which offers splendid views of Lake Washington and the University of Washington campus. Across the way is **Lakeview Cemetery**, final resting place Seattle's founding Denny family and two more contemporary personalities, martial arts expert and actor Bruce Lee and his son Brandon. From here, follow 15th north to East Howe Street and go left (west) past the **Grand Army of the Republic Cemetery.**

Two blocks past the cemetery, turn south onto Federal Avenue East, follow it two long blocks to East Garfield and turn right, shifting over to Tenth Avenue East. Follow this south past more elegant homes, then go west on East Highland Drive on block to the top of Broadway. On your right is a massive stone mansion that once belonged to **Sam**

Hill, one of the most colorful characters in the history of the Northwest. Son-in-law of a railroad baron, he built the Columbia Gorge Scenic Highway in Oregon, and a replica of Stonehenge above the Columbia River near Goldendale, Washington. A mansion near Stonehenge, which was never finished, has been converted into the Maryhill Museum of Art which—despite its remoteness—is one of the most-visited museums in the West.

But we're way off course. From Sam Hill's house, head south on Broadway and just keep following it for as many blocks as amuses you. It initially passes through a residential area and then becomes takes you through a lively, off-beat counter culture area. It's Seattle's **gay and lesbian district**, busy with body-piercing parlors, leather shops, gay boutiques and a good selection of interesting cafés and coffee houses.

As you approach the corner of Broadway and Pine, note the statue of local legend **Jimi Hendrix,** kneeling with his guitar and silently entertaining passersby. It's in front of the office of AEI Music. This is a good turnaround point. Go east on Pine for three blocks to 12th Avenue, which will take you north back to Volunteer Park.

10 *FREMONT "TROLL STROLL"* • *From the History House through the Fremont neighborhood. The hike, level to gently inclined, begins at the History House at Aurora Avenue North and North 34th Street, and covers a couple of miles, depending on your attention span. GETTING THERE: The Fremont neighborhood is along the Lake Washington Ship Canal just west of Lake Union. The only correct way to enter this area is to cross the exceedingly blue Fremont drawbridge over the Washington Ship Canal. To reach it from downtown, go north on Westlake Avenue (skirting the western edge of Lake Union), then cross the drawbridge, where the route becomes Fremont Avenue North. Turn right onto 34th and go one block to the History House under the Aurora Bridge abutment.*

If Broadway is Seattle's counter culture neighborhood, Fremont is its wacky and eccentric left bank. It all began some years ago when merchants and residents discovered that they occupied the center of the universe. To herald this discovery, they proclaimed Fremont to be a republic, and adopted *delibertas quirkas* as its motto. In other words, its a fun, upbeat and deliberately zany area that's fun to explore. For more on the district, see Chapter thirteen, page 200.

A good place to begin is the **History House,** a small museum devoted to neighborhood studies, beneath the Aurora Bridge at the corner of Aurora Avenue North and North 34th Street. It's on a corner lot enclosed by a fence wonderfully decorated with wrought iron figures of people, plants, bugs, ships, fish and Seattle landmarks. The museum is open Wednesday-Sunday noon to 5 and features rotating exhibits of various Seattle neighborhoods. If it's closed, pick up a copy of *The*

Walking Guide to Fremont, which more or less follows the route we outline below—although we've compressed ours somewhat. Along the route, Hysterical Makers describe things significant about the neighborhood. We like to call this the "Troll Stroll" because it begins with a visit to the famous Fremont Troll; see Chapter Two, page 62. Maybe the name will catch on.

From the History House, go two blocks up to Aurora Avenue North, where you'll find the Fremont Troll emerging from the dirt at the north abutment of the Aurora Bridge. Return to the History House and continue down to the waterfront beneath the Aurora Bridge anchorage. You'll encounter a small park area through which passes the **Burke-Gilman Trail,** a biking/walking route that we recommend below. Follow it a couple of blocks alongside the Lake Washington Ship Canal to the **Fremont drawbridge,** which is the "official" entrance to the Fremont Neighborhood. Take a stairway up to the bridge, pick up Fremont Avenue and go north. You'll shortly encounter the whimsical aluminum-cast **People Waiting for the Interurban** at Fremont and North 34th Street; it's one of Fremont's many pieces of public art. Locals frequently "dress" these figures with hats, T-shirts and even leis.

Turn west onto 34th and follow it several blocks to Phinney Avenue North and the **Redhook Ale Brewery** and **Trollyman Pub,** where you can sip some microbrews and inquire about tours. If it's Sunday, this stroll along 34th takes you through the heart of the **Fremont Sunday Market,** where everything from used clothing to collectibles to fresh produce is sold. From Redhook, go a block uphill on Phinney to North 35th, turn right and follow it three blocks to the actual center of the universe, marked by the **Fremont Rocket** at 35th and Evanston. Go uphill a block to the **statue of Lenin,** which an American teaching in Russia found toppled after the fall of the Soviet regime in 1989 and had shipped to Seattle.

Angle a block downhill on Fremont Place to Fremont Avenue, the business heart of the Fremont District with its funky boutiques, coffee houses and cafés. The shops and cafés extend for about three blocks uphill to North 38th Street, where you can do an about face and return to North 34th Street.

THE TEN BEST BIKE ROUTES

Seattle is a serious cycling city with many miles of traffic-free bike routes and separate bike lanes marked on many city streets. If you didn't happen to bring your two-wheeler along, you can rent a variety of bikes from Blazing Saddles near the waterfront 1230 Western Avenue at the foot of Harbor Steps; (206) 341-9994. Hours are 8 to 8 daily in summer and 9 to 5 daily except Tuesday the rest of the year. You get with your rental detailed instructions for five specific routes, or you can choose your own. For other rental places, look under "Bicycles—rental" in the Yellow Pages.

190 — CHAPTER TWELVE

1 **WEST SEATTLE** • *Shoreline ride around Duwamish Head to Alki Point. Almost completely level, just over ten miles round trip. It's best taken on weekdays because it's very popular with locals on weekends, particularly when the sun chooses to shine. GETTING THERE: Cross the tip of Harbor Island on the West Seattle Freeway or Spokane Street and go right onto Harbor Avenue.*

This route around the edge of the West Seattle peninsula offers awesome views across Elliott Bay to the Seattle skyline and then—as you round Duwamish Head—pleasing vistas across Puget Sound. It's also popular as a walking route since sections of it have separate walking/running paths.

Begin on Harbor Avenue SW, just north of the West Seattle Freeway. You won't have much of a view initially since you'll be traveling through a port industrial area. However, within less than half a mile, you'll emerge near the shoreline and that fine panorama across Elliott Bay begins. As you pass **Salty's on Alki** seafood restaurant, you'll begin pedaling through a waterfront park that extends along most of this shoreline. Benches, small fishing piers, swatches of lawn with picnic tables and little hidden sandy coves will appear as you pedal along.

After a mile or so, the biking and walking paths separate. (We noted that the cyclists were more conscientious than the pedestrians about keeping to their assigned paths.) As you pass **Armeni Park** and boat launch and round **Duwamish Head**, the city skyline falls behind and your vista becomes Puget Sound and—on a good day—the distant Olympic Mountains. Your route is now called Alki Way SW. The two-mile-long **Alki Beach Park** borders the shoreline here, and you'll enter the small community of Alki. It has several small cafés and one good bakery/coffee place, in case you feel the need for a break. We like to pause at **Alki Bakery** at Alki Avenue SW and 61st Avenue SW, which makes our list of Ten Best coffee stops in Chapter Four, page 107. Or if you're in the mood for a picnic, pick up an order of fish and chips at Alki Spud at 2666 Alki Avenue and carry your booty out to the beach. The Spud is listed in Chapter Four, page 103.

The separate biking/walking route ends just beyond here, although the beachside street, here called Beach Drive SW, is lightly traveled—except on sunny weekends. As you round **Alki Point,** where Seattle was first settled, you'll see Alki Point Lighthouse, which offers tours although its hours are limited. As you press onward, small homes and apartments line the beach and you'll begin losing your Puget Sound vistas. Watch on your right for tiny **Weatherwatch Park** at Beach Drive and SW Carroll, with a few benches and a obelisk with graphics on the history of the area. A few blocks beyond, you'll hit another stretch of open beach, and then the homes and apartments move beachside again, so this is probably a good place to turn around and head back.

Our favorite Seattle bike route finishes with a flourish, since you'll be pedaling right toward that great city skyline view on the return leg.

2 *THE BEST OF BLAZING SADDLES* • *From the foot of Harbor Steps on the Waterfront to Chittenden Locks, then back through Discovery Park. Fifteen miles; mostly level with two moderately steep hill climbs. GETTING THERE: Blazing Saddles is at 1230 Western Avenue at the foot of Harbor Steps just up from the waterfront; (206) 341-9994. Hours are 8 to 8 daily in summer and 9 to 5 daily except Tuesday the rest of the year.*

This is one of five "Best Rides" suggested by the Blazing Saddles bike rental firm; see Chapter Two, page 58. It provides a fine sampler of Seattle, particularly if you take the optional hill climb through Discovery Park and along the Magnolia Bluffs for awesome city and bay views. The easiest way to take it is one of Blazing's bikes, since the rental includes an easy-to-follow direction finder and a little bike-mounted computer that tells you how fast you're going and how far you've got to go. If you have your own bike, transfer the directions below onto a detailed street map and you may be able to stay on course.

Since it weaves through an assortment of interesting areas, the route is too complicated to describe here. It's best to do it aboard a Blazing Saddle bike with the detailed direction sheet on your handlebars. We'll just offer a few highlights: It starts at the firm's office at the foot of **Harbor Steps** and goes northward northwest along Alaskan Way, following the route of the cute little Waterfront Streetcar. After about a mile, you'll pedal into **Myrtle Edwards Park,** a pleasant stretch of waterfront greenery. Myrtle blends into **Elliott Bay Park.** At the end of the park, you'll pick up the Pier 91 Bike Route which skirts the perimeter of a large industrial and cargo area.

A few twists and turns will deliver you to the backside of **Chittenden Locks.** From here, you can pick up that optional hill climb and huff and puff up to **Discovery Park.** Sitting on a bluff above Puget Sound, this is the site of the former Fort Lawton Military Reservation.

You'll get some fine views from up here, and they'll get better. Heading south through the park and, you'll follow your direction sheet to **Magnolia Bluffs** for great vistas west over Puget Sound and southeast to the city. A downhill run takes you to **Elliott Bay Marina.** If you need a lunch break, try **Maggie Bluffs.** It and the more dressy **Palisade** restaurant above offer fine views of the city, filtered through the masts at the marina. From here, follow the waterfront back to your starting point.

3 *SOUTH PORT AREA* • *From Pioneer Square to the Museum of Flight at Boeing Field. All level; about thirteen miles round trip. GETTING THERE: Head south from downtown on First Avenue to Pioneer Square.*

There's nothing scenic in this busy industrialized port area. However, it's a good place to ride on weekends if you just want to crank off a lotta miles on an almost completely level surface. And it's a good way to get to the Museum of Flight (Chapter Two, page 33) while getting in a good workout. We specify *weekends* for this route because you probably don't want to compete with a lot of freight trucks that keeps these roads busy on working days.

Begin on First Avenue South and start pedaling southward from the Pioneer Square area. You'll shortly encounter the new home of the Seattle Seahawks (due for completion in 2002) and the imposing new brick-fronted Safeco Field, where the Seattle Mariners play. his section doesn't have bike lanes—a good reason to take this ride on a weekend, when traffic's lighter.

At the corner of First Avenue and Royal Brougham Way (opposite Safeco), turn west and drop down to Alaskan Way, where you'll pick up a marked bike lane. The route takes you through a busy port area and eventually becomes East Marginal Way. A couple of miles from your starting point, you'll pass under the Seattle Freeway viaduct that leads to West Seattle and Alki Point. If you want to add on a few extra miles, you can turn right onto Spokane Street (staying off the viaduct, which doesn't permit cyclists or pedestrians.) Go right onto Harbor Island and you can pedal about this large port complex, which won't be busy on a weekend.

Back on East Marginal Way, you'll lose the bike lane as you press southward. After about half a mile, watch for a sign on your right for the Diagonal Avenue South Public Shoreline Access. Follow it to an appealing little public tucked among the cargo storage facilities. It's on Duwamish Waterway and a short walking trail will take you down to waterside. (See Chapter Nine, page 149 for more on the park.)

Continue southward on East Marginal Way. After about a mile, it merges with First Avenue South, then the two separate, with First Avenue forking to the right. Get into the left lanes and continue straight ahead on East Marginal; otherwise, you'll wind up on a freeway. Just below here, you'll begin pedaling through the large Boeing Aircraft complex alongside Boeing Field, where you'll see an assortment of airplanes parked about. And of course for a really great assortment, pedal on down to the Museum of Flight at the lower end of Boeing Field.

4 *ELLIOTT BAY WATERFRONT* ● *From Pioneer Square to Elliott Bay Marina. Completely level; about eight miles round trip. GETTING THERE: Follow Seneca or Madison streets from downtown to Alaskan Way.*

Most of this route is so simple that it doesn't require much detailing. For the first leg get to the lower end of the waterfront at the base of **Pioneer Square.** Assuming you're bring your bikes here via car, you'll find plenty of parking lots in the area, particularly around the

Washington State Ferry Terminal at Pier 50 (Coleman Dock). From here, head northwest along Alaskan Way, following the route of the **Waterfront Streetcar.** There's a separate walking/biking route alongside the tracks. If it's an off-season weekday, you might try the wide sidewalk alongside the Elliott Bay piers, although it's generally too busy with pedestrians.

Along the way, you'll encounter most of what people come to the waterfront for—**Ye Olde Curiosity Shop** at Pier 54, several seafood restaurants, **Bay Pavilion** on Pier 57 with its shops and cafés, the very appealing **Waterfront Park** between piers 57 and 58, and the **Omnidome** and **Seattle Aquarium** on Pier 58. Just beyond, the many steps of the **Pike Place Hillclimb** lead up to **Pike Place Market** although you probably won't want to lug your bike up there.

From here, the route practically duplicates our North Waterfront walking route above on page 182. The only option is that you may want to add another mile and a half by following the fenced **Pier 91 Bike Trail** around the perimeter of a large Seattle Port District cargo and industrial complex. It bulges inland from piers 90 and 91 in Smith Cove, just beyond **Elliott Bay Park.** Your perimeter route will put you back on the waterfront near **Elliott Bay Marina,** which is your turn-around point.

If you don't want to duplicate that cargo/industrial complex ramble on the return route, head inland from Elliott Bay Marina, then go right onto the broad sidewalk of the **Garfield Street-Magnolia Bridge,** which is a viaduct over Smith Cove. At the lower end, go right briefly onto Elliott Avenue, then right again onto Galer Street and follow it toward the waterfront. You'll shortly encounter the waterfront biking/walking trail again; go left into Elliott Bay Park.

5 *LAKE WASHINGTON WEST SHORE* • *From Seward Park to Denny Blaine Park. Practically level; about twelve miles round trip, including a single 2.4-mile loop around Seward Park. GETTING THERE: Follow Rainier Avenue about four miles southeast of downtown, go left (east) onto Orcas and follow it less than a mile into Seward Park.*

This route probably is best for fat-tired bikes because it's rather rough in spots. The beginning loop around Seward Park—while asphalt—is rather pebbly and the paved path along Lake Washington's west shoreline is broken and lumpy from tree roots seeking to rise to the surface. In fact, many riders usually adjourn to adjacent Lake Washington Boulevard and Lakeside Avenue. Signs on the boulevard advise motorists that bicyclists have the right-of-way.

This route begins with a loop around **Seward Park,** a fat green thumb that extends into Lake Washington. A good starting point—as you pedal or drive into the park—is at a shoreside parking lot just beyond a picnic shelter. The path, labeled "emergency vehicles only," starts at the far end of the parking lot. It's a pleasant route, with the lakeshore on one side and thick trees on the other. After you've completed your loop—by pedaling into another parking lot near a Normandy style cross-timbered park building—veer to the right to pick up the lakeside biking/walking path, heading north along Lake Washington Boulevard.

You'll pass elegant shorefront homes, although you have the best view because they're across the boulevard. You'll encounter those tree-root speed bumps along here, and you may find yourself frequently standing in the saddle, or wishing that you had. Other than the bumps, this is certainly a pleasant pedal, since the entire lakeshore is essentially a park strip with grass and lots of trees. If you choose to use the street, which isn't heavily traveled on weekdays, you'll find sections of it almost completely canopied with trees.

Pressing northward, you'll pedal past **Sayers Park** and then **Coleman Park,** just short of the **Lake Washington Floating Bridge** that carries Interstate 90 eastward. As you pedal beneath the bridge's west anchorage, your route becomes Lakeside Avenue and then, as you pass **Leschi Park** the name changes again to Lake Washington Boulevard. Don't be confused; just keep pedaling close to the water. Our route ends at **Denny Blaine Park** just short of the **Evergreen Point Floating Bridge,** where Lake Washington Boulevard spirals steeply into a heavily wooded neighborhood, and then travels through **Washington Park.** You can continue on if you wish, although it's a very tough climb!

6 *UNIVERSITY VILLAGE TO GREEN LAKE* • *About seven miles round trip, including a 2.8-mile loop of Green Lake. It's mostly level, except for one semi-tough good hill climb on Ravenna Boulevard. GETTING THERE: To reach your starting point, head north from downtown Seattle on I-5, go east on Freeway 520 then, before you reach the Evergreen Point Floating Bridge, take the Montlake exit to the University of Washington campus. Midway through the campus, fork left onto 25th Avenue NE and you'll soon see University Center shopping mall on your right.*

This route begins in the University District, then angles northwest to Green Lake, one of the city's most popular parks. (If you're bikeless, you can run the route in reverse by driving to the Green Lake area and rent bikes from **Gregg's Green Lake Cycle.** It's at the juncture of Ravenna Boulevard, Green Lake Way and NE 70th Street; (206) 523-1822. There's free parking in Green Lake Park.)

University Center is a good starting point because it has plenty of parking, and you can fuel up on caffè latte at a Starbucks before starting out. From the shopping mall, pedal north on 25th Avenue NE to the second traffic signal, then turn left onto NE 54th Street. Curve around the bottom of **Ravenna Park,** then pick up Ravenna Boulevard NE and follow it northwest. It's an attractive route with a landscaped median strip, passing through a grand old tree-shrouded residential area. It's a great cycling route since the inside lane is reserved for bikes only. It's also a tough route, since you'll be pedaling uphill.

Mercifully, you'll top a rise and begin going downhill. Stay alert as you approach 15th Avenue NE since you'll have to zig right and then zag left to stay with Ravenna Boulevard. You'll zip under Interstate 5 then, within a quarter of a mile, blend onto Green Lake Way. The neighborhood surrounding **Green Lake Park** is an appealing little village of small cafés and shops. If you're in need of a personal fueling stop, take a break at Zí Pani café and bakery at the corner of Green Lake Way and NE 72nd St. It offers specialty coffees, baked goods and both indoor and outdoor tables for consuming them.

From here, peddle lakeside in large Green Lake Park. You'll encounter a 2.8-mile combined walking/biking trail around the lake with a separate lane for cyclers. Note that cyclists are supposed to go counter-clockwise to avoid colliding with one another. After looping the lake for as many times as pleases you, return to Green Lake Way and head back to your starting point.

7 FISHERMEN'S TERMINAL TO MAGNOLIA BLUFFS •

About eight miles; mostly level or gently hilly, with one steep grunt up to Discovery Park. You can combine it with the "Discovery Park Ramble" below for a total of twelve to fourteen miles. GETTING THERE: Take Elliott Avenue northwest from downtown, blend onto 15th Avenue West and take West Emerson exit just before 15th crosses the Ballard Bridge.

This route takes you from the West Coast's largest commercial fishing terminal to the popular Chittenden Locks, thence to Discovery Park and Magnolia Bluffs, where you'll share great vistas with some of Seattle's grandest homes. **Fishermen's Terminal** on Salmon Bay is a good starting point for several reasons. There's ample free parking here, you can visit a working fleet of nearly 700 commercial fishing boats and you can fuel up at any of several cafés here.

Having done this, head north and west from the fishing terminal on Commodore Way alongside the **Lake Washington Ship Canal** that links lakes Union and Washington with Puget Sound. After about 1.4 miles, cycle to the right into **Commodore Park** and cross a bridge to **Hiram Chittenden Locks**, which we visited in Chapter Two, page 39. You'll have to either park and lock or walk your bike, since cycling isn't permitted on the grounds of the locks or adjacent **Carl English Botanical Gardens**.

After exploring the area, return to Commodore Way, go north briefly, turn left (south) onto Lawton Lane and follow it southeast as it curves into Gilman Avenue West, which parallels Commodore Way with a railroad track between them. After about half a mile, make a hard left onto Fort Street then fork left onto Government Way, following signs to **Discovery Park**. This is a steep climb—the toughest part of this route. (We made it, although you can wimp out and push your bike.) You can explore the park by following the "Discovery Park Ramble" bike route below.

Having either pedaled or bypassed the park, go south along its eastern edge on 36th Avenue West, then go right on West Emerson Street to follow the park's southern edge. Turn left (south) onto Magnolia Boulevard and follow this route through the **Magnolia Bluff** neighborhood past some of Emerald City's most opulent homes. These mansions block some grand views of Elliott Bay and Puget Sound for much of the way. Then the vista opens up dramatically to mere mortals as you pedal through long and slender **Magnolia Park** at the edge of the bluffs. As you clear the end of the park, Magnolia makes a right hand turn at stop sign; continue straight ahead through the stop on Howe Street, stay on it four about four blocks, then take a half-right onto Thorndyke Avenue West. This travels alongside a port industrial area and **U.S. Naval Station,** and you can pick up the **Pier 91 Bike Route** which skirts the edge of this area. You can tack on a couple of extra miles, although it's a rather industrialized and not very interesting route.

Continue north on Thorndyke, which kinks slightly left to become West 20th Avenue, which in turn merges into Gilman Avenue. Turn right onto West Emerson and follow it east, back to Fishermen's Terminal.

8 *DISCOVERY PARK RAMBLE* • *Gentle hills with a couple of semi-steep climbs; about five miles, plus an additional 1.5 miles if you pedal up from Fishermen's Terminal. This route is best done on a weekend since Discovery Park and its approaches can be busy with traffic on weekends, especially sunny ones. GETTING THERE: If you're starting from within the park, follow directions for the "Discovery Park Loop" walking trail above, on page 185.*

Discovery Park is Seattle's largest public park, occupying the 534-acre site of Fort Lawton, established in 1894 to protect the city from enemy attack. Some military inholdings—mostly housing units—are still there, although most of the park is open to the public. Our bike route through the park comes with options. You can follow the first section of the "Fishermen's Terminal to Magnolia Bluffs" route above, then pedal into Discovery Park on Government Way. Or you can go directly to the park from Fishermen's Terminal by going northwest on Emerson, north (right) onto Gilman, left on Fort Street and then half left onto Government Way. A third option is to drive directly to Discovery Park, unleash your bikes in the large visitor center parking lot and start from there. For more on Discovery Park and the visitor center, see Chapter Two, page 46.

Once at the visitor center, you can pick up cycling and park maps for modest fees. From here, follow the main park road (the only one open to public vehicle traffic) northwest, headed for **Daybreak Star Cultural Arts Center**. This route can be busy with traffic—particularly on weekends—so pedal with caution. After you've passed the North Parking Lot, the route takes you on a steep sweep down to Daybreak Star. For details on this native peoples' center with its fine art gallery, see Chapter Two, page 62. And make sure you walk out to a vista point for fine views north to Shilshole Bay Marina, west across Puget Sound to the Olympics and south to West Seattle.

From Daybreak Star, head south on a pave road that's closed to motor vehicles. It ends after about half a mile at Utah Avenue near a military housing area. Turn right and follow the road down to **West Point Lighthouse**. The facility is closed to the public although you can view it from without and poke about sandy beaches here. Pedal back from the beach—it's a bit of a climb—and explore the rest of the park.

If you take a road south from Utah Avenue (about a a fourth of a mile beyond the road you followed from Daybreak Star), you can explore old Fort Lawson's Historic District and wind up at a picnic area. (It will be obvious on the park map.) From here, you can continue past a picnic area, exit the park and wind up on West Emerson Street and a brief jog east will take you to the head of Magnolia, where you can pick up the second half of the "Fishermen's Terminal to Magnolia Bluffs" route above. Or continue prowling about the park and eventually return to the visitor center parking lot.

9 BURKE-GILMAN TRAIL: GAS WORKS PARK TO LAKE FOREST PARK • *About twenty miles round trip, mostly level. It's all separated from traffic although there are some busy intersection crossings. GETTING THERE: From downtown, go north on Westlake Avenue along the western edge of Lake Union and cross the Fremont drawbridge. Immediately beyond the bridge, turn right onto North 34th Street and follow it beneath the Aurora Bridge. It becomes North Northlake and skims the edge of the park.*

Burke-Gilman is one of Seattle's most popular recreation trails, so this trip is best planned for a weekday. It begins at Gas Works Park and travels ten miles to Lake Forest Park on the northern tip of Lake Washington. If you really feel ambitious, you can pick up the **Sammamish River Trail** which follows that stream another twelve miles to **Marymoor County Park** in Redmond.

Neither route requires much description, since they're pretty obvious once you get onto the paths. Both are marked on the large *AAA Seattle map*, and they're described in *Short Bike Rides: Western Washington*, the cycling guide we recommended at the top of this chapter.

To start all of this, unleash your bikes at **Gas Works Park** which offers plenty of free parking. Pick up the trail (which actually begins a few blocks back in Fremont) and head east. The trail stays close to the shore of **Lake Union,** and then swerves away to cut through the **University of Washington** campus. It pops out the north end then wraps around the northern edge of **University Village** shopping center. It follows NE Blakeley Street and then 39th NE.

After traveling a couple of miles through thick residential areas, it picks up the **Lake Washington** shoreline. A long pedal northward—mostly paralleling city streets—will take you alongside the shore and finally to **Lake Forest Park.** This isn't a park; it's a Seattle suburb. Burke-Gilman ends at the lakefront **Log Boom County Park.**

If your fanny and legs can stand more punishment, pick up the **Sammamish River Trail** here. It parallels Bothell Way and—less than two miles from Log Boom—it picks up the shoreline of the Sammamish River. By going west from the trail on NE 45th Street and asking directions, you can find your way to the **Columbine** and **Château Ste. Michelle** wineries and **Redhook Brewery.**

10 *VASHON ISLAND LOOP* ● *Level, with some moderate to steep hills; various lengths. GETTING THERE: Vashon Island is served by a passenger only ferry from Pier 50 near downtown, and from an auto-passenger ferry leaving the Fauntleroy Dock below West Seattle.*

Despite its location just offshore of Seattle and Tacoma, Vashon Island is a bucolic retreat, populated by weekenders, artists and a few urban commuters. The rural countryside and country lanes are suggestive of one of the San Juan Islands and it's popular with cyclists. Part of the fun of a Vashon cycle is the ferry trip. One can commit to a multi-day cycling trip here, since Vashon Island is busy with small towns, interesting cafés and bed & breakfast inns. Between these touches of civilization are thick forests, rolling pasturelands and berry patches.

We won't suggest a detailed itinerary here, except to warn you that the first leg up from the ferry dock is a tough uphill pull. Once you've accomplished that, you can choose from a complex network of roads ranging from semi-busy highways to quiet lanes. Chapter Four of our *Washington Discovery Guide* has a section on Vashon Island, with listings of restaurants and inns. See the listing at the end of this book. *Short Bike Rides: Western Washington* does a thorough job of outlining a complex and interesting route about the island. You can find it at area book stores, or contact Globe Pequot Press, P.O. Box 833, Old Saybrook, CT 06475. (WEB SITE: www.globe-pequot.com)

A variety of mere nothings gives more pleasure than uniformity of something.
— **Jean Paul Richter**

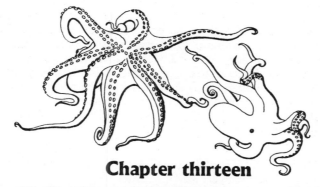

Chapter thirteen

ASSORTED LISTS
THAT DON'T FIT INTO OTHER LISTS

Seattle is a rich mix of attractions, flavors, sights and sounds. This chapter is intended to gather up all those loose ends that just don't seem to fit anywhere else.

ODD ENDS: A MISCELLANEOUS TEN BEST

Have we missed anything? This catch-all list catches Seattle's most interesting one-of-a-kind things.

1 THE BEST NEWLY GENTRIFIED NEIGHBORHOOD:
Belltown • *The area immediately north of downtown, bounded roughly by First and Fifth avenues, Virginia Street and Denny Way.*

This is Seattle's version of SOMA, San Francisco's south of Market area, busy with trendy shops, cafés, pubs, boutiques, galleries and an occasional design studio. Once an urban slum, it's the city's most recent area to feel the hand of gentrification, as aged brick buildings are either restored or removed to be replaced by high rise office buildings. It was still undergoing rehab as we wrote this, so sections are still haven to Seattle's homeless, who have shifted over here from Pioneer Square, which has simply become too touristy for the street people. Most of the dining and shopping action of Belltown is confined to a rather limited area, along a few blocks of First and Second avenues, between Lenora and Vine streets.

The region is part of a larger section called the Denny Regrade, named because a large bluff called Denny Hill was leveled during the early twentieth century to make room for the city's northward expansion. Much of it was sluiced into Elliott Bay in a kind of hydraulic cut and fill, using powerful monitors (water hoses) that had been employed by California miners to reach gold-bearing gravel veins. After eight years of pumping water from Lake Washington to blast away Denny Hill, it was leveled and the tailings gave Elliott Bay gained an additional eighty-five acres of shoreline.

2 THE MOST INTRIGUING NEIGHBORHOOD: Fremont •

The district along the northwest shore of Lake Union. GETTING THERE: The only correct way to enter this area is to cross the exceedingly blue Fremont drawbridge over the Washington Ship Canal. To reach it from downtown, go north on Westlake Avenue (skirting the western edge of Lake Union), then cross the drawbridge, where the route becomes Fremont Avenue North. Having done so, find a place to park, for this is a walking neighborhood.

Several decades ago, residents of the small Fremont district became aware that their neighborhood was the center of the universe. The source of this revelation has never been established, but these fortunate citizens decided to mark their good fortune by not taking it very seriously. Several locals erected a 52-foot rocket at the corner of North 35th Street and Evanston Avenue to mark the universe's exact center. An American veteran teaching in Russia found a toppled statue of Lenin during the 1989 collapse of the Soviet Union and arranged to have it shipped to Fremont. It stands on the corner of North 36th Street and Fremont Place. And just two blocks east on 36th, a giant troll lurks under the north abutment of the Aurora Avenue Bridge, just waiting to get his hands on another Volkswagen. If you own one of those ugly new beetles, avoid this area.

Goaded by a good-humored merchants association, Fremont has become Seattle's Left Bank and Haight-Ashbury, with a fine little collection of bookstores, coffee houses, bistros, antique stores, pubs, organic food stores and international cafés. Fremonters have adopted as their motto *De libertas quirkas*—"The freedom to be peculiar." They sponsor a wonderfully wacky summer solstice parade with goofy floats and costumes (always including at least one manifestation of the troll), plus an Oktoberfest, "Trolloween" and sundry other annual celebrations. For a guided walk through the center of the universe, see Chapter Twelve, page 188.

3 *THE MOST ECLECTIC NEIGHBORHOOD* ● *The University District. GETTING THERE: This is the neighborhood immediately north and west of the University of Washington campus.*

Seattle's popular "U-District" is a typical university neighborhood with its collection of book stores, coffee houses, incense shops, bakeries and bistros. Seattle's version adds another dimension: It's the city's best ethnic restaurant row, with small Chinese, Japanese, Indian, Pakistani, Vietnamese, Thai, Greek, Russian and even Sherpa (the Himalayan at 4214 NE University Way).

4 *STRANGEST PIECE OF PUBLIC ART* ● *Christopher Columbus statue on the waterfront. FINDING IT: Old Chris is in Waterfront Park beside Alaskan Way, between piers 57 (Bay Pavilion) and 59 (Seattle Aquarium).*

Good grief, Chris, what happened to you? You've got a hole through your helmet (and possibly your head) and your body looks boldly bionic. And shouldn't you be wearing something more than a cape and a loincloth? This curious bronze Christopher Columbus statue is leaning on its sword, staring morosely across Elliott Bay from Waterfront Park. What's Chris doing here? We realize that the famous navigator didn't know where he was going, and didn't know where he was when he got there. But we thought he was looking for a shortcut to the Orient, not the fabled Northwest Passage through Puget Sound.

5 *THE BEST PLACE FOR JUNK FOOD* ● *Seattle Center food court in the Center House; (206) 684-7200. Most shops open at 11; various closing times. GETTING THERE: Seattle Center is just northwest of downtown, two blocks up from the waterfront on Broad Street. The Center House is in the middle of the grounds.*

Talk about a junk food feeding frenzy! Step into the Seattle Center House and take your pick—The Frankfurter, Pizza Haven, Karob Corner shish kabab and gyros, Subway sandwiches, Orange Julius, Starbucks Coffee, Philly cheese sandwiches, Seattle Fudge, Magic Dragon Chinese food, Steamers fish and chips, Quincy's Burgers and the caloric list goes on. If you want to be more adult about all this, you can adjourn to Michelangelo's Bistro and Bar for a serious drink and something Italian.

6 *THE BEST PLACE TO FISH WHEN YOU FORGOT YOUR FISHING GEAR* ● *Elliott Bay Fishing Pier and Happy Hooker Baite and Tackle. GETTING THERE: The fishing pier is in*

Elliott Bay Park on the waterfront, about a mile and a half northwest of Pike Place Market. It's reached via Alaskan Way and then a walking/biking trail through the park.

Whether or not you catch any fish, Elliott Bay Fishing Pier is a great place to enjoy views across Puget Sound and back toward the city skyline. In deference to Seattle's unpredictable weather, the pier has several rain shelters. And if you really do want to fish, the adjacent Happy Hooker will rent you tackle and sell you bait. You also can get soft drinks and snacks here.

7 THE BEST USE OF URBAN SPACE ● *Freeway Park, between Union and Spring Streets and Sixth and Ninth avenue. GETTING THERE: It's above I-5 just above downtown, behind the Washington State Convention and Trade Center.*

What do you do with an odd-shaped piece of leftover land after you've dug a freeway beneath it and surrounded it with high rises? If you're Seattle city planners, you create a little green space in the heart of downtown. It's a moderately impressive little park, with landscaping, a fountain, concrete risers and a curious sculpture as a focal point. Downtown skyscrapers—particularly the towering Two Union Square—rise above. The easiest way to reach it is to exit the south end of Convention Place, or climb a set of concrete steps from the corner of Pike and Hubbell Place.

8 THE MOST APPEALING INDOOR SPACE ● *Contention Place, between Pike and Union streets and Eighth and Ninth avenues. GETTING THERE: It's on the eastern (upper edge) of downtown, partially tucked beneath I-5.*

Convention Place is an impressive space for a couple of reasons. It's terraced levels and lofty ceilings make it one of the most attractive indoor spaces in the city, and it represents an ingenious use of space that overwise would be lost to a freeway. Sections of Convention Place are tucked beneath I-5, although you never realize it as you explore its attractive interior.

Another clever application of urban space was the creation of Freeway Park (see above), which wraps around the center's eastern side. Convention Place is home to the Washington State Convention and Trade Center, a visitor center of the Seattle Convention and Visitors Bureau, several office complexes and retail outlets. Art work graces the walls and floors of the huge central corridor, which actually is a series of terraces, linked by escalators. With several open seating areas and food takeouts, it's a great place to pause and take a break from whatever it is that brought you to downtown Seattle. If you came for visitor information, the visitor's bureau is on the lower level, at the eastern end of a side corridor.

9 *THE MOST STRIKING INDOOR ART WORK* • *"Crystal Cascade" by Dale Chihuly in Benaroya Hall, 200 University St. GETTING THERE: Benaroya Hall is home to the Seattle Symphony and this sculpture is near the University and Third Avenue corner.*

This stunning piece, fashioned from hand-blown white glass and steel, twists and cascades from the ceiling of the city's smart new performing arts center. Not a chandelier, it glitters stunningly from carefully placed spotlights. While it's quite beautiful, it can suggest—if you're in a negative mood—an elongated head of Medusa.

10 *THE BEST PLACE TO FIND EVERYTHING YOU NEVER WANTED* • *Fremont Sunday Market, in the Fremont Neighborhood. It's along North 34th Street between Fremont Avenue North and Phinney Avenue North. GETTING THERE: From downtown, go north on Westlake Avenue (skirting the western edge of Lake Union), then cross the Fremont drawbridge. Take an immediate left onto North 34th Street and you'll be at the market. PARKING TIP: It's difficult to find a spot during market days, although you can continue past the market for a block or two and turn right into one of the Burke office complex lots. Signs ask only that you not park in marked reserve spaces.*

Every Sunday, this eclectic public market occupies half of 34th street for two blocks (turning it temporarily into a one-way street) and spills into a pair of parking lots. What does the market offer? What *doesn't* it offer! Browse among its hastily set up booths for curios, collectibles, antiques, outright junk, used clothing, tired old cameras and typewriters, some really ugly lamps, handcrafted jewelry and pottery, emu oil, herbs, incense, cut flowers and old LPs in case you've not yet gotten a CD. Browsing can work up an appetite, so you can nosh from several ethnic food booths and a Great Harvest Bread Company outlet. Several booths also sell fresh fruits and vegetables.

THE TEN BEST PLACES TO PEOPLE-WATCH

Seattle is a great people-watching city, from its sidewalk cafés to its waterfront walks to its downtown shopping centers. What follows is the city's Ten Best places to sit and do nothing, providing an opportunity to slow down, take the weight off your feet and watch the rest of the city hurry past. People- watching is like being a couch potato in public, without the distraction of a TV set.

1 *HARBOR STEPS* • *Off First Avenue at the base of University Street above the waterfront. It's beside Wolfgang Puck Café and just below the Seattle Art Museum.*

Our favorite people-watching place is fashioned as a series of concrete terraces descending from First Avenue to Western Avenue just above the Seattle waterfront. A fountain accompanies you downhill, gushing merrily at one level, disappearing beneath the concrete and reappearing in a different format on a lower terrace. It's a grand place for viewing the waterfront, the ship traffic on Elliott Bay and the towering highrises of downtown Seattle behind you. If you feel the need for caffeine, a Tully's Coffee outlet is on a lower level near Western Avenue, with several tables outside. If you feel the need to shop or dine, several places are terraced alongside the Harbor Steps, including the wonderfully garish Wolfgang Puck's; see Chapter Four, page 88. And if you want to rent a bike, Blazing Saddles is just around the corner on Western Avenue; see Chapter Two, page 58.

2 CITY CENTRE FOYER • *1420 Fifth Ave.; (206) 622-6465. GETTING THERE: This shopping complex is downtown, rimmed by Fifth and Sixth avenues and Pike and Union streets. Our people-watching venue is just inside the Fifth Avenue entrance.*

Several tables and chairs occupy the foyer of this stylish downtown shopping center, beneath an impressive three-story atrium. It's a fine place for relaxing and watching the beautiful people heading for City Centre's trendy shops or a power lunch at the Palomino Café. And should you need something to sip or nibble, a Starbucks outlet is adjacent to this public seating area.

3 CONVENTION PLACE AND FREEWAY PARK • *Upper edge of downtown between Pike and Spring streets and tucked partially beneath I-5 freeway.*

Convention Place is one of Seattle's most attractive spaces and Freeway Park represents an ingenious use of urban space. Between the two—since Freeway Park essentially wraps around the eastern side of Convention Place—you can find lots of places for people-watching. You can relax on concrete risers in the park beneath the dramatically curved tower of Two Union Square and watch the passing parade (along with the nervously puffing office workers since buildings here are non-smoking) or retreat inside Convention Place, where you'll find several seating areas. Our favorite is a cluster of tables and chairs at the south end of level two. Above you, reader boards flash little bits of wisdom, sometimes in several languages. There are several takeouts nearby, within Convention Place and Two Union Square.

4 IL FORNAIO DELI • *In Pacific Place at 600 Pine St.; (206) 264-0993. GETTING THERE: Il Fornaio is on the ground floor of Pacific Place, a downtown shopping complex rimmed by Pine Street, Olive Way and Sixth and Seventh avenues.*

Some of Seattle's beautiful people and a lot of the ordinary ones stream through Pacific Place, downtown's most upscale shopping center. Il Fornaio's upscale deli occupies the heart of the ground floor as a kind of outdoor café under glass—a fine place to sit and sip a cappucino, savory bakery items or a hefty deli sandwich, while watching the passing parade of credit card clutchers. The firm also has a large, attractive restaurant adjacent.

5 PUBLIC PLAZA AT FOURTH AVENUE AND PINE STREET • *Downtown Seattle.*

This large wedge of a park in the shadow of highrises has several benches where you can sit and watch the constant stream of downtown pedestrian traffic. If it's a warm day or if you're just feeling silly, you can walk a wet path through the plaza's unusual double cascading fountain.

6 SEATTLE CENTER HOUSE • *Seattle Center. GETTING THERE: Seattle Center is just northwest of downtown, two blocks up from the waterfront on Broad Street. The Center House is in the middle of the grounds.*

Seattle Center, site of the 1962 World's Fair, has two good people watching places—outside the Seattle Center House, and inside. From tables near the front entrance or from a small park strip nearby, you can watch the folks stroll about, listen to the kids happy screams on the Fun Forest amusement park rides, and stare skyward at the profile of the Space Needle, looking like a great flying saucer that sprouted awfully long legs. Inside, you can park at one of the tables in the large food court, enjoy some junk food and perhaps watch a live show on the adjacent stage.

7 STARBUCKS AT UNIVERSITY VILLAGE • *In University Village Shopping center just north of the University of Washington Campus. GETTING THERE: The center is in northeast Seattle. Take I-5 north, go briefly east on Freeway 520, then exit north onto Montlake Boulevard, which goes through the heart of the campus. Take a double left turn onto 25th Avenue NE and the shopping center is on your right.*

If you're young—in heart at least—the large outdoor seating area of this Starbucks is a good girl-and boy-watching place. Students of the nearby University of Washington like to converge here with their caffé lattes, their textbooks and their friends.

8 UNION SQUARE • *Downtown, bordered by Sixth and Avenue and Union and University streets.*

Not to be confused with the more famous version in San Francisco, this Union Square is a sunken courtyard rimmed by modern highrises in the heart of the downtown area. With landscaping and an artificial stream that cascades alongside a terraced walkway, it's an inviting place for sitting and people-watching. Don't plan on working on your summer tan, however. Those surrounding highrises keep it in almost perpetual shade.

9 *WESTLAKE CENTER FOOD COURT • Pine Street between Fourth and Fifth avenues downtown. Weekdays 9:30 to 9, Saturday 9:30 to 8 and Sunday 11 to 6.*

This fast food venue on the third mezzanine level of Westlake Center has seating along the balcony rail and on an outdoor deck three blocks above the street. You can thus people-watch either indoors our out. The balcony seats offer imposing view of surrounding highrises and street scenes three floors below.

10 *WATERFRONT PARK • Just south of the Seattle Aquarium and Omnidome, on Pier 58. GETTING THERE: Take any of several downtown streets to Alaskan Way; the park is below and just south of Pike Place Market.*

You can watch the passing parade of tourists along Alaskan Way or enjoy views across Elliott Bay from this large waterfront park. It's between piers 57 that contains the Bay Pavilion shopping complex, and Pier 59 which is home to the Seattle Aquarium and Omnidome, so you can expect a plentiful supply of strolling tourists. A series of concrete risers, picnic tables and concrete risers offer plenty of places to sit. It was undergoing renovation as this book went to press, so it should be quite attractive when you arrive. Among its attractions are an interesting squared fountain and a curious robotic bronze of Christopher Columbus; see above.

A CITY CELEBRATES: THE TEN BEST FESTIVALS

The big event in Seattle is Seafair, spread over three weeks from mid-July into early August. It tops our list of the city's Ten Best Festivals. The other top nine are listed as they appear on the calendar. To learn more about events listed below—and others—call the Seattle-King County Convention and Visitors Bureau at (206) 461-5840.

1 *SEATTLE SEAFAIR • Three weeks, from mid-July to early August; (206) 728-0123.*

The Seafair is a busy dazzle of parades, craft shows, sports events, food fairs and ethnic festivals held throughout Seattle. Major events include unlimited hydroplane races across Lake Washington and an aerial close-order drill performed by the Navy-Marine Corps Blue Angels. Book your lodgings early if you plan to be in town during this lively time.

2 OPENING DAY OF YACHTING SEASON • *First Saturday in May; (206) 325-1000.*

The Seattle Yacht Club leads the way and the skies billow with canvas as hundreds of boats sail from Lake Union to Lake Washington. As many as 250,000 people line the banks to watch. One of the highlights is the Windermere Cup rowing race through Montlake Cut. **Maritime Week** also is held in May, with tugboat races, boat displays and other aquatic activities, conducted between piers 48 through 70 at the Elliott Bay waterfront; (206) 443-3830.

3 NORTHWEST FOLKLIFE FESTIVAL • *Memorial Day weekend at Seattle Center; (206) 684-7300.*

Nearly 200,000 people crowd into Seattle Center each Memorial Day Weekend to watch more than 5,000 international performers in one of America's largest free festivals. Singing, dancing, arts and crafts demonstrate Emerald City's great cultural diversity. **Pike Place Market Festival** also occurs that weekend, with a street fair, international, foods, music and crafts.

4 SEATTLE INTERNATIONAL FILM FESTIVAL • *Late May to mid-June at several local theaters; (206) 324-9996.*

More than 140 films attract more than 100,000 cinema fans in America's largest international film festival. The focus is on independent American and foreign movies.

5 PIONEER SQUARE FIRE FESTIVAL • *Pioneer Square area in June; (206) 622-6235.*

Historic fire rigs are displayed at this lively festival that marks the burning of early Seattle in 1889. Costumed performers, food booths and craft vendors had spice to this street fair.

6 FREMONT CELEBRATIONS • *Summer Solstice Parade in late June and Trolloween on October 31; (206) 547-7440.*

The Fremont neighborhood, Seattle's self-proclaimed center of the universe, stages several wacky celebrations each year. Foremost among them are the **Solstice Parade** on the Saturday nearest summer solstice, and the **Trolloween celebration** on Hallowe'en. Residents dress up in outlandish outfits—or sometimes no outfits at all—and create goofy floats for these processions. Expect a Trolloween appearance by the famous Fremont Troll; see Chapter Two, page 62.

7 *A BITE OF SEATTLE* • *Seattle Center in mid-July; (206) 684-7200.*

More than fifty local restaurants, thirty specialty food vendors, a dozen or more coffee roasters and twenty-five Washington state wineries invite the public to sample their culinary wares. Entertainment is provided by area musical and dance groups.

8 *BUMBERSHOOT FESTIVAL* • *Seattle Center over Labor Day weekend; (206) 281-7788.*

Local and internationally known musicians, artists and craftsmen star in one of America's largest cultural festivals, drawing as many as 250,000 patrons. A "bumbershoot," of course, is an umbrella and participants hope none are needed, since this festival is spread through Seattle Center's seventy-four acres.

9 *EARSHOT JAZZ FESTIVAL* • *Three weeks in October-November; (206) 547-9787.*

Almost anyone can be within earshot of this large jazz festival, since it's held at various locations throughout the city.

10 *CHRISTMAS IN SEATTLE* • *Various locations from Thanksgiving through New Year's.*

Seattle celebrates the holidays with a variety of activities, starting with the Bon Marché Holiday Parade and Westlake center tree lighting around Thanksgiving. Seattle Center dons thousands of lights and sets up a miniature "country Christmas" village. The season's highlight is the Christmas Ship Festival, a parade of lighted boats along Elliott Bay and on lakes Union and Washington. On New Year's Eve, the Space Needle is ignited with thousands of lights at the stroke of midnight.

THE TEN BEST SPECIALTY GUIDES TO THE SEATTLE AREA

Of course, you are holding in your the best possible guide to Seattle. Here are ten others, with a more specialized focus. Most are available only at bookstores in the Seattle area, or by special order. We've listed the publishers' mailing addresses so you can order copies before you head for Emerald City. However, check before you send a check; there may be mailing and shipping charges and of course prices are subject to change. The books are listed in no particular order, except possibly alphabetically.

1 BEST PLACES SEATTLE • *By Giselle Smith. Sasquatch Books, 615 Second Ave., Suite 260, Seattle, WA 98104-9841; $18.95. (WEB SITE: www.sasquatchbooks.com)*

This thick book combs Seattle with fine literary teeth, presenting lists of its attractions, restaurants, lodgings, cultural offerings and shopping areas.

2 BREAKFAST IN SEATTLE • *By Marilyn Martin Dahl and Kay Vail-Hayden. Johnston Associates International, P.O. Box 313, Medina, WA 98038; $9.95.*

This slim book lists of dozens of places—other than the city's thousand coffee stops—to start your day.

3 NATIONAL TRUST GUIDE: SEATTLE • *By Walt Crowley. Preservation Press, 605 Third Ave., New York, NY 10158-0012; $19.95.*

If you like history and architecture, pick up a copy of this comprehensive, illustrated guide that covers the city's downtown area and various neighborhoods.

4 NEWCOMER'S HANDBOOK FOR SEATTLE • *By Amy Bellamy. First Books, P.O. Box 578147, Chicago, IL 60657; $14.95. (WEB SITE: www.firstbooks.com)*

You like Seattle so well that you want to stay? This guide lists neighborhoods, schools, shopping areas and other items of interest to present and future residents.

5 PORTRAIT OF SEATTLE • *Photos by Charles Krebbs. Graphic Arts Center Publishing Company, P.O. Box 10306, Portland, OR 97296-0306; $12.95.*

This softcover is filled with exceptionally attractive photos of Seattle, with none of those phony Space Needle shots with blown-up moons in the background.

6 SEATTLE CHEAP EATS • *Sasquatch Books, 615 Second Ave., Suite 260, Seattle, WA 98104-9841; $15.95. (WEB SITE: www.sasquatchbooks.com)*

This book lists three hundred places to dine without denting your wallet or purging your purse. Restaurant listings are cross-referenced by food type and location.

7 *SEATTLE CITY WALKS* • By Laura Karlinsey. Sasquatch Books, 615 Second Ave., Suite 260, Seattle, WA 98104-9841; $16.95. (WEB SITE: www.sasquatchbooks.com)

Brought your walking shoes? This guide outlines sixteen walks in Seattle and environs, with photos, guide maps and historical-architectural commentary.

8 *SEATTLE NOW AND THEN* • By Paul Dorpat. Tartu Publications, P.O. Box 85208, University Station, Seattle, WA 98103-1208; $17.95.

The author writes an historical column for the *Seattle Times* and this book is a compilation of his city vignettes, illustrated with historic and contemporary photos.

9 *SHORT BIKE RIDES: WESTERN WASHINGTON* • By Judy Wagonfield. The Globe Pequot Press, P.O. Box 833, Old Saybrook, CT 06475; $13.95. (WEB SITE: www.globe-pequot.com)

Brought your bike? More than a dozen Seattle area bike rides are included in this guide to western Washington bike routes. Each is accompanied by a map.

10 *ZAGAT SURVEY* • 4 Columbus Circle, New York, NY 10019; $9.95. (WEB SITE: www.zagat.com)

Zagat combines Seattle with Portland in this typically brief, witty and opinionated survey of restaurants.

EASY LISTENING: THE TEN BEST RADIO STATIONS

What turns you on when you turn on your radio? Mellow sounds, light rock, jazz, classics or Garth Brooks? Our choices, while quite varied, reveal that we don't like hard rock or rap and that we tilt toward more mellow sounds.

1 *KPLU—FM 88.5* • Our favorite is this National Public Radio station that features light jazz and blues, plus the usual newsy and informative NPR features.

2 *KUOW—94.9 FM* • National Public Radio news and talk.

3 *KWJZ—FM 98.9 FM* • Smooth jazz.

4 *KYCW—96.5 FM* • Country, traffic and sports.

5 *KBSG—97.3 FM* • Pops oldies and traffic reports.

6 *KBCS 91.3 FM* • Public supported station that features American and international folk music.

7 *KIRO—710 AM* • News, sports and talk.

8 *KVI—570 AM* • News and talk.

9 *KIXI—880 AM* • Oldies pops.

10 *KJR—850 and 950 AM* • Sports.

THE WORST OF EMERALD CITY

We saved the worst for last in this chapter, and the first of the worst deals with Seattle's transportation problems.

1 *THE WORST SINGLE THING ABOUT SEATTLE* • *No, it's not the rain. It's the lack of a serious public transit system.*

Seattle and Los Angeles have only one thing in common—thankfully. Several decades ago, planners felt that freeways could solve their transit problems and now today's often gridlocked commuters and visitors are stuck with their bad judgment. Gimmicks like underground bus tunnels and express lanes and shift directions between morning and afternoon rush hours are only poorly applied Band-Aids. Diamond lanes are a good idea if there's two of you, although it's often difficult to maneuver over to them during rush hour traffic, and then to maneuver back out when you reach our exit. It's particularly tricky if you're a visitor not familiar with the street system.

San Francisco has BART and Metro Muni, Portland has MAX, and San Diego has a fine light rail system, plus the Coaster commute train. Belatedly, Emerald City *is* getting serious about transit that is both mass and rapid. Voters approved a levy in 1996 and the first elements of a combined greater Seattle area light rail and main rail system (using existing train tracks) we begin offering service in 2005.

Meanwhile, a word of caution to visitors: Don't try to go anywhere during the morning and evening rush hours. It's not just the freeways. Popular surface streets can become congested as well. (Just ask any innocent who decides to go to Southcenter Mall during the rush hour. At peak commute periods, suburban streets and highways can become just as clogged as those in the city.) Of course, traffic jams are particularly bad when it's raining. Too many motorists haven't figured out the physics of stopping distances as they relate to wet asphalt; see the next listing.

2 THE WORST TIME FOR TRAFFIC TANGLES • *During a rainstorm, particularly after a dry spell.*

Seattle area residents must have figured out by this time that it rains a lot here—as much as forty inches a year. Yet, whenever it rains, motorists hurry along as usual, accidents rise and traffic becomes a mess. It's particularly bad on freeways such as I-5 and I-90 during the rush hour. C'mon guys, haven't you yet figured out that rain mixes with oil deposits on the highways, forming a slippery goo? And that it's particularly bad after a dry spell, when oil from vehicles has had a chance to build up? We offer a simple solution for visitors and anyone else who doesn't have to commute: When it rains, find a comfortable café or bar and wait out the rush hour.

3 THE WORST FREEWAY COMPLEX • *Interstate 5 downtown.*

This spaghetti tangle must drive tourists to tears, particularly those approaching from the south. To get downtown on exit 165, you must exit to the left, which most motorists don't expect on a freeway. And if you get too far left, you'll be peeled into an express lane and away you go, off to Everett. If you decide to continue to the next exit, marked "Pike Place Market," you must work your way across the freeway and exit to the right—too far right, in fact. The route takes you on the wrong side of the freeway and through several complex turns before pointing you toward the market.

4 THE WORST DOWNTOWN FREEWAY ONRAMP • *Denny Way from Seattle Center to southbound Interstate 5.*

We hope the person who designed this interchange has been drummed out of the highway planning department. If you head east on Denny Way and then follow I-5 signs south (Minor Avenue), you'll be in for a rude surprise when you hit the freeway. Within less than a quarter of a mile, you need to shift over *four lanes* to avoid getting peeled off onto three consecutive exit-only ramps. Try *that* caper during the evening rush hour!

5 THE WORST STREET ON WHICH TO GET STUCK GO-
ING THE WRONG DIRECTION • *Aurora Avenue between downtown
Seattle and Washington Memorial Bridge.*

Before the days of Interstate 5, Aurora Avenue was converted into a
ground level expressway to hurry old Highway 99 traffic through
downtown Seattle. This essentially created a barrier between the east
and west sides of the eastern Queen Anne district north of downtown.
If you innocently blunder onto Aurora, you can't turn around until you
reach the Lake Washington Ship Canal northbound or Mercer Street
southbound, and these turn-arounds are rather complex. And if you
don't bail out quickly enough while southbound, you'll suddenly disap-
pear underground and emerge—mole-like and blinking in confusion—
on the Alaskan Way Viaduct. Before you know it, you'll be in the south
Seattle port district when all you really wanted to do was get across
Aurora several miles back.

On the other hand, Aurora does provide a quick route through
town and out of town, and we've used it frequently in this book to get
you from points A to B.

6 THE WORST VIOLATORS OF TRAFFIC LAWS • *Bike
messengers.*

Downtown bicycle messengers flit through thick traffic like suicidal
humming birds, essentially ignoring such things as red lights, one-way
streets and the right-of-way of other vehicles and pedestrians. Yet
we've never seen one of them cited, although Washington's vehicle
code requires that cyclists obey the same traffic laws as motorists. The
Seattle Police Department does employ officers on mountain bikes, although we've never seen one attempt to intercept a bike messenger. A
cop on a mountain bike chasing a bike courier—now *that* would be a
sight to see!

7 THE WORST PLACE TO REACH AT SEA-TAC INTER-
NATIONAL AIRPORT • *The North Terminal.*

Just how far north is this place, anyhow? You can't get to the North
Terminal—also called the North Satellite—by car, taxi or public con-
veyance. (The first time we needed to use it, our cab driver didn't even
know there *was* a North Terminal.) To reach this elusive satellite of
Sea-Tac, you must lug your luggage through the main terminal, go up
and down a couple of escalators, catch an underground subway, and
then return to an upper level to check in. There's also a South Satellite,
served by the same subway, which is halfway to Tacoma. Pity the poor
folks who have to use these different terminals during a tight plane
change.

8 *THE DUMBEST PIECE OF PUBLIC ART* • *In Myrtle Edwards Park. GETTING THERE: Myrtle Edwards Park is between Elliott Bay Park and the Waterfront Streetcar barn. Drive northwest on Alaskan Way to a parking lot beside the car barn, then walk into the park.*

This huge "assemblage" plopped onto a field of gravel doesn't stretch the meaning of art; it ridicules it. Titled "Adjacent, Against and Upon," it consists of three large slabs of concrete—one with a hefty boulder sitting beside it, the next with a boulder leaning against it and the third with a boulder sitting on it. With foolishness such as this, it's no wonder that some taxpayers object to publicly funded art. (To be fair, Seattle has some wonderful public art and we think Christopher Columbus—above on page 201—is kinda cute. But *this* thing...)

9 *THE MOST MISLEADING VISITORS' BUREAU CLAIM* • *"It doesn't really rain a lot in Seattle."*

C'mon guys, you've got a glorious city in a great setting, with fine restaurants, outstanding museums, plentiful shopping, excellent public parks and great waterways. You won't scare visitors away by admitting that Seattle is a wet city. We'll come anyway.

To quote from a Seattle King County News Bureau release: "Seattle is 44th on a listing of U.S. cities by rainfall amounts with an average of 37 inches a year. It gets less rain than Mobile, Alabama, or Miami, Florida." But how many cities get *less* rainfall than Seattle? Portland, San Francisco, Denver and all other major Western cities are drier. The climate is wetter throughout the South and along the Atlantic Seaboard, so of course most of those cities get more rainfall than Seattle.

Still, thirty-seven inches is a lotta rain, kids! (According to the U.S. Weather Bureau, it's thirty-eight inches.) What the news release should say is: "Yes, it rains a fair amount in Seattle and that's why our setting is so beautiful. Most of that rain falls from late fall through spring, so if you come in the summer, leave the bumbershoot home and enjoy our glorious vistas."

10 *THE WORST THING YOU CAN DO AT A SEATTLE SEAHAWK'S GAME* • *Wear a San Diego Chargers, Oakland Raiders, Kansas City Chiefs or Denver Broncos cap.*

Seattlites are a pretty friendly lot, so the worst you'll probably get is a glare or two. Don't expect good service from the beer man, however.

The traveler sees what he sees; the tourist sees what he has come to see.
— **Gilbert K. Chesterton**

Chapter fourteen

LEAVING SEATTLE
BEYOND EMERALD CITY

Most visitors to this area—probably including yourselves—come not for Seattle alone. You'll want to explore more of this fascinating region of water, wooded hills and snowcapped peaks that is western Washington.

This chapter offers a sampler to this area—our ten favorite lesser-known getaways. Nine are charming little towns and one is an awesomely beautiful wilderness area. You can find more on these and other interesting places in our *Washington Discovery Guide,* which has detailed chapters covering all of the state. It's available at book stores everywhere, or you can order it on the web at *amazon.com* or *bn.com.*

TEN BEST REASONS FOR GETTING OUT OF TOWN

All of these lures are within a few hours' drive of Seattle. We've avoided the obvious; everyone knows about Mount Rainier, Mount St. Helens and the Olympic Peninsula. But how may of you have been to an oyster shucking shed, or visited a town flanked by more than two hundred metal sculptures? We begin with an exceedingly charming little port town:

1 **WESTPORT** • *On the Pacific Ocean at the south entrance to Grays Harbor; about 100 miles from Seattle. GETTING THERE: Go south from Seattle on I-5 and west on State Highway 8 from Olympia, which blends into U.S. 12 and takes you to Aberdeen. From there, follow State Highway 105 to Westport. FOR INFORMATION: Westport-Grayland Chamber of Commerce, P.O. Box 306 (2985 S. Montesano St.), Westport, WA 98595-0306; (800) 345-6223 or (360) 268-9422. (WEB SITE: www.techline.com/~westport/; E-MAIL: westport@techline.com)*

Tiny, slightly scruffy and completely charming, Westport is our favorite "overlooked getaway" from Seattle. Despite its appealing location on a tip of the entrance to Grays Harbor, it has been bypassed by the tourist mainstream—or at least by fancy resorts. Mom and pop motels are abundant; major hotels are missing. This may be an undisguised blessing. It has been spared the commotion and tackiness of more popular coastal retreats.

Westport is primarily a fishing port, both commercial and pleasure, and the town justifiably calls itself the Salmon Capital of the World. It's also popular for whale watching when the great beasts pass just offshore, southbound from November through February, and north in March and April.

As you approach Westport, don't be put off by the drab looking scatter of small homes, businesses and motels along the main road. The appealing part comes at the very end when you drive into the town as you're about to run out of land. Its charming old business district looks out over **Westport Marina** to Grays Harbor. Wood frame storefronts house the usual shops, boutiques, cafés and requisite frozen yogurt outlets. The look, except for the frigid yogurt, is 1950s seaside. Across Westhaven, a good sized squadron of pleasure and commercial boats doze in their slips. Park and stroll along the marina promenade, noting oval plaques depicting famous and contemporary ships and boats. They include Captain Robert Gray's *Columbia Rediviva*, aboard which he discovered the Columbia River's mouth, plus early native plank canoes and assorted fishing vessels.

You'll want to pause at the **Westport Historical Maritime Museum** at 2201 Westhaven Dr.; (360) 268-0078. It's open daily 10 to 4 from Memorial Day through Labor Day; Thursday-Monday noon to 4 the rest of the year, with a modest admission charge. Housed in a Nantucket-style 1939 Coast Guard station, the museum displays historic seafaring regalia, pioneer artifacts, old photos and an operating Fresnel lighthouse lens. Continue beyond the museum on Westhaven past the downtown area and marina to Neddie Rose Drive, where you'll encounter a viewing tower, offering vistas of the harbor and open sea. Turn right and follow Nellie Rose past a couple of RV parks to a traffic circle and another viewing platform. For a brief cruise on Grays Harbor, catch the **Westport-Hoquiam Ferry** which provides passenger service from the waterfront to Hoquiam and Ocean Shores; (360) 268-0047. Westport offers an abundance of charter fishing and whale watching cruises. Contact the chamber of commerce address above, or just check with the many cruise operators at the harbor.

Not surprisingly, most of the restaurants here feature seafood. While you won't find much fare or salmon puddled in raspberry pureé, you can get descent food at inexpensive prices. Some of our favorites are **Barbara's by the Sea** at 2323 Westhaven Dr., (306) 268-1329; Pelican Point Restaurant at 2681 Westhaven Dr. (corner of Neddie Rose), (360) 268-1333; and Gay Nineties style Sourdough Lil's at 301 Dock St. (Nyhaus), (360) 268-9700.

You'll find an abundance of relatively inexpensive motels on the highway leading into town, plus the inexpensive **Elma-Grays Harbor Youth Hostel** at 6 Ginny Lane in nearby Elma; (360) 482-3119. Our favorite hideaway here is the **Harbor Resort** right beside the water off Nettie Rose Drive; (360) 268-0619. It has kitchen units with view decks and motel type rooms.

2 INDEX • *This tiny town is just north of Highway 2 on the route to Stevens Pass in the Cascades, about fifty miles northeast of Seattle. GETTING THERE: Take I-5 north, then exit onto State Highway 522 above Kirkland and follow it northeast to U.S. 2 at Monroe. Head east and you'll shortly encounter Gold Bar, Wallace Falls State Park and then Index.*

This former mining camp with a funny name sits beneath the monolithic mass of Baring Mountain, alongside the sparkling current of the north fork Skykomish River. With an infectious weathered charm, Index is the kind of place that tempts even the hurried traveler to linger.

A settlement emerged from this wilderness in 1891, when Amos Gunn opened a way station. He laid out the town two years later, then the railroad arrived in 1893. Index began booming toward the end of the nineteenth century with the discovery of gold in the area. By 1900, it boasted a water works, lumber mill, scores of stores, a newspaper, dance hall and even a hospital.

Progress has since gone elsewhere, although the town has weathered the lean years well. It offers an appealing collection of prim wood frame buildings, such as the old style **City Hall** with a slender totem out front. Step into the **Mount Index Tavern and Beer Garden** for a game of darts, and maybe a snack and beer on a deck over the river. The **Index General Store,** staffed by exceptionally friendly folks, functions as the local visitors bureau. It also shelters a great little bakery; try some of the huge molasses cookies that once were popular in lumber camps. Ask for an historic walking tour brochure and stroll the town's quiet streets. Or pick up picnic fare and have lunch at **Doolittle Pioneer Park.**

Picket Historical Museum across from the town hall on Avenue A is open weekends noon to 3, Memorial Day through September. It's exhibits—nicely arrayed and uncluttered—include pioneer relics and historic photos tracing the town's early days. Fisherpersons like to wet their flies in the next-door river, and hikers can get a trail map from the store.

If you're tempted to linger longer, check into a century-old roadhouse, **Bush House Country Inn** at 300 Fifth Street at Index Avenue. This 1898 restored inn with three cupolas popping from its roof sits dramatically against a mountain wall, with an attractive garden out front. The interior is done in dark wood wainscotting, with a fieldstone fireplace, historic photos and pastel paintings.

While you're in the neighborhood, check out **Gold Bar,** another old mining town that's not quite as interesting but worth a pause. And definitely worth a pause is nearby **Wallace Falls State Park** where you can hike up to a brace of waterfalls on the Wallace River.

3 *LA CONNER • This early American style town is west of I-5 about sixty miles north of Seattle. GETTING THERE: Head north on I-5, take exit 221 at Conway and follow signs west. FOR INFORMATION: La Conner Chamber of Commerce, P.O. Box 1610, La Conner, WA 98257; (888) 642-9284 or (360) 466-4778. (WEB SITE: www.laconner-chamber.com; E-MAIL: info@laconnerchamnber.com)*

La Conner is a nicely preserved example of a rural late nineteenth and early twentieth century village—not Victorian but no-nonsense wood-frame American. It sits prettily along the narrow Swinomish Channel between the mainland and Skagit Island. The downtown area offers an impressive assortment of shops, boutiques, galleries and trendy cafés. La Conner's shops offer a good mix of artwork, antiques and American folk crafts. Steep side streets will lead you to a tilted neighborhood of fine old homes and to an the nicely done **Skagit County Historical Museum** at 501 Fourth St.; (360) 466-3365. It's open Tuesday-Sunday 11 to 5, with a modest admission fee.

Our favorite La Conner dining spots are the cute little **Calico Cupboard Café** at 720 S. First St., (360) 466-4451; and **Lighthouse Inn** at 512 First St. (on the waterfront, near Morris), (360) 466-3147. If you like microbrews, check out **La Conner Brewing Company** at 117 S. First St.; (360) 466-1415. The town's fanciest lodging is **La Conner Country Inn** at 107 S. Second St.; it's an attractive shingle-sided country-style inn with individually decorated rooms. The inn's **Palmer's Restaurant & Pub** serves Northwest and continental fare, with full bar service.

4 *MOUNT BAKER • A National Forest recreation area about 150 miles north of Seattle. GETTING THERE: Head north from Seattle to Bellingham on I-5, then follow State Route 542 west. FOR INFORMA-*

TION: Mount Baker Ranger District, 2105 Highway 20, Sedro Woolley, WA 98284; (360) 856-5700.

The northernmost volcano in the Cascade Range, Mount Baker isn't as famous as Mount Rainier and Mount St. Helens, although it's equally attractive. It offers some of the most striking alpine scenery in the entire Northwest. Ordinary cities like Bellingham and Mount Vernon are made attractive by having Mount Baker as a backdrop. The mountain itself is tucked into the remote northwestern edge of Washington, not really on the way to anywhere. That's why it's missed by many travelers.

Like most of its volcanic sisters, 10,775-foot Baker is asleep but not dormant. An ash eruption in 1843 started a huge forest fire. Well over a century later, in 1975, a sudden hiss of volcanic steam melted glacial ice to form a new lake in the crater. The peak was named for Captain George Vancouver's first mate, Joseph Baker, who spotted the promontory as their ship sailed past in 1792. Indians had a more interesting name for it—*Koma Kulshan* or "Broken One," referring to an ancient eruption that shattered part of the summit.

The only land approach is on the Mount Baker Highway, which takes you through the small town of **Glacier,** where you can find a couple of places to eat and sleep. (There are no facilities on the mountain) You'll find no glaciers here; the name comes from nearby Glacier Creek.

Climbing toward the peak, you'll pass the **Mount Baker Ski Area** then, a couple of twisted miles above, you'll emerge onto a broad parking area at **Artist Point,** atop a lofty ridge. The high Cascades emerge suddenly from hiding and surround you with their jagged sawtooth ridges and snow-smothered peaks. Waves of granite sweep away in every direction. Mount Baker is a massive presence, standing across a deep glacial-carved valley. Opposite Baker and even more imposing is 9,127-foot **Mount Shuksan,** an incredibly ragged ridge of granite.

Trails beg you to explore these heights further. For a relatively easy walk, take the **Artist Ridge Trail** in a one-mile loop toward Mount Shuksan. Interpretive signs explain the area's geology. A favorite masochists hike is on **Table Mountain Trail.** It switchbacks more than a thousand feet up an old lava flow that has eroded into a butte. Plan a couple of hours for this two-hour pant; views from the top are worth the effort. More trails reach from Artist Point into the inviting Mount Baker Wilderness.

5 OYSTERVILLE ● *On the Long Beach Peninsula in southwestern Washington, about 165 miles southwest of Seattle. GETTING THERE: Go south from Seattle on I-5 to Longview, then follow State Highway 4 along the Columbia River to its junction with U.S. 101. Follow Highway 101 south to Ilwaco, then go north on State Route 103 to Oysterville.*

FOR INFORMATION: *Long Beach Peninsula Visitors Bureau, P.O. Box 562, Long Beach, WA 98631; (800) 451-2542 or (360) 642-2400.*

The Long Beach peninsula is Washington's most popular ocean resort, busy with the usual seaside tourist gimmicks and attractions. North of here, toward end of that peninsula is a town of quite a different sort. Oysterville is a small collection of weathered buildings—including a few Victorians—that make up Oysterville National Historic District.

This quiet gathering of old homes tucked beneath huge shade trees is a refreshing departure from the intensive tourism of Long Beach. Many of the old commercial structures have been converted to private homes; some are marked with signs indicating their age and former use. The town was born in 1854, and a year later it became the seat of Pacific County. It held that post "until the South Bend raiders came on Sunday morning, February 5, 1893, and carried away the records."

Definitely worth a pause is the 1892 **Oysterville Church,** a small New England-style chapel on your left as you enter town. It's a real charmer, with an elaborate red and white witch's hat bell tower, kerosene lamps, a pot bellied stove, wooden pews and a still-functioning pump organ. Call (360) 665-4268 to find out when it's open. Try to come on a Sunday in July or August, when music vespers are held at 3 p.m. Near the church is the bell-towered **Oysterville School,** built in 1908 and active until 1957. It's now a community center.

From the historic district, follow Oysterville Road toward the bay to **Oysterville Sea Farm,** where you can buy fresh and smoked oysters and clams. Hours of this rustically nautical shack are 11 to 5, daily from June to October, then weekends and holidays the rest of the year; (360) 665-6585. In a large processing shed adjacent to the sales room, you may see workers shuckin' and jivin' freshly harvested oysters.

Turn left onto Main Street in front of the Sea Farm and you'll shortly rejoin Highway 103. Within a couple of blocks, you'll encounter historic **Oysterville Store.** It's now mostly a mini-mart and souvenir shop, although it retains the wooden floors and pot-bellied stove of an old general store. It's open daily 9 to 5:30; (360) 665-4766.

Pressing north from Oysterville, you'll pass under a canopy of ancient evergreens, and then run out of road at **Leadbetter Beach State Park** at the tip of Long Beach Peninsula. Within the park, the thick forest yields to grassy dunes and marshes. Leadbetter is essentially a nature preserve with no camping or picnicking facilities. Lots of trails wind among the grasslands and lead to mudflat beaches. You can fetch a trail map from a brochure rack at a parking area. Part of Willapa National Wildlife Refuge, this is a fine place for birdwatching and for plucking wild blackberries and domesticated strawberries and huckleberries.

Returning from Leadbetter Beach, stay to the eastern edge of the peninsula on Sandridge Road instead of following Highway 103. You'll shortly encounter tiny **Nahcotta,** with a mix of old false front and a few modern stores and homes. If you feel the need for more oysters, pause at **Jolly Roger Oysters** at Nahcotta's weathered waterfront (left down 273rd Street). The oyster fleet at anchor, with the bay behind and thick woods of Long Island and the mainland beyond, provides a tranquil scene.

North of here, you'll enter the state's largest cranberry bog area. Most of them are inland, particularly off Cranberry Road, north of an **Ocean Spray** cranberry processing facility. In late fall, when the bogs are flooded to facilitate harvesting, the millions of berries floating on the surface form fascinating patchworks of red. The rest of the year, they're merely square sections of vines and mud, like leafy rice paddies. Although Ocean Spray doesn't offer tours, you can visit the **Cranberry Museum and Gift Shop** on Pioneer Road. Watch for the road to your left as you head south on Sandridge Road. Part of a cranberry growers' cooperative research unit, it's open Wednesday, Thursday and Sunday 10 to 3 and Friday-Saturday 10 to 5; (360) 642-2031. The facility consists mostly of a gift shop with a few cranberry exhibits and a display window into a cranberry laboratory. You can take a half-mile self-guided tour of adjacent experimental cranberry bogs daily from 8 to dusk.

6 *PORT GAMBLE • On the northern tip of the Kitsap Peninsula about thirty miles northwest of Seattle. GETTING THERE: Take Seattle-Bainbridge Island ferry, then go north from Bainbridge Island on State Highway 305, crossing to the Kitsap Peninsula. Then go north from Poulsbo on State Highway 3. FOR INFORMATION: Kitsap Peninsula Visitor and Convention Bureau, P.O. Box 270, Port Gamble, WA 98364; (800) 416-5615 or (360) 297-8200. (WEB SITE: www.visitkitsap.com)*

A charming transplant from New England, Port Gamble offers a wonderful collection of old false front, early American and Victorian buildings. It was founded in 1853 as a sawmill town and lumber shipping port by Captain William Talbot, A.J. Pope and Cyrus Walker. They styled their settlement after their hometown of East Machias, Maine, even importing maples and other New England hardwoods. The Pope and Talbot lumber mill was the longest operating sawmill in America, turning out lumber until it was closed in 1995. You'll still see activity down at the waterfront mill site, since it's a log storage and shipping area.

Still a "company town," Port Gamble is operated as an historic trust by the Pope Resources Company, and it has been declared a national historic site. The town is impeccably groomed, with more than a dozen nineteenth century homes sharing one great rolling green lawn.

The only remaining commercial activity is the Port Gamble Country Store building, which also houses a pair of museums. **Of Sea and Shore Museum** is open daily 11 to 4 in summer, weekends only the rest of the year; (360) 297-2426. It consists of an amazingly large collection of sea shells and other sea critters. Behind and below the store is the outstanding **Port Gamble Historic Museum,** open daily 10 to 4 in summer; closed the rest of the year; (360) 297-8074. This is one of the finest small town museums in the state, with detailed replicas of an early Port Gamble Hotel lobby, Cyrus Walker's elegantly furnished bedroom, a hand-hewn cedar board native dwelling, and a full-scale mock-up of Captain William Talbot's shipboard cabin.

The store itself is worth a browse. Once serving the needs of the lumbermen, it still has the look of a general mercantile. However it caters more to tourists today, selling folk crafts and gift items.

7 *PORT TOWNSEND* ● *On the Olympic Peninsula fifty miles northwest of Seattle. GETTING THERE: Take the Bainbridge Island ferry from Seattle, drive north on State Highway 3 to Port Gamble, cross Hood Canal on State Highway 104, then go north on Highway 19, following signs to Port Townsend. FOR INFORMATION: Port Townsend Chamber of Commerce, 2437 E. Sims Way, Port Townsend, WA 98368; (888) 365-6978 or (360) 385-2722. (WEB SITE: www.pt.guide.com; E-MAIL: ptchamber@olympus.net)*

Gracefully aging Port Townsend is one of the most appealing towns in Washington and certainly the most intriguing on the Olympic Peninsula. Its main street, on a low coastal shelf, is an outdoor architectural museum, with one of the West's largest collections of nineteenth century brick, cut stone and false front buildings. They house boutiques, galleries and several restaurants. Cluster-globe street lamps add a final touch to this Gay Nineties scene. Elegant Victorian homes stand in neighborhoods on the bluff above.

Preening contentedly with its yesterday look, this small town has more than seventy preserved buildings. This structural treasure trove came from a brief and prosperous career as a key shipping point in the Strait of Juan de Fuca.

Port Townsend was established in 1851 as a lumber shipping center. Within three decades, it had become the chief port of entry for Puget Sound, even hosting consulates from several nations. Toward the end of the century, cargo ships began bypassing the town, steaming straight to new transcontinental railheads in Tacoma and Seattle. Port Townsend soon went to sleep. And as Rip Van Winkle discovered, in hibernation there is preservation.

To learn more about the town's past, stop by the **Jefferson County Museum** occupying the three-story 1892 city hall at 210 Madison St. (near Water St.); (360) 385-1003. It's open Monday-Saturday 11 to 4 and Sunday 1 to 4 in summer; weekends only in the off-season. Also check out the **Jefferson County Courthouse** at Jefferson and Walker. Built in 1892 and still in use, this Romanesque-Gothic cut stone creation looks more like a medieval castle than a county office building. You can pick up a map at the chamber that will guide you past several historic buildings and handsome Victorian homes.

While you're in the area, drive out to **Fort Worden State Park** and Conference Center at 200 Battery Way, Port Townsend, WA 98368; (360) 385-4730. This is a busy historical package. Established to protect the entry to Puget Sound, it's one of the most intact late nineteenth century military installations in the Northwest. The parade ground is lined with restored plantation-style buildings, housing a conference center, vacation housing units and other facilities. Its **Puget Sound Coast Artillery Museum** is open daily 11 to 4 in summer, weekends 11 to 4 in fall and spring; closed December and January. **Port Townsend Marine Science Center** is open Tuesday-Sunday noon to 6 in summer, weekends noon to 4 in spring and fall; closed November-March.

Some our favorite dining spots are **Blackberries** in Building 210 at Fort Worden, (360) 385-9950; **Belmont Restaurant and Saloon** in downtown Fort Townsend at 925 Water Street between Taylor and Tyler, (360) 385-3007; and the cheerfully decorated **El Sarapé** at 628 Water Street near Madison, (360) 379-9343.

The area has a good assortment of motels and inns, plus lodgings in former military apartments and houses at **Fort Worden**; call (360) 385-4730. Port Townsend also is noted for fine bed & breakfast inns, most occupying grand old Victorian. A couple of our favorites are the **Ann Starrett Mansion** at 744 Clay Street near Adams, (800) 321-0644 or (360) 385-3205; and **The James House** at 1238 Washington St., (360) 385-1238.

8 *ROSLYN* • *About eighty miles east of Seattle, off Interstate 90. GETTING THERE: Head east on I-90 over Snoqualmie Pass, then turn north toward Rosyln at exit 80. FOR INFORMATION: Tiny Roslyn has no visitor center, although your can get information from the nearby Cle Elum Chamber of Commerce, P.O. Box 43 (211 E. First St.), Cle Elum, WA 98922; (509) 674-5958.*

This ancient and properly tattered old coal mining town became a tourist draw in the early 1990s when it was became the fictitious town of Cicily, Alaska, for the popular TV series, *Northern Exposure*. Tourism waned after the show was canceled in 1995. However, even if it hadn't found TV fame, this weathered 1855 coal mining town worth a stop, with an exceptionally handsome string of weathered false front stores along its main street. In the eyes and actions of local tourist promoters, Roslyn *still is* Cicely, and many of its shops sell *Northern Exposure* souvenirs.

Serious *Northern Exposure* trekkies will want to head for the Northwestern Improvement Company building at First and Pennsylvania. Once the company store for the coal mines, it housed the show's fictitious radio station KBHR. The **Memory Makers** souvenir shop in the building offers an alarming variety of *Northern Exposure* T-shirts and other curios—more now than when the show was active. The radio station signs are still intact. Another familiar *Northern Exposure* site is the **Roslyn Café** with a curious camel mural on its brick exterior. However, a moose, not a camel, was the show's trademark. It strolled past the café during each show's opening episode. Moose memorabilia are still quite popular at the souvenir shops, particularly at **Cicily's Gift Shop** at 112 Pennsylvania. Unfortunately, the original moose, like the TV series, it has since expired.

The **Roslyn Museum** on Pennsylvania, which was spruced up through contributions from the *Northern Exposure* crew, features a pleasant disarray of pioneer regalia. It's open daily 1 to 4 in summer and by appointment in the off-season; (509) 674-5958.

9 *RAYMOND* • *About forty-five miles southwest of Seattle at the head of Willapa Bay. GETTING THERE: Take I-5 south from Seattle to Chehalis, and head for the coast on U.S. Highway 6; Raymond is at the junction of highways 6 and 101. FOR INFORMATION: Raymond Chamber of Commerce, 524 N. Third St., Raymond, WA 98577; (360) 942-5419.*

Founded as a lumber shipping port at the turn of the twentieth century, Raymond hasn't changed much since then. It's rather charming, with awning-covered sidewalks in its wood-frame downtown area, a handful of false front stores and a couple of historical murals.

However, this isn't the reason that Raymond makes our list of Ten Best discoveries in western Washington. The town's most striking attraction is the **Raymond Wildlife-Heritage Sculpture Corridor.** It consists of more than two hundred metal sculptures scattered about town and along Highway 101 for nearly five miles. Most are silhouettes, designed and drawn by area artists and then cut from sheet metal by Tacoma Steel. Another artist used scrapes from these cuttings to fashion thirty three-dimensional sculptures. The various art works represent everything from wildlife to fishermen to family scenes.

As State Route 6 hits U.S. 101, go right for a block and then turn left at the next signal onto Heath Street, headed for the new **Willapa Seaport Museum** at Heath and Alder; (360) 942-5666. The museum is open Wednesday-Sunday noon to 4. Exhibits focus on the Willapa Bay area's seafaring, oyster-harvesting and lumbering industry. To explore the town's compact business district, go back two blocks to Fifth Street and follow it past a three-block-long city park. It's something of an outdoor museum, with a collection of antique wagons, farming and lumbering equipment and several nicely-done wooden carvings. Opposite the outdoor equipment collection is **Dennis Company Trading Center** at Fifth and Blake, marked by an imposing 85-foot mural of an old time logging scene. Built in 1912 by Stewart

Lake Dennis, this is still a busy hardware and mercantile, with a few historic exhibits among the merchandise. Hours are Monday-Saturday 7:30 to 5:30 and Sunday 10 to 3.

Another charming town of Willapa Bay is nearby **South Bend**, also offering a weathered old business district. If you have itchy feet or bikes aboard, you can follow the four-mile **Raymond/South Bend Biking-Walking Trail** along Willapa Bay between the two communities. Once in South Bend, check out its **Pacific County Museum** at 1008 W. Robert Bush Drive (Highway 101); (360) 875-5224. It's open daily 11 to 4, with exhibits on local history. **Robert E. Bush Park** in the heart of downtown offers harbor views, picnic tables and an interesting lifesize wooden carving of Robert Bush, a local boy who won the Medal of Honor as a Navy corpsman during World War II.

10 STEILACOOM • *About forty miles southwest of Seattle; just west of Tacoma. GETTING THERE: Follow I-5 south through Tacoma, then take exit 128 and follow Steilacoom Boulevard west. FOR INFORMATION: Tacoma-Pierce County Visitor & Convention Bureau, 1001 Pacific Ave., Suite 400, Tacoma, WA 98402; (253) 627-2836.*

Established in 1854, Steilacoom was Washington's first incorporated community, and it looks its age. The small downtown area offers an enticing collection of false front and brick stores. With carefully-tended flower baskets hanging from vintage lamp posts, it's as prim as a pin. Not surprisingly, it has been declared a national historic district. Settlement in the area actually predates the town. Captain Lafayette Balch established Point Steilacoom just up the beach in 1851. Later that year, John B. Chapman founded the rival community of Steilacoom City, on the town's current site.

To learn of this charming old town's past, pause at the **Steilacoom Historical Society Museum** at 112 Main St.; (253) 584-4133. It's open Tuesday-Sunday 1 to 4. Definitely worth a visit is the **Blair Historic Hardware and Drug** at Lafayette and Wilkes streets; (253) 588-9668. It's open weekdays 9 to 4, weekends 8 to 4. Free. Built in 1895 as a combined hardware and drug store, it's now mostly a small café and ice cream parlor (see listing below). Many of the original hardware and drug items are on display, and the café's bakery lurks behind old style post office boxes. Also check out the **Steilacoom Tribal Cultural Center** at 1515 Lafayette St. (corner of Pacific); (253) 584-6308. Hours are Tuesday-Sunday 10 to 4.

Just north of downtown, a continuation of Lafayette Street takes you to **Sunnyside Beach,** with both sandy and grassy areas and a swimming bay. There's a parking lot just above with a modest all-day parking fee. If you're hungry, you can dine simply at **Blair Drug** or quite grandly at **E.R. Rogers Restaurant** at 702 Commercial Street, corner of Wilkes; (253) 582-0280. This elegantly restored Queen Anne Victorian features Northwest cuisine.

The public is the only critic whose opinion is worth anything at all.
— **Mark Twain**

Chapter fifteen

READERS' FORUM
AND NOW, IT'S YOUR TURN

Now that you've learned all about Seattle and its attractions, we'd like your input. We invite you to submit your own list of what's best in Emerald City, using the form that follows. (You can photocopy these pages or write your selections on a piece of paper, if you don't want to dismember the book.) Of course, we don't expect you to come up with a nomination in each category. Any and all entries will be welcomed. You can choose some of the same selections that we have, or you can dare to disagree.

All who send us at least fifteen selections will receive a free copy of the next edition of *Seattle: The Best of Emerald City.* They can be in any category you wish. Send your selections to:

Pine Cone Press, **Inc.**
631 N. Stephanie St., PMB 138
Henderson, NV 89014
YOU CAN FAX YOUR LIST IF YOU WISH, TO (702) 558-4355.

READERS' SURVEY FORM

YOUR FAVORITE THING ABOUT SEATTLE _____

_____

THE BEST ATTRACTION _____

THE BEST "HIDDEN" ATTRACTION _____

THE BEST SEATTLE ACTIVITY _____

THE VERY BEST RESTAURANT _____

THE BEST ASIAN RESTAURANT _____

THE BEST OTHER ETHNIC RESTAURANT _____

THE BEST SEAFOOD RESTAURANT _____

THE BEST SPECIALTY OR THEME RESTAURANT _____

_____

THE BEST BREAKFAST CAFÉ_____

THE BEST OUTDOOR DINING AREA _____

THE BEST VIEW RESTAURANT _____

THE BEST "COFFEE STOP" _____

THE BEST FREE ATTRACTION _____

THE BEST CHEAP RESTAURANT _____

THE BEST CHEAP MOTEL/HOTEL _____

THE BEST HOTEL _____

THE BEST BED & BREAKFAST _____

THE BEST PERFORMING ARTS GROUP _____

THE BEST NIGHTCLUB _____

THE BEST MOVIE THEATER _____

THE BEST COCKTAIL LOUNGE _____

THE BEST IRISH PUB _____

THE BEST LOBBY BAR _____

THE MOST ROMANTIC BAR _____

THE BEST THEME BAR _____

THE BEST HISTORIC BAR _____

THE BEST VIEW BAR _____

THE BEST BREWPUB PUB _____

THE BEST PLACE TO SNUGGLE _____

THE MOST ROMANTIC RESTAURANT _____

THE BEST SEATTLE VISTA _____

THE BEST PHOTO ANGLE OF THE CITY _____

_____

THE BEST SHOPPING MALL _____

THE BEST SPECIALTY STORE _____

THE BEST HIKING/WALKING PATH _____

THE BEST BIKE ROUTE _____

THE BEST PEOPLE-WATCHING PLACE _____

THE BEST ANNUAL FESTIVAL _____

THE BEST SEATTLE NEIGHBORHOOD _____

THE BEST RADIO STATION _____

THE WORST THING ABOUT SEATTLE _____

_____

THE BEST SIDE TRIP FROM SEATTLE _____

OTHER "BEST" NOMINATIONS NOT ON THIS LIST:

_____

_____

_____

_____

_____

_____

NEW CATEGORIES YOU'D LIKE TO SEE IN THE NEXT EDITION?

_____

_____

_____

_____

- -

THANKS FOR CONTRIBUTING TO OUR SURVEY!

Please list your name and address if you want to receive a free copy of the next edition of *Seattle: The Best of Emerald City.*

Name _____

Address _____

City/state/ZIP _____

Please send this form or a facsimile to:
Pine Cone Press, *Inc.*
631 N. Stephanie St., PMB 138
Henderson, NV 89014
or FAX it to (702) 558-4355

INDEX: Primary listings indicated by *bold face italics*

A Contemporary Theatre, 131
AAA Washington Travel Store, 17
Active Singles Life newspaper, 159
Adult Entertainment Center, 156
Ainsworth & Dunne Wharf, 28, 182
Air service, 15
Airport Plaza Hotel, 118
Alexis Hotel Seattle, *122*, 180
Alki Bakery, 107, 190
Alki Beach Park, 23, 190
Alki Spud Fish & Chips, 103
Allen, Paul, 14, 36, 38
American Backpackers Hostel, 118
Amtrak, 16
Anthony's Fish-Bar, 103
Anthony's Pier 66, 72
Argosy Cruises, 29, *56*, *86*, 179
Armeni Park, 190
Assimba restaurant, 115
Athenian Inn, *90*, 99, 178
Atlas Foods, 90
Avenue One restaurant, 152

B acon Mansion B&B, 126
Bagley Wright Theater, 131
Bahn Thai, *77*, 153
Ballard, 21, 26
Bangkok House, 77
Bank of America Tower, 61
Barnes & Noble, 175
Bay Pavilion, 20, 29, 179, 193
Beacon Hill, 183
Beans & Machines, *107*, 180
Beer Sheva Park, 24
Bellevue Square, 170
Belltown, 21, *199*
Belltown Pub, 141
Benaroya Symphony Hall, 15, *32*, 131, 203
Beth's Café, 91
Bicycle messengers, 213
Big Time Brewery/Ale House, 141
Bill Speidel's Underground Tours, 29, 59

Blake Island State Park, *58*, 179
Blazing Saddles, *58*, 180, 191
Blue Moon Tavern, 146
Boeing, William, 14
Boeing assembly plant tour, 60
Boeing Field, 22, 24
Bohemian Café, 134
Bon Marché, 20
Bookstore, The, *146*, 149, 180
Briazz cafés, 95
Bumbershoot Festival, 208
Burke Museum of Natural History and Culture, 45, *51*
Burke-Gilman Trail, 189, *197*
Bus service, 16
Bush Garden, 77

C afé Starbucks, 106
Campagne restaurant, *68*, 88, 124
Camping, 18
Capitol Hill, 22, 187
Carl English Gardens, 195
Cascadia Restaurant, 68
Catfish Corner restaurant, 115
Center for Wooden Boats, *45*, 48, 111
Central, The, *95*, 146
Chambered Nautilus B&B Inn, 127
Champ Theater Adult Superstore, 157
Chandler's Crabhouse, 99
Chapters Coffee House, 107
Chelsea Station B&B Inn, 127
China Gate, 78
Chinook's at Salmon Bay, 47, *73*
Chittenden Locks, 39
Christmas holiday activities, 208
Chutney's restaurant, 82
Cilantro restaurant, *78*, 180
Cineplex Odeon, 136
Cinerama Theater, 137
City Centre, 20, *170*, 204
City Centre Cinema, 137
Cle Elum, 223
"Coffee craze", 107

Comedy Underground, 134
Commodore Motor Hotel, 118
Crocodile Café, 134

Dad Watsons Restaurant, 142
Dahlia Lounge, 69
Danny Woo Garden, 30
Daybreak Star Cultural Arts Center, 27, 46, *62*, 111, 162, 197
DeLaurenti Italian store, 176
Desert Fire, 96
Diagonal Avenue Public Shoreline Access, 24, *149*
Dimitriou's Jazz Alley, 134
Discovery Park, 27, *46*, 112, 185, 191, 195, 196
Duwamish Waterway, 24

Earshot Jazz Festival, 208
East Win Restaurant, 116
Eastgate Motel, 119
Egyptian Theater, 137
El Gaucho, 135, *153*
Elephant and Castle Pub, 142
Elliott Bay, 11, 12, 13, 43, 44, 56, *192*
Elliott Bay Book Company, 175
Elliott Bay Marina, 28, 183, 191, 193
Elliott Bay Park, 28, 183, 191, 193
Elliott's Oyster House, *73*, 179
Empty Space Theatre, 132
Erotic Bakery, 158
Etta's Seafood, 74
Experience Music Project, 15, *38*

Fantasies Unlimited Arcade, 158
FAO Schwarz, 175
Fenix & Fenix Underground, 135
Ferry service, 16
5th Avenue Theatre, 132
First Class Limousine, 150
Fishermans Restaurant, *99, 179*
Fishermen's Terminal, 27, *47*, 112, 167, 195
5 Spot café, The, 92
Floating homes, 168, *185*

Flying Fish restaurant, 72
Fort Worden State Park, 223
Four Seasons Olympic Hotel, 122
Freeway Park, 30, *202*
Fremont neighborhood, 21, 137, 188, *200*
Fremont Outdoor Cinema, 137
Fremont Rocket, 189
Fremont Sunday Market, 189, 203
Fremont Troll, *62*, 188
Fullers restaurant, *69*, 124, 153

Galerias restaurant, 83
Gameworks, 47
Gas Works Park, *63*, 162, 197
Gaslight Inn/Howell Street Suites, 127
Gates, Bill, 10, 14, 36, 56
Gay and lesbian district, 188
Georgian Room, The, *70*, 122, 154
Giao's restaurant, 78
Glacier, town of, 219
Gold Bar, 218
Golden Gardens Park, 26
Gordon Biersch Brewery-Restaurant, *96*, 142
Gourmet Sausage Company, 116
Grand Illusions Cinema, 138
Green Lake Park, 26, *48*, 112, 186
Green Tortoise Hostel, 119
Guild Theater, 138

Harbor Island, 23
Harbor Steps, 180, 191, *203*
Hendrix, Jimi, 38, 133, 188
Henry Art Gallery, 45
Hill House Bed & Breakfast, 126
Hing Hay Park, 40
Hiram Chittenden Locks & Carl S. English Jr. Botanical Gardens, 27, *39, 113*, 191, 195
History House, *62*, 188
Hi-Spot Café, 92
Ho Ho Seafood Restaurant, 79
Hooters, *147*, 158
Hotel Edgewater, 28, 32, *123*, 182
Hotel Monaco Seattle, 123

Hotel Vintage Park, 123
Hunt Club, The, *70*, 125, 154

Il Fornaio deli, 204
Il Terrazzo Carmine, 82
Index, town of, 217
Inn at the Market, 124
International District, 20, 30, *39*
Intiman Playhouse, 131
Ivar's Acres of Clams, 29, *74*, 179
Ivar's Fish Bar, 105

Jack's Fish and Chips Spot, 105
Jefferson County Museum, 222
Jet Motel Park 'n Fly, 119
Jitterbug café, 93
José Rizal Park, *34*, *151*, 165
J&M Café and Cardroom, *96*, 143

Kells Irish Restaurant & Pub, 82
Kerry Park, 163
KeyArena, 56, 131
King County, naming of, 12
King's Barbecue House, 40
Klondike Gold Rush National Historical Park, 29, *40*, 113, 181
Kobe Terrace Park, 30, 40

La Conner, 218
Lake Union, 21, 168, 185, 198
Lake Washington, 8, 21, 22, 24, 56, 168, 185, 193, 198, 200
Lampreia, 70
Larry's Green Front Café, *93*, 97
Lenin statue, 189
Lincoln Park, 24
Little Chinook's, 32, 73, *102*
Lockspot Café, 103
Lowell's restaurant, *100*, 104, 178
Lusty Lady, The, 157

Macrina Bakery & Café, 94
Mad Pizza, 87
"Made in Washington" stores, 174
Mae Pim Thai restaurant, 114
Maggie Bluffs Grill, *94*, 183, 191

Magnolia Bluffs, 27, 191, 196
Marion Court, 97
Maritime Heritage Center, 48
Market Heritage Center, 29, *64*, 179, 180
Maximillien in the Market, 100
McCormick & Schmick's, 74, 100
Merchants Café, 89
Microsoft, 10, 14, 36, 38
Mildred's Bed & Breakfast, 128
Monorail, 18, 166
Moore Hotel, 119
Mount Baker, 218
Mount Rainier, 161, 168
Murphy's, 145
Museum of Flight, 24, 33, *50*, 163
Museum of History & Industry, 25, *51*
MV Challenger B&B, 128
Myrtle Edwards Park, 28, 183, 191

Nahcotta, 220
New Orleans restaurant, *80*, 135
Nike Town, 174
Nikko restaurant, *79*, 126
Nishino restaurant, 83
Nordic Heritage Museum, 26, *52*
Nordstrom, 20, *171*
Northern Exposure TV series, 223
Northgate Mall, 171
Northwest Chamber Orchestra, 132
Northwest Seaport, 48

Occidental Mall & Park, 42, 181
Odyssey, the Maritime Discovery Center, 29, *52*, 182
Of Sea and Shore Museum, 221
Omnidome, 29, *49*, 193
On the Boards theater, 132
Original Starbucks, 108
Owl 'n' Thistle Irish Pub and Restaurant, 135
Oysterville, 219

Pacific Northwest Ballet, 133
Pacific Place, 20, *170*
Pacific Place Cinema, 138

Pacific Science Center, 28, *41*, 56
Painted Table, The, *71*, 122, 154
Palisade Restaurant, 31, *71*, 143, 155, 183, 191
Pampas Room (at El Gaucho), 135
Paramount Theater, 131
Parking, 17
"People Waiting for the Interurban" statue, 189
Phó Bác restaurant, 116
Phó Hoà restaurant, 116
Pike Place Hillclimb, 29, 179, 180
Pike Place Market, 20, 29, 30, *36*, 111, *172*, 178, 193, 207
Pioneer Square, 19, 20, 29, 41, *42*, 113, 174, 178, 180, 192
Pioneer Square Fire Festival, 207
Pioneer Square Saloon, 143, 181
Planet Hollywood, 89
Port Gamble, 221
Port Townsend, 222
Public transit, *17*, 211
Puget Sound Maritime Museum, 53
Pyramid Alehouse, 144

QFC supermarket chain, 176, *184*
Queen Anne Hill, 21
Queen Anne Hill B&B, 128

R & L Home of Good Bar-B-Q, 86
Rainfall, *10*, 214
Rainier Square, 20, *64*, *172*
Rasa Malaysia restaurant, 117
Ravenna Park, 26, 187, 194
Raymond, town of, 224
Ray's Boathouse, *75*, 101
REI outdoor store, 32, *173*
Renton, 22
Roslyn, 223
Rover's restaurant, *80*, 152
Roy's restaurant, *89*, 126
RV parks, 18

Sacred Circle Gallery of American Indian Art, *62*, 111
Safeco Field, 23, 30, *57*, 182
Saigon Teriyaki, 117

Salisbury House, 129
Salty's on Alki, 23, *75*, 101, 190
Sanitary Public Market, 179
Santa Fe Café, 84
Sazerac restaurant, *71*, 123
Sea Garden Seafood Restaurant, 76
Sea Shanty, 105
Seattle Aquarium, 29, *43*, 179, 193
Seattle Art Museum, *53*, 54, 180
Seattle Asian Art Museum, *54*, 167
Seattle Cellars, 175
Seattle Center, 18, 20, 28, 182, 201, 205, 208
Seattle Children's Museum, *54*, 56
Seattle Fallen Firefighters Memorial, *64*, 181
Seattle Fishermen's Memorial, 47
Seattle Hostel International, 119
Seattle Int'l Film Festival, 207
Seattle Lodging Guide, 17
Seattle Metropolitan Police Museum, 29, *55*
Seattle Opera, 56, 131, *133*
Seattle Repertory Theatre, 133
Seattle Seafair, 207
Seattle Seahawks, 30, 182, 214
Seattle Symphony, 32, *131*
Seattle Visitors Guide, 16, 17
Seattle waterfront, 20, 43
Seattle's Best Coffee, 108, 150
Seattle-King County Convention & Visitors Bureau, 16
Seattle-Tacoma Airport, *15*, 213
Shafer-Baillie Mansion, 129
Shanghai Garden, 76
Sheraton Seattle, *124*, 145
Shilshole Bay Marina, 26
Sisters Café, 87
Skagit County Museum, 218
Sleepless in Seattle movie, 56, 99, 148, 168
Smith Cove Park, 149, 183
Smith Tower, 29, *49*, 181
Sorrento Hotel, 124
South Bend, 225
Southcenter Mall, 172
Space Needle, 28, 31, *55*, 161, 166

Space Needle Restaurant, *98*, 155
Spanish Table, The, *176*, 179
Speakeasy Café, 136
Spirit of Washington Dinner Train, 59
Starbucks Coffee, *8*, 14, 31, 67, *106*, *108*, 162, 171, 178, 194
Steamers Seafood cafés, 104
Steilacoom, 225
Stranger newspaper, 157
Szmania's restaurant, 81

Taboo Video, 156
Taco del Mar, 117
TenRen Tea Company, 40
Terrace Garden, 97
Three Girls Bakery, *87*, 179
Ticketing information, 130
Tillicum Village salmon bake, 29, *58*, 179
Tír Na Nóg, 146
Top Gun restaurant, 86
Top Lounge (Space Needle), 147
Torrefazione Italia, 109
Totem House Seafood, 104
Train service, 16
Tula's Restaurant, 136
Tully's Coffee, *9*, 67, *106*, *109*, 180, 204

Union Square, 205
University District, 21, *45*, 194, *201*
University of Washington, 25, *45*, 194, 198
University Village, 26, *173*, 194
Uptown Theater, 138
Uwajimaya supermarket, 40
U.S. Coast Guard Light Station, 24

Varsity Inn, 94
Varsity Theater, 139
Vashon Island, 198
Victor Steinbrueck Park, 162, 178
Victoria Clippers, *56*, 28, 182
Victoria's Secret, 158
Vincent's Guest House, 120

Vintage Park Hotel, 150
Virginia Inn, 144
Visitor services, 16, *30*
Volunteer Park, *61*, 187
Von's Martini-Manhattan Memorial, 144

W Seattle hotel, *125*, 145
Wallace Falls State Park, 217, 218
Wallingford, 21
Washington Park, 25, 194
Washington State Convention and Trade Center, 30
Washington State Ferry Terminal, 29, 179, 193
Waterfall Garden Park, 29, *65*, 113, 151, 181
Waterfront Park, 29, 151, 179, *206*
Waterfront Streetcars, 18, 28, *59*, 179, 182, 193
Weatherwatch Park, 190
West Point Lighthouse, 197
West Seattle, 23, 33, 165, *190*
Westin Seattle, 125
Westlake Center, 20, *173*, 206
Westport, 216
Wild Ginger Asian Restaurant and Satay Bar, 79
Wild Salmon Seafood Market, 47
Wing Hay Park, 30
Wing Luke Asian Memorial Museum, 30, 40, *65*
Wolfgang Puck Cafe, *88*, 180
Woodland Park Zoo, 26, *44*
World Trade Center, 182
World Wrapps, 102

Yanni's Greek Cuisine, 81
Ye Olde Curiosity Shop, 20, 29, *49*, 114, 179, 193
Yesler, Henry, 12, 29, 42, 51, 181
YMCA, 120
Youth hostels, 119
Yummy House Bakery, 40

Zí Paní Breads & café, 98

REMARKABLY USEFUL GUIDEBOOKS FROM
Pine Cone Press

Critics praise the "jaunty prose" and "beautiful editing" of Pine Cone Press travel, wine and relocation guides by Don and Betty Martin. They're available at bookstores throughout the United States and Canada.

ARIZONA DISCOVERY GUIDE

This guide covers attractions, scenic drives, hikes and walks, dining, lodgings and campgrounds in the Grand Canyon State. A "Snowbird" section helps retirees plan their Arizona winters.   *— 408 pages; $15.95*

ARIZONA IN YOUR FUTURE

It's a complete relocation guide for job-seekers, retirees and "Snowbirds" planning a move to Arizona. It provides essential data on dozens of cities, from recreation to medical facilities.   *— 272 pages; $15.95*

THE BEST OF DENVER AND THE ROCKIES

Discover the very finest of the Mile High City, from its Ten Best attractions, museums and parks to its leading restaurants and lodgings, and then explore attractions of the nearby Rockies.   *— 256 pages; $16.95*

THE BEST OF THE WINE COUNTRY

Where to taste wine in California? Nearly 300 wineries are featured, along with nearby restaurants, lodging and attractions. Special sections offer tips on selecting, serving and storing wine.   *— 336 pages; $13.95*

CALIFORNIA-NEVADA ROADS LESS TRAVELED

This is a "Discovery guide to places less crowded." It directs travelers to interesting yet uncrowded attractions, hideaway resorts, scenic campgrounds, interesting cafes and other discoveries.   *— 336 pages; $15.95*

LAS VEGAS: THE BEST OF GLITTER CITY

This impertinent insiders' guide explores the world's greatest party town, with expanded "Ten Best" lists of casino resorts, restaurants, attractions, buffets, shows and much more!   *— 256 pages; $15.95*

NEVADA DISCOVERY GUIDE

It covers all of Nevada, with a special focus on gaming centers of Las Vegas, Reno-Tahoe and Laughlin. A special section advises readers how to "Beat the odds," with casino gambling tips.   *— 416 pages; $15.95*

MORE BOOKS & ORDERING INFORMATION ON THE NEXT PAGE